Global Hong Kong

Globalizing Regions

Globalizing Regions offers concise accounts of how the nations and regions of the world are experiencing the effects of globalization. Richly descriptive yet theoretically informed, each volume shows how individual places are navigating the tension between age-old traditions and the new forces generated by globalization.

Australia – Volume One
Anthony Moran

Global Hong Kong – Volume Two
Gary McDonogh and Cindy Wong

Forthcoming:

On Argentina and the Southern Cone – Volume Three
Alejandro Grimson and Gabriel Kessler

The Koreas – Volume Four
Charles Armstrong

China and Globalization:
The Social and Political Transformation of Chinese Society –Volume Five
Doug Guthrie

Morocco – Volume Six
Shana Cohen and Larabi Jaidi

Global Iberia – Volume Seven
Gary McDonogh

Ireland – Volume Eight
Tom Inglis

The Globalization of Israel: McWorld in Tel Aviv, Jihad in Jerusalem – Volume Nine
Uri Ram

Global Indonesia – Volume Ten
Jean Gelman Taylor

Global Iran – Volume Eleven
Camron Michael Amin

Global Hong Kong

GARY MCDONOGH AND CINDY WONG

DS
796
.H757
M347
2005
v. rest

Routledge
Taylor & Francis Group
New York   London

Published in 2005 by
Routledge
Taylor & Francis Group
270 Madison Avenue
New York, NY 10016

Published in Great Britain by
Routledge
Taylor & Francis Group
2 Park Square
Milton Park, Abingdon
Oxon OX14 4RN

Printed in the United States of America on acid-free paper
10 9 8 7 6 5 4 3 2 1

International Standard Book Number-10: 0-415-94769-3 (Hardcover) 0-415-94770-7 (Softcover)
International Standard Book Number-13: 978-0-415-94769-5 (Hardcover) 978-0-415-94770-1 (Softcover)
Library of Congress Card Number 2005004156

Library of Congress Cataloging-in-Publication Data

McDonogh, Gary W.
    Global Hong Kong / Gary McDonogh and Cindy Wong.
        p. cm. -- (Globalizing regions series ; v. 2)
    Includes bibliographical references and index.
    ISBN 0-415-94769-3 (hb : alk. paper) -- ISBN 0-415-94770-7 (pb : alk. paper)
    1. Hong Kong (China)--History. 2. Globalization. I. Wong, Cindy H., 1961- II. Title. III.
Series.

    DS796.H757M347 2005
    951.25--dc22   2005004156

Taylor & Francis Group
is the Academic Division of T&F Informa plc.

Visit the Taylor & Francis Web site at
http://www.taylorandfrancis.com

and the Routledge Web site at
http://www.routledge-ny.com

Whether distracting or helping us, the next generation has been with us in Hong Kong, China, Greater Philadelphia, and Chinatowns around the world.

With love, we dedicate this book to Larissa Jiit-Wai McDonogh-Wong and Graciela Jiit-Heng McDonogh-Wong.

Acknowledgments

Over the years that we have lived, worked, and taught in and about Hong Kong, we have been helped by many people and institutions. These include our home institutions, Bryn Mawr College and the College of Staten Island, City University of New York, for both financial support and the intellectual challenges posed by students and faculty. Thanks to the CIES Fulbright Exchange Program and the Program in American Studies at the University of Hong Kong we were able to spend the year of the transition in Hong Kong, 1996–1997. We also thank Hong Kong Baptist University, where Wong taught.

As we have assembled our ideas and written this text, others have guided us in terms of general discussions and specific readings and comments. Certainly, we thank Jacob Wong Hing Cheung, Wong Yuen-Ling, Wong Yuen-Ching, Carola Hein, Shirley Wong, Paul Smith, Don Barber, Ying Zhu, Kevin Chuc, Gina Marchetti, Lin Qian, Alan Smart, and others for questions large and small. Emily Kahoe and the University of Pennsylvania Cartographic Modeling Laboratory provided crucial maps. Our initial outside readers, series editors, and David McBride, Angela Chnapko, and Linda Manis at Routledge have been truly supportive through-out this process.

Our gratitude as well to Del Ramers of Bryn Mawr Visual Resources who helped us digitalize our illustrations.

Introduction
Why Hong Kong?

A small, mountainous island (Hong Kong), a Chinese peninsula (Kowloon, New Territories), and other assorted islands: This place with a total surface area of only 1100 square kilometers (423 square miles) seems an unlikely focus for the study of globalization, even if it houses some seven million inhabitants. Yet Hong Kong, in its history, people, cultures, spaces, and connections, stands as a remarkably vital microcosm of globalization. Through the heritage of its colonial past (1842–1997), its postcolonial challenges, the opportunities of the world's "freest economy," its vibrant films and striking urbanism, Hong Kong and its peoples have emerged as an iconic twenty-first century global city. After centuries of contact and conflict, the globalism of its citizens is evident in politics, commerce, mass media, and movement; Hong Kongers have participated in many processes of globalization over time. In an Archimedean sense, Hong Kong provides a place to stand and to contemplate the movement of the world.

Hong Kong has been intrinsically "global" since it took shape 165 years ago at the edges of two world empires — China and Great Britain. Eight years after the Handover of 1997 that formally returned this crown colony to Chinese control, the

Hong Kong Special Administrative Region (HKSAR) and its citizens live in a hybrid system that balances the colonial past and China's present and future (although this way of life is only "guaranteed" until 2046). Moreover, the legacies of multiple populations and landscapes forged under colonialism — in which a handful of Britons (and other colonized subjects) thousands of miles from home ruled a burgeoning but divided Chinese population — continue to pose new questions. Some of these arise from the definition of "Chineseness" itself, distinguishing and relating Hong Kong peoples, Mainland Chinese, and overseas Chinese. Other issues arise from strategies for growth in Hong Kong, whose GDP has passed US$200 billion amid competing economies of the Pacific Rim. Family, memory, investments, media, and telecommunications also bind transnational émigrés around the world to Hong Kong's global future in ways we must explore.

This overview of Hong Kong suggests that any understanding of globalization must take into account changing and even divergent meanings of that term. Hong Kong emerged at the intersection of world systems (Wallerstein 1974), when the political economic interests of expanding European maritime colonial empires confronted the millennial development of imperial China. As shown in chapter 2, Hong Kong played a pivotal role in the trade of opium — produced in colonial India, sold by Western merchants for debilitating use in China — that united those worlds. After the convulsions of World War II and the Chinese Revolution, Hong Kong became part of the global production system of the Pacific Rim, as investment, industries, and jobs left Western nations for less expensive production in Japan, Hong Kong, and eventually China and Southeast Asia. In recent years, Hong Kong citizens have moved

Figure I.1
The Skyline of Hong Kong in the 1990s (photograph by the authors).

beyond production to become managers of production, especially for nearby South China. Their dynamic roles in trade, finance, investment, currency, and information have made the Hong Kong Special Administrative Region (HKSAR) a center for the international service economy: "Asia's world city," as tourist slogans proclaim.

Hong Kong also provides insights into varied ideas of "world cities," as developed by Friedman (1974), King (1990, 2003), Sassen (1994, 2002), Swyngedouw and Baeten (2001), and others (See Huang 2004). This label often evokes postmodern images of a nodal position in an electronic global economy, or of cities competing for primacy in a global playing field, both of which we explore in this volume. King argues that the colonial city was the forerunner of today's global metropoles, adding another dimension to the significance of Hong Kong's historical development (1990; see Abbas 1997; Meyer 2001). Moreover, as Sassen reminds us, globalization does not create merely an end product — that is, a separate space — but entails pervasive processes that shape structures, spaces, and lives in the city itself (1994, 2002; see Swyngedouw and Baeten 2001).

Yet, we must also understand globalization in terms of people. Hong Kong was constituted by Chinese and British colonial immigrants. The latter, as sojourners, brought language, laws, imperial connections, and mixed populations to the divided city. Meanwhile, diverse Chinese people in Hong Kong maintained and transformed ties to Southern Chinese culture and society. Others — Eurasians, South Asians, Filipinos, and "Americans" — complicate the history and life of the territory. Meanwhile, Chinese movement through Hong Kong to destinations around the world has created a diasporic, often familial network that must be read in counterpoint to any Western projections of globalization (Ong 1999; Smart and Smart 1999; Wong 1999; Meyer 2001; Smith 2001).

Finally, we read globalization through flows of knowledge and images (Castells 1996, 1997, 1998; Appadurai 1996). Global cities are global not only because of their connectedness, but also because they have a presence and salience that separates them from competing destinations and locales. Hong Kong is no longer an exotic colonial outpost or a symbol of decadent capitalist modernity — images that permeated earlier Western and Chinese discourse. Instead, it now represents a creative city of speed and flash, known for its exciting films, its soaring buildings, and its frenzied pace. It also represents a crucible of change, where observers seek clues about how Chinese and Western heritages and divergent agendas may mesh in the future (Clark 1996; Morley and Robins 1997; Lee 2003; Callahan 2004; Brasher 2004b) (See Figure I.1).

Architectural historian Vittorio Magnago Lampugnani once wrote that "Hong Kong is an enormous monument to the transitory" (1993: 11). Yet, as shown throughout this book, Hong Kong and its people embody many continuities of family, place, culture, action, and creativity. Hong Kong has not only become an important world city whose people continue to adapt creatively in the twenty-first century, but it also offers insights into what globalization may mean over time for other regions and peoples of the world (Yahuda 1996; Ritzer 2004).

RESOURCES AND METHODS

To explore multiple perspectives on global Hong Kong, this book synthesizes spatial studies, history, anthropology, and media and cultural studies. Through these, we consistently seek to explain political and economic development in terms of people who construct and interpret their environment and through more abstract national, regional, and global contexts. We also read space through the more concrete places of landscape, architecture, and settings for human interactions and expression. The "tour" of the HKSAR in chapter 1, for example, shows how the changing form and use of the built environment intersects with the rich history and sociology of the HKSAR, themes that are reexamined in chapters 4 and 6. Later, we resituate Hong Kong within its regional context (South China), compare it to some other related cities of the booming Asian Pacific Rim, and finally return to the human connections of a diasporic Hong Kong. Nevertheless, in all these readings, we value people — individuals and families — as agents in constructing and reflecting on their global lives and meanings, and as producers of cultural texts.

History entails a critical reading of a diversity of representations and debates that undermines any simple narrative of a place or people. Beginning from the contrasting perspectives of Chinese and British encounters that divide the historiography of Hong Kong, we explore the words and ideas of diverse scholars and witnesses who have imagined and acted on that history. Annual government reports, "counterreports" from academic and political observers, archives, newspapers, and secondary sources constitute an extensive literature in Chinese and English on many topics, events, and people. We offer an overview here, illuminating continuing political, economic, and sociocultural processes while suggesting other sources to which readers may turn.

Our training in anthropology, media studies, and cultural studies insists that we explain Hong Kong culture and identity as ongoing products of people and circumstances. Culture also grounds debate among multiple interpretations and rights to these interpretations. Thus, we ask repeatedly who speaks for Hong Kong, how, and why? Who worries about Hong Kong as a political problem? What does it mean to see Hong Kong primarily as a global center of intensely modern economic skills? What does it mean to read Hong Kong — inside or outside the SAR — as a postmodern metropolis of global consumption, a mall that extends from Sir Norman Foster's glossy new airport and a future Disneyland into the crowded streets of Central, Causeway Bay, or Tsim Sha Tsui? And what, in turn, does it mean to feel excluded from these visions?

In presenting Hong Kong, we have also given special attention to cinema as a primary urban art form that has projected

Hong Kong onto a global screen. Filmmakers and critics already have worked extensively with these cultural products that reflect and reconstitute the changing conditions of Hong Kong (Law Kar 1997; Teo 1997; Abbas 1997; Fu and Dresser 2000; Bordwell 2000; Yau 2001). Still, one must not confuse representations or analyses with the experience of Hong Kong peoples themselves. Thus, we suggest how films that will be available to readers worldwide offer clues to social and cultural meaning, yet must be read in the context of different visions, issues, and audiences (Wong and McDonogh 2001ab; McDonogh and Wong 2001). In addition, Internet resources offer keys to Hong Kong's global network and tools for extending our work through official Web sites (see Discover Hong Kong for examples of images) and sites of discussion, such as exlegislator Christine Loh's Forum (see Civic Exchange Web site).

Since the dynamism of global Hong Kong transcends space, documents, and visual culture, we continually integrate Hong Kong families, folklore, language, events, and food into this book. Our own divergent backgrounds — as a Hong Kong born and raised Chinese woman who has studied American and global communication, and a Euro-American man who has looked at Hong Kong within a comparative framework of urban form and policy — have shaped our reading of Hong Kong and its significance for global issues through residence there and reflection abroad. These differences have opened discussions about features of a complex metropolis that convey different meanings depending on where one stands. Still, while providing answers about what globalization means, we have tried to allow Hong Kong and its people to pose questions as well.

The chapters that follow explain Hong Kong on an ever-widening stage, exploring different meanings and experiences of globalization, culture, and agency. The first chapter introduces the "time and place" of Hong Kong, including its global presence and local physiognomy. It illustrates how features of globalization permeate even a single social construction of urban place, the Walled City of Kowloon. The three subsequent chapters reconstruct the historical development of the colony and SAR. Chapter 2 reads the first century of Hong Kong as a divided colonial space where China and Britain encountered each other and something new emerged. Chapter 3 covers Hong Kong's transformations from the 1930s to the 1960s, shaped by Japan's rise as a world power, its defeat, and the reconstruction of Cold War Hong Kong across the border from a newly Communist regime in China. It ends with the riots of the 1960s, which marked a watershed in identity and governance for the colony. Chapter 4 explores the critical transitions of the last four decades, including, but not ending with, the 1997 Handover.

The final chapters reframe the context of Hong Kong. Chapter 5 illuminates Hong Kong's relations to South China, including the former Portuguese colonial enclave of Macau, the central city of Guangzhou, and the new Special Economic Zone of Shenzhen that has exploded across the Hong Kong border. It ends with a comparison of this region to the dynamic northern Chinese global metropolis of Shanghai. Chapter 6 expands regional comparison to some other Asian "tigers" and their transformations, illustrated by global–local development in Taipei, Singapore, and Bangkok, giving special attention to relations to Hong Kong and Greater Chinese connections. Finally, we move from Hong Kong as a point of global encounter to the outside world as influenced by Hong Kong, examining Chinese diasporas, Chinatowns, and flows of goods, images, and information.

This book does not showcase original research or elaborate arguments. Instead, it provides what we hope is an engaging, synthetic introduction to a complicated place, its inhabitants, and its implications for an understanding of contemporary globalization. As such, this book provides a foundation to guide readers forward with regard to the issues we have examined and others — relations of gender, environment, or law — that we have only touched on. The bibliography and filmography, as well as Web links provided at the end of the book, are intrinsic tools of this project. They are an assemblage of materials available to English-language audiences to enrich readings of Hong Kong, to provide richer visual materials, and to explore the many issues that this vibrant metropolis raises. These data and interpretations from Hong Kong, in turn, should offer new perspectives on what global connections and strategies mean to cities over time and in changing contexts.

Reading Hong Kong in Place and Time
One

"Here — at her own doorstep — China and here — after traversing half the world — England, abruptly confront their antitheses. Here two peoples, each profoundly confident of its own superiority, meet face to face." (Sayer 1975: 129)

The introduction suggested Hong Kong's unique role as a "laboratory" for globalization in the last two centuries. This chapter makes these insights concrete by introducing places and people in more detail, situating Hong Kong in time and space. It begins with two contemporary episodes that have reminded citizens of Hong Kong and people around the world of Hong Kong's global centrality after attention to the Handover faded. The first is the 2003 outbreak of SARS (Severe Acute Respiratory Syndrome), a disease that probably originated in nearby Guangdong but spread to Hong Kong and then to the rest of the world. Human interactions transmitted SARS — people attending weddings, visiting homes, traveling on business — and underscored Hong Kong's role as a bridge between worlds, intensified by many daily international flights. A second, ongoing question arose in the summer of 2003 around Mainland China's attempts to strengthen ideological control of Hong Kong through laws on subversion. Responses, via marches, editorials, and conversations, have continued ever since. Citizens have taken to the streets to define their rights and values in ways that neither the colonial regime nor the negotiated rule of "One Country, Two Systems" had anticipated. While seemingly more local, Hong Kong's reactions echo debates within China and embody global questions about "Western democracy" that arise from its history as an outpost of British law in Asia, albeit a colonized city where "freedoms" were circumscribed.

This chapter also explores Hong Kong space, time, and people through a tour of the territory that provides a context for subsequent chapters. The chapter ends with the Walled City of Kowloon as a microcosm within a microcosm that illustrates how experiences and interpretations of a single place over time can have global implications. A relic of nineteenth century treaty negotiations that left Chinese sovereign territory within the British controlled "New Territories," this settlement took on new meanings as Chinese refugees flooded Hong Kong after the 1949 Chinese Revolution. Apparently outside both colonial and Chinese authority, the Walled City became a vertical shantytown whose towers harbored residences, factories, schools, legal and illegal enterprises, and entertainment. Its population surpassed thirty thousand, but was crammed onto six acres — three million people per square mile! — while it gained mythic fame as a warren of vice and danger. Only Hong Kong's prospective return to China permitted a Sino–British decision to tear down the Walled City, but its legend survives within cyberspace and science fiction.

HONG KONG AS A GLOBAL SPECTACLE: SARS AND ARTICLE 23

SARS arrived in Hong Kong from China in the spring of 2003. While treaties severed Hong Kong from southern China in the nineteenth century, it remains part of that ecosystem (Marks 1998). People and goods have continually crossed borders (about four million people cross between Hong Kong and China at Lo Wu every month). Epidemics are even less likely to observe political boundaries. Within months, SARS killed some 300 people in Hong Kong and spread across the world, despite quarantines that attempted to isolate the region (See Loh and Citizens Exchange 2004; Thomas 2004).

SARS probably originated in Southern China. In 2002 and 2003, rumors already abounded about a strange strain of pneumonia in the contiguous Guangdong province, but most people in Hong Kong gave little attention to it, except to observe that people were consuming a great deal of vinegar as a folk cure. Health experts have identified the fertile tropical lands and booming cities of South China as a hotbed of infectious diseases — although the reasoning that people there live closer to animals or eat a varied palate of wild game hardly distinguishes this zone from many other areas of the world.

Historically, the third Bubonic Plague pandemic had spread via Hong Kong in 1894, often turning Chinatown connections into suspected nodes of contamination (Shah 1991; Echenberg 2002; Mohr 2005). Later influenza labels betray a geography of culpability as envisioned by the West; the first "Hong Kong flu" pandemic in 1968 caused more than thirty thousand deaths worldwide. Before SARS, regional avian flu epidemics in 1997 and 1998 had also received global publicity as thousands of chickens were slaughtered and vital supply lines were cut between Hong Kong and the People's Republic of China (PRC); epidemiologists and journalists still watch this changing disease as another potential "Asian" threat to global health.

Thanks to the aggressive investigation of Hong Kong scientists and global health workers, the human story of SARS has been well-mapped. In March 2003, a Mainland Chinese doctor who had been treating patients with this atypical pneumonia crossed from Guangdong province to Hong Kong for a wedding. He stayed on the ninth floor of the Metropole Hotel in Mong Kok. While there, he unknowingly infected seven other guests on the same floor: three from Singapore, one from Vietnam, two from Canada, and one local. The local guest later entered Prince of Wales Hospital in Sha Tin, where he infected medical personnel, workers, other patients, and visitors; more than 100 medical personnel eventually became infected with the disease. At the end of March, a patient from the Prince of Wales Hospital transmitted the disease to a private high-rise housing cluster in Kowloon Bay, Amoy Gardens, where 300 people were infected. By April 15th, 321 SARS cases had been diagnosed in Hong Kong. Schools closed and people avoided crowded places, venturing into the streets wearing protective masks amid constant flurries of cleaning. Quarantines, meanwhile, made escape difficult. In the end, the World Health Organization (WHO) documented 1755 SARS cases and 299 deaths in Hong Kong before the epidemic faded (WHO Web site).

The infected international visitors created a worldwide chain of SARS cases that followed family connections and hospital contacts. Here, the social meanings of Hong Kong's century-old connections with Southeast Asia (Nanyang), North America (Gum Shan/Golden Mountain), and Great Britain took on tragic meanings as new victims sickened and died. The WHO eventually documented 8076 cases in 28 countries (nearly 20 percent among health care workers) and 799 fatalities (see WHO Web site).

SARS highlighted Hong Kong's economic and social integration with the rest of the world. As people traveling to, from, and through Hong Kong became suspected carriers of this mysterious yet deadly disease, Hong Kong fell into an economic slump. Tourists and business visitors avoided the city, emptying hotels and restaurants. Hong Kong business-people could not attend a watch convention in Basel, while the University of California barred Hong Kong students from its summer program. Some even worried about the safety of packages and goods shipped from the port. Chinatowns worldwide also saw a drop in their business, despite local endorsements by politicians and celebrities. In Toronto, where the disease arrived via a Chinese woman from Hong Kong, some questioned immigration policies as well.

Globalization also entails a flow of information. While the first case of SARS did not occur in Hong Kong, the territory boasted more open, accurate reporting procedures than China, which most believed concealed the seriousness of outbreaks in Beijing and other areas. Since the Hong Kong Health Authority could identify the first patients of the outbreak, its data pro-vided crucial information about the disease and its spread. In 2004, as researchers watched for recurrences amid new concerns about the avian flu, Hong Kong went on high alert as a regional information and laboratory center for the WHO. By Summer 2005, however, officials discussed the possible disappearance of SARS as an epidemic (Yardley 2005) despite the WHO's concerns for the future.

The "global" impression, then, is that Hong Kong has infrastructures, both informational and medical, that are closer than other cities of China or the region to what the West has recognized as legitimate, scientific, and functional. Because of its colonial history and its capitalist success story, Western (and other) governments have construed Hong Kong to be more enlightened and more honest than so-called Third World cities; Hong Kong is a place with which the world can do business. Yet the SARS crisis was still shaped by its links to the ecosystem and the people of South China.

A few weeks after the quarantine measures were finally lifted, Hong Kongers again claimed a global spotlight through massive demonstrations on July 1st, the sixth anniversary of the Handover, to oppose the passage of Article 23 — the Anti-Subversion Law. Here, global observers questioned not Hong Kong's safety, but China's willingness to maintain the "one country, two systems" model that had been negotiated to preserve Hong Kong's distinct political and economic character after reunification. Nonetheless, public protest had its roots in colonial history as well as talks in the 1980s that produced the Basic Law, which established Hong Kong's status within the PRC.

The clause in question had a troubled history. After the June 4, 1989, Tiananmen Square protests, in which Chinese troops quashed a student/populist occupation of China's most visible symbolic place, an amendment to create an antisubversion and national security law was added to the Basic Law, as drafted under the aegis of the 1984 Sino–British Joint Declaration establishing Hong Kong's return to China. Since the Handover, Hong Kong is constitutionally required to uphold Article 23; however, this law was never codified. Neither the administration nor the Legislative Council ever drafted a bill to define it. In 2003, however, the SAR government, under its postcolonial Chief Executive Tung Chee-hwa, proposed a draconian bill that meant that crimes such as subversion, treason, and sedition against the state could result in life imprisonment. Peaceful demonstration itself could be banned; someone could be charged with sedition if she handled publications merely "likely to induce a person to commit" subversive acts. In its initial version, the article would have banned in Hong Kong any organization banned in China, such as the Falun Gong religious group. Moreover, this law would have permitted police to search without a warrant in the case of issues of national security.

The British colonial administration also had used police, censorship, and more subtle manipulations to suppress popular uprisings. During the 1925 General Strike (probably unknown to most 2003 protestors), for example, the colonial government manipulated news and organizations (Tsai 1993). Colonial *Hong Kong Reports* routinely noted that all films were reviewed by a "Panel of Film Censors" before being screened. In fact, the 1997 Hong Kong International Film Festival highlighted this fading colonial function with a program entitled "I Have a Date with Censors" that showcased films banned or altered for political reasons.

Despite this colonial legacy — sometimes concealed by colonial education about British benevolence — the potential enforcement of Article 23 struck many Hong Kong Chinese as a threat imposed by Beijing through the pro-China Hong Kong administration. It violated expectations of individual freedom under British common law, even though Great Britain had never incorporated Chinese masses in Hong Kong as full citizens. The Chinese government, moreover, has never gained the trust of the Hong Kong people in jurisprudence or human rights. Drafted with little public consultation during difficult social times, the bill sparked widespread unease. Still, the administration and the Secretary of Security Regina Ip sought hurried passage by July 9, 2003. On July 1st, however, over five hundred thousand people marched in Hong Kong to protest. Ip lost her post and Tung withdrew the bill until further consultation, with the blessing of China.

Readings of these events traveled far beyond Hong Kong. *Time Asia* read the story as a monumental event for China itself:

> It was the largest pro-democracy protest anywhere in China since 1989. No matter how the authorities respond — be it defiance, compromise or capitulation — the marchers have made one of the most effective statements of popular will ever in the history of the People's Republic. At stake is whether the world's next superpower will tolerate a democratic model of development in one of its supposedly showcase cities. . . .
>
> The irony for Hong Kong, and China, may be that such a crisis could end with a rejuvenated, more confident city that is once again viewed internationally as a dynamic center of culture and commerce. Contrary to Beijing's and perhaps Tung's fears, increased freedoms for Hong Kong may mean greater stability in the territory. (Fitzpatrick 2003)

Time Asia's interests went beyond democracy and human rights: "Multinational corporations and international investors would be reassured that rule of law exists, public opinion matters, and due process is observed — in short, that Hong Kong is not just another Chinese city" (Fitzpatrick 2003). For many in Hong Kong, however, Hong Kong is a uniquely Chinese "global city," or even "Asia's World City," never just *another* Chinese showcase city.

Repercussions of Chinese control continue to haunt Hong Kong. In 2004, for example, Beijing insisted that only those who are "patriots" for China may be elected to office in Hong

Kong's increasingly contested legislative and executive races (Kahn 2004). By April 2004, the PRC government issued explanations about the HKSAR's ability to interpret its law, especially on the issue of popular election. Building on the "success" of the march on July 1, 2003, the oppositional Democratic Party started to demand direct popular election of the Hong Kong legislature and the Chief Executive in the next election then scheduled for 2007. In the language of the Basic Law, changes to election rules demand assent from a two-thirds majority of the Legislative Council, the Chief Executive, and the National People's Congress Standing Committee. On April 6, 2004, the Standing Committee met and decided that since the PRC is a "one-system" unified state, the Mainland government would have the ultimate power to decide such a change of law. It stressed that the "actual situation" of Hong Kong needed to be understood and changes implemented under the principle of "gradual and orderly progress." An editorial from *Hong Kong Economic Journal* stated: "For people who are fighting for democracy, in the next few years they will be faced with the realities of a 'bird cage' politics. Beijing has consolidated its power to control the change in electoral laws. If the Democrats want to have concrete political gains, they have to start a dialogue with the mainland government" (April 7, 2004, p. 1).

Mainland China would not allow Hong Kong full power on legislative matters any more than it would allow such a request from Tibet. Public demonstrations followed, while three outspoken prodemocracy radio hosts left Hong Kong, allegedly facing threats. Protests erupted again — on July 1, 2004, three hundred thousand or more people again took to the streets to demand a wider franchise. Nonetheless, democratic leaders have not been able to build on this energy in legislative elections. And China continues to offer new persuasions in its vision of a racial/familial and culturally harmonious Greater China — bringing its 2004 Olympic medalists, for example, to Hong Kong after the Athens Olympiad to incorporate Hong Kongers into China's success.

Hong Kong people enjoy a semidemocratic political structure left by the British who initiated such changes, knowing that they had to leave in 1997. But China now has the final say. This, in many ways, mirrors Hong Kong's experience under British rule, where people enjoyed a certain degree of freedom, but with the British holding the final say. The "bird cage" has never left Hong Kong, leaving the Western press trying to make sense of it. A *New York Times* editorial makes this clear:

> Such clumsy overreaching by China's leaders is ultimately self-defeating. It imperils Hong Kong's stature as a financial center, which is partly predicated on the rule of law. It also serves to fuel the pro-democracy movement, which deserves the support of the outside world, especially Britain, which pushed for Hong Kong's autonomy when it agreed to the handover. If other countries appear not to be concerned about the fate of the territory's people, the Chinese government will feel little compulsion to abide by its commitments. And there will be even less reason to expect that the nation's economic liberalization will ever pay democratic dividends to the one billion other people in China. (April 23, 2004)

We do not equate globalization with how the West has perceived Hong Kong. Nor is it simply a process of differentiation from China or an alternative to Mainland models. Instead, the events we have chronicled underscore the creative tension of Hong Kong's positions. Global contacts and experiences have meant that most people in Hong Kong see themselves as different from Chinese on the Mainland, in Taiwan, or overseas. Be it their colonial education, their free economy and consumption of goods and ideas from around the world, or a belated exposure to limited democracy, many in Hong Kong believe they have a relatively more open, enlightened government than that of the state to which they belong. Nonetheless, anyone who has ever visited Hong Kong notices that it is a very Chinese city, although many social and cultural practices resemble those of other metropolitan global cities like New York, London, or Tokyo. Globalization in Hong Kong, then, embodies similarity and difference, intersections and hybrid creations of new forms of life that permeate the city and the lives of its citizens.

PLACING HONG KONG

Despite the way it is often discussed, Hong Kong is not a city per se. Hong Kong actually designates both the 30 square mile (80 square kilometer) island of Hong Kong (from the Cantonese *Heung Geung* [Xianggang in Mandarin], meaning "Fragrant Harbor") and the entire territory, encompassing the Kowloon Peninsular to the north and the New Territories, which includes 230-plus outlying islands. Together, these constituted the land of the Crown Colony from 1898 to 1997 and the contemporary administrative unity of the HKSAR. The core urbanization of the north coast of the island was baptized Victoria (today's Wan Chai, Central, and Sheung Wan), and the harbor also bears the name of the British monarch. Roughly one-fifth of the total population resides on the island (mainly on the north coast) and another 31 percent across the harbor in Kowloon. The government, which owns all land (with rare exceptions), has controlled development by leasing plots for terms ranging from 75 to 999 years

Population distribution recognizes the impact of geography as well. While the deepwater harbor brought trade and wealth to Hong Kong, the steep slopes of the island kept its growing population from occupying much of the island. Hence, over the past 150 years, Hong Kong has become vertical, taming the slopes with money and technology, building ever higher buildings on flat land and reclaiming space from the harbor. The competing towers of Hong Kong and its vibrant population density — averaging 6,480 persons per square kilometer (similar to New York City and Paris), but peaking at 55,020 per square kilometer (Kwun Tung, Kowloon) — epitomize the urbanism of the contemporary global city. Kowloon has achieved and maintained even higher density than Hong Kong.

Since World War II, legal and illegal settlements in formerly rural spaces and infill reclamations of shorelines (a process that began earlier in Central) have expanded land for buildings. Legal developments, whether public housing estates or new elite centers, often replicate the verticality of central Hong Kong, spires of urbanization surrounded by the remnants of agricultural land or framed against the South China Sea. Nonetheless, despite the push to build, much of Hong Kong's territory remains open space. Twenty-three country parks and fifteen special areas cover 41,852 hectares of "nonbuildable" spaces and those maintained for recreation and environmental preservation — 40 percent of the HKSAR's total surface area.

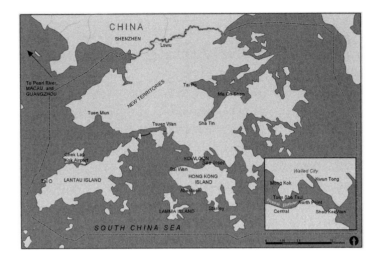

Figure 1.1
Map of Hong Kong. (Courtesy of Cartographic Modeling Laboratory of the University of Pennsylvania.)

Perhaps the most emblematic image of Hong Kong is that of the Central framed by the harbor and the Peak, seen from Kowloon (Figure 1.1). Lit by fireworks or adorned with thousands of lights for New Year's displays, Central offers an unmistakable but ever-changing landscape. Fifty years ago, this cityscape still would have incorporated old colonial-style buildings with arched porticos and balconies on warehouses, as well as public and commercial buildings, interrupted by the more modernist landmarks of the Hongkong and Shanghai Bank and Bank of China. In the last few decades, however, this landscape has been rebuilt, at times more than once, seeking ever higher rents and prestige from limited space. "Historical" buildings like the 1912 neoclassical Supreme Court building (now the Legislative Council), the International Style Central

Market, crowded Chinese stalls along narrow rising streets, and even the 1960s City Hall (a performance space rather than a governmental one) have been dwarfed by masses of tall buildings. Here, major Hong Kong and international businesses have their headquarters in some of the most expensive commercial real estate in the world, surrounded by exclusive shopping centers, hotels, restaurants, and clubs. Central also provides a connecting point for mass transit systems (including ferries to Kowloon and other islands), subways, buses, minibuses, trams, highways, and a dense web of overhead passages connecting the skyscrapers above the street (see images on the Discover Hong Kong Web site).

Like many global "downtowns," Central grows quiet at night when offices close. The rowdier Lan Kwai Fong, slightly uphill, developed roughly twenty years ago as a cosmopolitan night spot with a special appeal for expatriates (S. Cheng 2001). Yet, movies, restaurants, and other entertainment also light up Wan Chai, Causeway Bay, and Kowloon. A more striking transformation of this central space occurs on Sundays, when public spaces, the overhead passages connecting buildings, and even the open ground floor of the modern Hongkong and Shanghai Bank building teem with thousands of expatriate maids, mainly from the Philippines, who gather with their friends on their day off, feeling unwelcome in malls or other places that expect consumption. These women, nearly two hundred thousand in the new millennium, have become mainstays of dual career families but escape their demands at home one day a week to come together, sit on the ground, share food, gossip, play music, and domesticate public spaces. Anthropologist Nicole Constable, who has studied Filipino maids in Hong Kong, highlights the conflict in this occupation of space as

Hong Kongers complain about "a nightmare with the atmosphere of a third-rate amusement park" (1997: 4). Filipinos, in turn, see these complaints as attempts to hide Hong Kong's dependence on their labor (Escoda 1994).

Above Central, the Mid-levels and higher zones on the Peak have been elite residential areas since colonizers claimed special rights to their cooling breezes, even if summer typhoons and mudslides have threatened construction on these slopes. Walking upward, one passes the Anglican Cathedral, the American Consulate, the Roman Catholic Cathedral, the Governor's House, and the Hong Kong Botanical Gardens. Although the Peak's onetime racial segregation has disappeared (see chapter 2), the further up one goes, the more exclusively residential and residentially exclusive it becomes, with fewer and fewer commercial activities before the tourist complex at the summit. In other areas of the territory, however, "unbuildable" hills became refugee and squatter areas, although many have been gradually replaced with public and private developments (see chapter 3).

Moving westward from the Central Harbor, past major department stores and voluminous restaurants, an outdoor escalator links Central to the residential Mid-levels near the University of Hong Kong. This combination of 20 escalators and 3 moving stairways travels 800 meters while moving 135 meters upwards. Its escalators snake downward between buildings to Central in the morning and run upward later in the day. Opened in 1993 at a cost of HK$240 million (US$30 million), it showed Hong Kong to be a wealthy city whose public works went beyond housing and welfare. Its intersection with commercial streets has generated its own new yuppie area, nicknamed SoHo for "South of Hollywood Road" (as well as being a reference to New York and London).

Such transnational references are not uncommon in a global city: A 1994 shopping and entertainment complex in Causeway Bay, for example, is named "Times Square" and a development in Kowloon is named "Hollywood Plaza." Yet, in a city whose population is nearly all Chinese, even expatriate and tourist areas cater to a predominantly Chinese clientele.

Further west, the Chinese immigrant population of the island settled in the mid-nineteenth century in today's Sheung Wan and Sai Wan. While Chinese villages and boat clusters existed before colonization, they tended to be in southern coastal areas. These new areas hosted immigrants who created a new "Chinatown" in Hong Kong. Sheung Wan still shelters important institutions such as Man Mo Temple, and streets here sometimes have retained a more "traditional" ambience with businesses that trade dried goods like shark fins, abalones, salted fish, and Chinese medicine. As ethnographer Frank Leeming noted, these are *nam-pak-hong* businesses, whose local space is an intermediary point in a trade of goods from China (and Korea for ginseng or Japan for mushrooms) to the South (*nam/nanyang*) or the New World (1977: 46–49). Hong Kong Chinese refer to the World War II–era three- and four-story buildings left in the area, where owners would live with their goods above ground floor businesses, as "Chinese buildings" (*Tong Lau*). Director Ann Hui's 1979 film *The Secret* captures and accentuates this atmosphere, as do the introductory location shots from the Hollywood film *Love Is a Many-Splendored Thing* (1955). Still, these residential and commercial edifices diverged from Chinese models even in the nineteenth century. Today, their effusive neon and project-ing signs dueling to control layers of space above the trams and buses of the streets below have created a cityscape as characteristic of Hong Kong as Central — and apparently as transient. The Western crossharbor tunnel has opened this area to rapid change, as sleek skyscrapers replace tattered buildings and gaudy signage.

To the east of Central, areas like Admiralty, Wan Chai, and Causeway Bay have undergone continuous development from prewar slums to mixtures of commercial, industrial, and residential high-rises that jumble classes and function, although Wan Chai still evokes images of the fictional bar girl Suzie Wong for some tourists (an imagery in which the Hong Kong Tourist Association is complicit). Today, the wings of the new Convention Center completed for the Handover jut into the harbor here, symbol of a new Hong Kong. Above Admiralty, onetime British barracks were replaced by 1990 with Hong Kong Park, a favorite scene for wedding photos on sunny weekends, and Pacific Place, an upscale mall anchored by the Japanese department store Seibu and Hong Kong's own Lane Crawford. The mall, in turn, is a podium for top hotels and is flanked by the Hong Kong Supreme Court and the British Council. Causeway Bay, another nearby bustling shopping and residential area, also includes Victoria Park, where Hong Kongers celebrate the mid-Autumn festival and Chinese New Year and also have commemorated Tiananmen Square.

Happy Valley, its historic cemeteries, and its racetrack lie to the South. East of Causeway Bay is North Point, famed as a center for Shanghainese exiles after 1949 (Richardson 1977). Eastbound trams reach Shau Kei Wan, a former fishing village antedating British colonialism. It is now engulfed by high-rises and corporate complexes that stretch ever further eastward along the subway and highways into lands populated by squatters only scant decades ago.

For decades, reaching the south side of Hong Kong Island entailed circumnavigating the island by boat or driving along winding mountain roads. Since 1982, the Aberdeen tunnel has linked this less-urbanized coast to Central in minutes. The South's major Chinese settlement is Aberdeen (*Heung Geung Jai* or "little Hong Kong"), another former fishing village and tourist site, whose massed boat dwellers and Jumbo Floating Restaurant have appeared in movies for decades. Most boat-dwellers have, in fact, moved ashore, and the nearby spit of land known as Duck Tongue Island (Ap Lei Chau) boasts high-rise middle class apartment towers clustered around a mall.

The other characteristic settlement pattern of the South is a sort of suburban development, transferring the "bourgeois utopia" of British suburbia to a colonial setting (Fishman 1987). This includes the residential resort Repulse Bay, the private home compounds of Shek O, and the more touristic Stanley, as well as the Hong Kong Country Club and the American Club. These exclusive areas lack major commercial development, much less the street life of urban Chinese neighborhoods. Pok Fu Lam, on the west coast, shares some of these characteristics but may change through development of the new Hong Kong Cyberport (see chapter 6).

While Hong Kong Island has historically controlled population, money, and prestige, it represents less than 10 percent of the land mass of the SAR. When China ceded Kowloon to the British in 1860, it more than doubled colonial territory and gave the British full control of both sides of the harbor. This sheltered harbor, whose navigation channels range from ten to twenty meters deep, provides a good vantage to control the nearby Pearl River and remains one of the world's busiest ports, although container wharfs and storage have been pushed further along the coast by urban development. More than ten thousand watercraft go through this harbor each day. Still, the pressures of land reclamation on both sides have reduced the channel to one kilometer at its narrowest, and raise questions about its ability to cleanse itself of pollution.

Kowloon today is more densely populated than Hong Kong, with more than two million people in 47 square kilometers. Its diverse neighborhoods range from the "garden city" of Kowloon Tong to the night market of Temple Street, another frequent tourist snapshot and movie backdrop (*C'est La Vie, Mon Cherie* 1993).

Kowloon Tong's single family homes and walled gardens again recall colonial suburbanization that borrowed British patterns. At Kowloon's southernmost tip is Tsim Sha Tsui, where most tourists stay. Before the subway opened in 1979, Tsim Sha Tsui was the most accessible point to Central: a short, pleasant Star Ferry ride connected them. Its stores, hotels, and amusements echo those of Central; indeed, the elegant Peninsula Hotel has been an elite center since its foundation, and high tea in its lobby remains a quintessential "colonial" experience in a postcolonial city. This area also hosts cultural facilities like the Cultural Centre, Museums of History and Science, the major urban mosque, and Kowloon Park.

Further northwest, Yau Ma Tei and Mong Kok (which literally means "Popular Place") represent the densest and busiest areas of the HKSAR, with street markets, factories, small businesses of all kinds (legal and illegal), and residents crammed on the top floors. These areas are busy, messy, loud, and, at times, disorderly; few Western expatriates frequent these streets. They have also served as a heartland for Hong Kong movies, both in terms of spectatorship and representation. Mong Kok theaters are famous for late-night showings and rowdy audiences; Yau Ma Tei houses both one of the oldest remaining cinemas in the SAR (now specializing in pornography) and a sleek new art cinema (Wong and McDonogh 2001a). Director Fruit Chan's *Durian, Durian* (2000) uses this area to portray the lives of recent illegal Chinese immigrants.

West Kowloon has been targeted for future and global development under a master plan designed by Sir Norman Foster, who envisions urbanization of open (industrial/shipping) lands under a swooping plastic canopy. Preeminent global museums like the Pompidou Center and New York's Guggenheim and MOMA have sought a place in this 100-acre site that "resembles an immense dragon and will become a symbol of the city to compare with the Eiffel Tower in Paris or the Sydney Opera House" (Bradsher 2005a). Such an architectural counterpoint to the Handover's Convention Center has been attacked by civic groups who view the plan as elite development that will not respond to pressing social needs. (See Civic Exchange and Friends of the Harbour Web sites for local comments.)

To the northeast of Tsim Sha Tsui lie Hung Hom, To Kwa Wan, and Kowloon City, where Kai Tak airport anchored a dramatic approach to the city until 1998. These are all densely mixed, medium-rise residential and commercial areas, and once included the Walled City (see below).

Beyond Kowloon, a different world once opened up that is hardly imaginable to anyone crossing Boundary Street today. The British acquired the New Territories on a 99-year lease in 1898. This 960 square kilometer "buffer against the Chinese" (including 176 square kilometers of islands) constitutes nearly 90 percent of Hong Kong's territory, with about half the population. Here, precolonial agricultural towns and fishing villages also have undergone rapid growth and cultural transformation (see Hayes 1977, 1983; Faure 1986; Faure, Hayes, and Birch 1984; Hase and Sinn 1995). When Wong was growing up in the 1960s, the New Territories still meant the countryside, with walled villages, rice paddies, and duckponds. Postwar development has created dynamic urban nuclei like Sha Tin, which, with its own "suburbs" like Ma On Shan, now houses one million people as well as the Chinese University of Hong Kong, a race track, and many malls. New towns (planned urban nuclei) extend along mass transit lines from Kowloon to the newly permeable Chinese border. For example, Tsuen Wan, a fishing and farming village founded in the seventeenth century, was known in the nineteenth century for pirates and the pineapples and fresh produce it sent to Victoria. By the twenty-first century, it has become a world center for cargo traffic, with a population passing five hundred thousand (Hayes 1993). High-rise private developments with names like Gold Coast and even a townhouse development called Palm Springs along the border complicate the socioeconomic panorama of contemporary New Territories development (Ruggeri 2002). Meanwhile, "traditional" villages like Kam Tim and the Tang clan also have changed, as agricultural land becomes real estate and women demand the rights they might hold elsewhere in Hong Kong (Lee and DiStefano 2002).

Finally, to the north lies China. Geologically, climatologically, socially, and culturally, Hong Kong is part of Guangdong and China. Yet, Hong Kong has been carved away by political processes, turning regional and national relations into complex webs of change (see chapter 5).

The "other" islands of Hong Kong vary in size, function, and history. The largest, Lantau, is actually bigger than Hong

Kong Island and closer to the Pearl River to the west. There, the old village of Tai O, with its stilt houses above a small waterway, seemed distant from sleek Central even in the late-twentieth century (Wong Wai King 2000). Lantau also hosts a large Buddhist monastery and the cosmopolitan suburbanism of Discovery Bay, accessible by water from the bustle of Central. Since the 1990s, the mega-project of the new airport, bridges, trains, and highways have transformed the physiognomy of the island, integrating it into the entire region. The future Hong Kong Disneyland (to be open in 2005) is also located on Lantau. Other islands, such as Cheung Chau, Lamma, and Peng Chau offer smaller and less busy landscapes amid country parks. Many islands are uninhabited and have served as bases for pirates, smugglers, and refugees over decades — hence their early Portuguese name, the Ladrones.

Geographical and social complexity should not obscure the small size of the HKSAR — between New York City (784 square kilometers) and Los Angeles (1202). Moreover, its dense urban fabric is further integrated by history, family ties, overlapping institutions, and mass media. Constant movement also integrates the city — the throngs in the streets and markets as well as an excellent mass transportation system that moves more than three million people every day. Despite a 100 percent tariff on cars (that are not produced locally), streets and highways are usually clogged. Even buildings seem to fall and rise anew with startling speed across the HKSAR.

At the same time, Hong Kong constantly participates in the world. Since 1997, connections by bus, ferry, and train have grown with China, while the new Chek Lap Kok airport, on Lantau, is one of the busiest in the world, handling thirty million passengers on sixty airlines each year (and two million tons of cargo). Yet, it has no "domestic" flights. The city and its varied places and peoples are both local and global, as we show in one final example.

THE WALLED CITY: GLOBALIZATION IN A SMALL SPACE

This book begins with Hong Kong as an intersection of two empires and ends with Hong Kong people and media dispersing through and imagining the larger world. Yet, globalization also transforms everyday life and place. Perhaps no place made this more evident than the Walled City of Kowloon, a miniscule (2.7 hectare/6 acre) space created by a loophole in 1898 treaty negotiations between China and Great Britain. Once possessing some of the most dense housing in the world, the site is now a landscaped park rendering homage to Ming and Qing traditions with scant recognition of the alternate city that rose there (Halter 2000). Where illegal skyscrapers once rose, new Chinese pavilions provide relaxation for the elderly while children race their bicycles and Filipina maids socialize. Video games, Web sites, and creative artists, however, have given the Walled City a new life as a virtual city for those who may never have seen it in a physical form (Figure 1.2).

From its inception, the Walled City was a place of cross-cultural interpretation and imagery transcending mundane reality. In the mid-nineteenth century, when Chinese constructed its walls after British destruction of an earlier Kowloon fortress, the site contained a school, a temple, and an administrative center and residences. More problematic for the British were the environs of the fort, with "numerous factories, shops and gambling dens in its narrow, evil-smelling roadways" (Wesley-Smith 1980: 18). As a local market center,

Figure 1.2
The Walled City of Kowloon, 1992 (photograph by the authors).

this zone attracted clients from Hong Kong Island even before China ceded Kowloon to Great Britain in 1860.

Problems grew with the 1898 New Territories lease. Having learned from their experiences with other treaty ports, the Chinese refused to relinquish the magistrate's domain. While Britain slowly extended its power in the leased territories, Chinese resistance turned the Walled City into an ambiguous interstitial space. As historian Peter Wesley-Smith concludes, "Hong Kong residents distrusted Chinese officials and objected strenuously to the fort and the suburban area, whereas to the Chinese in Peking the Walled City was a government installation, a visible symbol of imperial control constructed for the very purpose of discouraging British interference in the region" (1980: 18).

Over time, coastal reclamation pushed the space further and further inland, still surrounded by housing and businesses of the colonial metropolis. By the 1920s, it was a refuge for squatters. During World War II, the Japanese tore down its walls to rebuild nearby Kai Tak airport, but did not eliminate the site, which became more imposing with the influx of refugees after World War II. Attempts to evict its squatters in 1946 sparked riots in nearby Guangzhou (Canton). After 1949, further waves of refugees, who swamped Hong Kong's housing system, began to build upward, creating massed vertical towers, while the Communist takeover ruptured ties with Chinese sovereignty. Nonetheless, in the 1960s, attempts to resettle or reform the burgeoning settlement were met with formal protests in Beijing (Wesley-Smith 1980: 127–129).

In 1971, the census recorded 10,004 people living within the bounds of the former compound; at its height, the population of the area may have tripled that. Wesley-Smith's description of the area was dark, although curiously restrained about the multistory buildings that set it apart from other contemporary squatter settlements: "The mandarin's yamen is still there, and a temple, but the sense of spaciousness and almost solitude which must have existed before the second world war is now crowded out by twisting lanes, dark alleyways, malodorous open drains, clattering factories, brothels, gambling halls and drug dens, mangy dogs and dubious citizens" (1980: 129; compare Girard and Lambot 1993).

Yet, as ethnographers and journalists have shown, while the colonial government could not exercise complete regulation of the Walled City, neither was it the lawless zone outsiders read it to be. Residents received mail, firemen fought fires, sanitary engineers chlorinated wells, and police even patrolled its multilevel streets in the 1960s and 1970s. "Edges" of the site were demolished to promote safer landings at Kai Tak. Cooperative arrangements between resident organizations and local authorities partially laid the groundwork for later demolition (Wesley-Smith 1980: 130–135).

By the 1980s, the Walled City was doomed, a victim of British–Chinese rapprochement. In 1983, it received successive visits from both China's unofficial representative in the city (the head of the Xinhua News Service) and the Governor. After the 1984 Joint Declaration, its interstitial space evaporated. On January 14, 1987, the Hong Kong government and the Chinese Foreign Ministry announced plans to move and compensate residents and to clear the site, dealing with "a question left over from history" (cited in Wilkenson 1993: 71). Demolition and relandscaping were completed shortly before the Kai Tak airport closed. As a team of Hong Kong social scientists noted, the Chinese who lived there were more adaptable than the sovereignty issues that had created the place itself (Chan et al. 1991: 46, 64–66). Still, some residents protested as their buildings were systematically leveled.

When we visited the Walled City in the summer of 1992, only a few cats haunted dark corridors above the street level shops and temples. Yet the sheer verticality of the grassroots megastructure remained imposing, with ten- to twelve-story buildings propping each other up, honeycombed connections of multiple levels, and a rooftop forest of antennae from which one caught far too close a view of jets landing at the airport. This networked quality, which had given the Walled City a metaphoric function as well, was an artifact of postwar construction, as concrete buildings replaced wooden huts that were destroyed by fires in the 1940s. Resident Lam Shu Chuen asked, "How were these buildings erected without piling?

Well, you might consider it a miracle like Moses crossing the Red Sea. We used traditional Chinese ways. We excavated deep in the ground and then we built three storys. After that we built another three and then three more" (in Girard and Lambot 1993: 72; see Basler 1992; Ho 1993).

The Walled City was a symbolic as well as a social space. For Wong and her friends, for example, growing up on Hong Kong Island, it was a place that she saw from the outside and knew about, without ever visiting it. It was reputed to be an unlawful place, a haven for Triads (organized gangs with historical origins in anti-Manchu secret societies), prostitution, and drugs. Immigrants lived and worked there — notably, dentists from the Mainland, unlicensed in Hong Kong, who worked in this unregulated space. It also was famous for the production of fishballs, a compressed ground fish dumpling and staple Hong Kong street-hawker food. While this image seems jarring given the density and dirt there, one friend noted that "dirty was not that dirty in those days." That is, the Walled City recalled Hong Kong before its rise to a "world city."

In his 2004 memoir *Gweilo*, Martin Booth provided another vision of the Walled City from the perspective of a 1950s expatriate child growing up in Hong Kong: "It was to Hong Kong what the Casbah was to Algiers, with one exception: it was more or less closed to outsiders. . . . It was said that any European who entered it was never seen again unless floating out of it in the nullah (gutter) that served as a sewer" (cited in "Inside the Forbidden City" 2004).

Even those who attempted to reform the Walled City's people reinforced these images. Evangelist Jackie Pullinger, for example, who worked with drug addicts in the Walled City for years, conveyed images of darkness and depravity:

> I loved the dark city. I loved wandering down the narrow lanes
> which were like some exaggerated stageset. It upset me to see
> twelve- or thirteen-year-old prostitutes and to learn that these
> girls were not free, having been sold by parents or boyfriends.
> It troubled me to meet their minders — the aged *mamasans* who
> sat on orange boxes in the streets luring the Walled City voyeurs
> with promises of "she's very good, very young, very cheap."
> I noticed their hands, which were scarred on the back with
> needle marks from heroin injections which made the job
> bearable. Or maybe the job was to pay for the heroin. (1989: 7)

Heroin had replaced opium, and numbers had increased, but the images of the sold girl or dark and dank crowded residences evoke Chinese Hong Kong so clearly to generations of outsiders that the sense of "an exaggerated stageset" takes on dual meanings.

Chinese film imagery reinforced civic perceptions of the Walled City as well. Johnny Mak's 1986 gangster film *The Long Arm of the Law*, precursor to important works by John Woo and Ringo Lam in its violent choreography, shows Mainland soldiers entering Hong Kong for a bungled robbery attempt. After gunplay, sexual violence, and the murder of an undercover policemen, surviving gang members seek help from a physician in the Walled City. There, police trap them in a massacre of orgiastic violence, as bullets and blood pierce the walls of their refuge.

Before the Handover, however, the Walled City reappeared in a play that treated it as a site of Cantonese vernacular culture. In 1994, the Hong Kong Drama Society, Chinese Music Company and Dance Company coproduced a musical, *Walled City Rhapsody*, tracing the site from its origins to its demolition.

The musical recaptured the Walled City as a land of *sam but kuan* — not ruled by any of the three powers (China, Hong Kong, or Britain). Born with contact between China and the West, it was demolished with the departure of the West, while Qing officials, street peddlers, prostitutes, and fishball makers lived their lives there. Critics lamented the play's lack of historical context — but history was being erased as Hong Kong was rebuilt (Toe 1998).

Yet the Walled City did not disappear with its buildings. Japanese interest in this site of mysterious modernity led to an elegant volume on the Walled City in 1997 that included exquisitely detailed composites of multiple linked towers as well as historical and social data. Later, in a special issue of *Space and Design* dedicated to Hong Kong, critic Shin Muramatsu used his exposure to the Walled City through the video game Kowloon Gate to distill a tension between the past and the future in Hong Kong itself (see Kaima 1997; Kinashita 1997). The images of the game became Hong Kong "Gothic," which "might be described as a stratum of Chinese customs that the city has accumulated," where "what I might call 'Acceleration City' is the youthful power that acts destructively upon that stratum" (Muramatsu 1997: 12). For him, "The Hong Kong of 'Hong Kong Gothic' and the Hong Kong of 'Acceleration City' have in fact been alternating or overlapping in the course of history" (Muramatsu 1997: 12). While architect Kazuhiro Kajima proclaims later in the issue that "The Future Reveals itself in Hong Kong" (Kajima 1997: 50), references to the Walled City and links to Chungking Mansions evoke a tension between the old and the new, the Gothic and the ephemeral.

Chungking Mansions, an aging skyscraper on Nathan Road in Kowloon whose bottom floor houses a bazaarlike congerie of

Chinese and South Asian shops and stores, gained global fame with Wong Kar-Wai's 1994 film *Chungking Express.* Its upper floors house restaurants and cheap hotels serving immigrants from around the world; Africans, South Asians, and others mill around the elevators and food stands on the ground floor. Hong Kong people associate the building with South Asians, and stories abound about the complexities of ownership that keep this decaying building intact as newer skyscrapers are replaced around it. The film adds mystery and romance with its subplot of drug smuggling and betrayal, even as the director's rapid cuts and swirling action transmuted it into the aesthetics of a new, accelerated Hong Kong (Abbas 1997; Marchetti 2000).

Beyond video games, Japanese Webmasters also became involved in the creation of a virtual Walled City that attracted comments and visitors with its mixture of photos, memories, and information about the Walled City (the Virtual Walled City Web site is not currently available). In the site, architects, video gamers, tourists, and those nostalgic for a Hong Kong they will never see ("Is there nothing left of it?" lamented one Swedish correspondent) greeted occasional responses from Hong Kong residents who recalled it as a bad place, and even former inhabitants who complained of crowding and rats. This Web site included the atmosphere of the still-existing Chungking Mansions so as to embody the "scent of the Kowloon Walled City."

The cyberspacial Walled City expanded through American science fiction master William Gibson, who has modeled human places on it in his novels *Virtual Light* (1993), *Idoru* (1996) and *All Tomorrow's Parties* (1999). In the preface to *Idoru* (1996), Gibson credits his introduction to the Walled City to Japanese film director Sogho Ishii as part of a project for a science fiction film there. Photographs by Ryuji Miyamoto shaped Gibson's creation of a hyperdense illegal slum on the Golden Gate Bridge in *Virtual Light*. By *Idoru*, Gibson had encountered other secondary sources for the buildings and the Walled City metamorphosed into a cyberplace:

> buildings or biomass or cliff face looming there, in countless unplanned strata, nothing about it even or regular. Accreted patchwork of shallow random balconies, thousands of small windows throwing back blank silver rectangles of fog. Stretching either way to the periphery of vision and on the high, uneven crest of that ragged façade, a black fur of twisted pipe, antennas sagging under vine growth of cable. And part of this scribbled border a sky where colors crawled like gasoline on water. (1996: 131–132)

Gibson's transmutation of the real city into the virtual, the experience of Hong Kong into a metaphor, divorces the Walled City from its historical sense of place and people. Indeed, a casual Internet search finds the term "walled city" applied to clustering and dividing programs that may be completely unrelated to any Hong Kong history despite the evocative overlap. The Hollywood blockbuster *Batman Begins* (2005) also evokes the Walled City in the grim urban form of "the Narrows" as a city within the towering city of Gotham, again transmuting the now-disappeared site. For us, however, the Walled City, changing in form, personnel, meaning, and reality over two centuries, embodies fundamental features of the globalization of Hong Kong that are developed throughout this book. The creative destruction of the city — the transformations of space and people that occur with speed and dramatic shifts in trajectory — and the intersection of images and ideas of Hong Kong, local and global, allow it to be present to people who may never have visited the city. While Hong Kong is a small place, it has been and continues to be a point from which the world is not only viewed, but changed.

Two

Hong Kong has always been an unlikely place. Born of the China trade in the most dubious circumstances, it was scorned by its colonizers as a "barren rock" that would "never become a mart of trade." This 19th century forecast only goes to show that the perils of political prediction have a long pedigree. But it had its uses, for in a way it may have steeled the inhabitants of Hong Kong to a way of life that was always going to pit them against the odds. (Chief Secretary Anson Chan, Hong Kong Report 2000: 1)

For more than a century, the image of a "barren rock" has haunted Hong Kong. This phrase identified the island as a once-uninhabited, unused space completely *re*-created under British colonialism. Lord Palmerston, British foreign secretary at the time of possession, initially denigrated Britain's prize as "a barren island with hardly a House on it" (cited in Kai Cheung Chan 1993: 455). This dismissal took on a variety of imperial overtones over time. An 1893 British guidebook claimed that "for ages prior to the year 1841, it existed only as a plutonic island of uninviting sterility, apparently capable of supporting the lowest forms of organisms. To-day it stands forth before the world with its City of Victoria and a permanent population of over two hundred thousand souls — a noble monument to British pluck and enterprise" (*Hong Kong Guide* 1893: I).

A reader would hardly suspect that nearly all this population was Chinese; much less that Chinese had lived, worked, and ruled in this area for centuries before the British arrival. A 1924 English guidebook was more bluntly dismissive: "Hongkong has no history prior to its occupation by the British" (*Hong Kong* 1924: 1). Later, while the civil servant–historian G. R. Sayer recognized possible dual prefaces to the history of the island — "the story of British intercourse with China before the occupation and the story of the island before the occupation," — he added that, "With the latter I have little concern" (1980: 5).

Chinese and other historians have worked to refute this pervasive image (see Lo et al. 1959; Yu and Liu 1993, 1995). In the 1993 *Other Hong Kong Report* (one of an important series of collections whose scholarship and political questions go beyond the government *Hong Kong Report*), Chan Kai-Cheung systematically refuted this pervasive myth by a review of settlement evidence since the Bronze Age. He paid special attention to incorporation of the area into Chinese politics, including its role in the final months of the Southern Song and the later forced evacuation of the whole coast in the seventeenth century that created an appearance of emptiness (1993: 455–483). Liu Shuyang's Mainland history of Hong Kong, published for the Handover, devotes its first twenty pages to the area before "British Occupation" (1997: 1–23; see H. Lo 1959; Yu and Liu 1993). Today, visitors to Hong Kong's refurbished History Museum must ascend to the Opium Wars and British occupation, while the initial exhibits on the ground floor offer a long saga of formation from geological processes through the Qing dynasty and Hong Kong folklife.

Tensions over this myth of origin exemplify the conflicting claims to ownership that have appeared repeatedly in Hong

Kong. Claims that Hong Kong was a product of British intervention reinforced its status as a Crown Colony. For the Chinese, for whom the Opium Wars inaugurated years of shame only partially assuaged by the 1997 Handover, this claim was not only a wrong-headed example of British imperialism, but also a violation of continuities of land, people, sovereignty that Hong Kong shares with China.

Still, neither empire prized this hybrid consistently. For the British, Hong Kong remained a "hardship" posting through the 1990s, with ample housing allowances for civil servants posted there and provisions to educate their children in England. Meanwhile, as critic Poshek Fu notes, Chinese (Mainland) elites described Hong Kong as "beyond the pale of civilization," a "cultural desert" even as the colony developed in the twentieth century (2003: 51). Colonial Hong Kong represented both a site of profound global clashes of place, power, and meaning and a divided city, embodying Frantz Fanon's characterization of the colonial city as "a world cut in two" where "the two zones are opposed, but not in the service of a higher unity" (1963: 38).

Ultimately, citizens of Hong Kong have refuted the image of a barren rock by claiming their own history, as is evident in the initial citation from Anson Chan Fang On-Sang, Chief Secretary before and after the Handover. That a polity characterized by "Borrowed Time, Borrowed Place" (Hughes 1976 from author Han Suyin) or an "Aesthetics of Disappearance" (Abbas 1997) — to cite two pre-Handover titles — continues to grow and change in the new millennium reminds us that globalism itself must be read from multiple vantage points. Still, even for Chinese who live there, Hong Kong can seem a placeless place, a space of transience rather than commitment, of future rather than past (Abbas 1997). As Chan continues, in fact, her vision of history flows into a world where place disappears and the Hong Kong Special Administrative Region (HKSAR) becomes "Asia's City for the Cyber Century. Hong Kong is gearing up to take its place in a world without walls" (2000: 2).

This chapter reviews Hong Kong's origins and its colonial development in its first century. To illuminate the intersections of Imperial China and Imperial Britain, we begin with opium, the key symbol and commodity of early contacts. In trade, in war, and in the financing and life of the colony thereafter, opium was present from the birth of the colony through World War II. The chapter then goes on to discuss the people and issues of the first century of the colonial city in two broad portraits: Hong Kong as a divided city through the 1880s, after the British also had taken Kowloon, and early-twenti-eth-century Hong Kong, a more established urban society complicated by race, class, gender, and hybridity. In the latter period, for example, elite Chinese began to formally advise the Governor, while other Chinese took to the streets to protest actions by Britain, Japan, and the United States.

OPIUM AND EMPIRE

The Opium War (Yapian Zhanzheng), directed by Xie Jin, premiered in Beijing on July 1, 1997. Its director called it a "special gift for the motherland and the people . . . to ensure we and our descendants forever remember the humiliation the nation once suffered" (see the Opium War Web site). This lavish film featured elaborate scenes of the 1839 burning of opium in Guangzhou that served as a pretext for British war against China. Heroes and villains are clear: the film depicts

Queen Victoria stating that "We must teach them a lesson on free trade." Nor was it the first Chinese film on the war; in 1943, filmmakers in Japanese-occupied Shanghai were forced to make a film for the centenary of the Opium Wars. As Poshek Fu notes, the film *Eternity (Wanshi liufang)* proved sufficiently ambiguous to let viewers critique the contemporary opium trade in Shanghai, dominated by Japanese suppliers, despite its ostensibly anti-British story (2004: 108–118).

Such cinematic narratives underscore deep divisions of historical consciousness. For Europeans, Americans, and others who traded in it, opium created private fortunes and sustained empires. For Chinese, the Opium Wars represented struggles over land, trade, and human welfare: the beginning of the "Century of National Humiliation."

Opiates, refined from the poppy *Papaver somniferum*, include the alkaloid morphine as an active component. Taken in various forms, from laudanum (opium mixed with alcohol, a popular nineteenth-century Western tonic) to heroin (refined from morphine for injection), opium produces a sense of peace and escape. It is also physically and psychologically addictive and debilitating over time. While Muslim traders introduced opium into China by the eighth century, widespread leisure use probably only appeared in the eighteenth century, when East Asians mixed it with tobacco for smoking — an ironic meeting of global addictions. Despite Chinese Imperial prohibitions, tobacco had spread into China from the New World via the Portuguese colony of Macau a century earlier. In 1729, the Qing emperor forbade opium use, too. But European traders still carried on the trade, transporting it from South Asia to China.

China, at this time, was a major global economy and had developed multiple strategies to control relations with the

West, whether in commerce, politics, or ideology. In the sixteenth century, China had permitted the Portuguese to build a fortress settlement, Macau, on a small peninsula at the mouth of the Pearl River (see chapter 5). From this post, Europeans could trade under restrictive conditions through Guangzhou/Canton. During this time, China consolidated its political, social, economic, and cultural unity in the South and developed profitable trades with the West, Japan, and other parts of Asia.

In the next century, the Chinese empire went through a difficult political transition. The decline of the Ming Dynasty was followed by the rise, consolidation, and assimilation of the Qing dynasty, Manchus who conquered Beijing (1644–1911). This initially led to reduced contacts with outsiders, especially along the coast. Europe, meanwhile, had entered a new phase of expansion after Iberian colonization of the New World in the fifteenth and sixteenth centuries. In the century before the establishment of Hong Kong, Great Britain and France had struggled for sovereignty in Europe, North America, the Caribbean, and India. Trade meshed with new imperialism at home and abroad, epitomized in the formation of British India and plantation economies throughout the world. In the eighteenth century, Britain also sought entry into restricted Chinese markets, especially given the silver China held and the export products — tea, silk, and porcelain — that Britons increasingly desired. The Chinese emperor, however, rejected the 1763 trade mission of Lord George Macartney that sought to expand trade beyond Guangzhou and redress trade imbalances.

Opium, however, ensured an addicted consumer who would defy government edicts. It was already a global commodity. Most opium for use in Britain — made famous by literary figures such as De Quincey, Coleridge, and Wilkie Collins — came from Turkey (Milligan 1995). As Britain extended its political control over India in the eighteenth century, the East India Company gained a monopoly on opium there (which it held till 1813), increasing its production through company-sponsored farming. A complex trade evolved: British textiles went to India, eviscerating local production. From India, opium went to China, and tea could come back to England, constituting a warm, unnourishing mainstay for industrializing England. Meanwhile the slave plantations of the Caribbean shipped sugar to England to sweeten the tea (Mintz 1985). Americans also bought opium in Turkey for the China trade, while South Asian Parsis explored alternative sources in India. By 1838, opium was the crux of "probably the largest commerce of the time in any single commodity" (Michael Greenberg cited in Blue 2000: 34).

For Britain, the opium trade created the *hongs* and *taipans* (the great trading companies of Hong Kong and their influential owners). Jardine Matheson, founded by two Scotsmen, Hutchison Whampoa, Swire, and others would come to shape the economies of property and consumption in Hong Kong for decades. Traders initially operated between Macau and seasonal residences (factories) in Guangzhou before Hong Kong existed. Opium also created a British bureaucracy, beginning with appointment of Lord Napier as superintendent of trade and following with his successor, Royal Navy Captain Charles Elliott. Both figured prominently in the confrontations leading to war and colonization.

The Chinese government rejected both the economic disadvantages of the trade and its social consequences, banning opium smoking again in 1796 and making importation illegal in 1800. The smuggled good, though, remained immensely profitable to Westerners working with corrupt Chinese. Trade soared to 30,000 chests annually in 1838, enough for 1.5 to 2.5 million addicts. Each chest held forty balls covered with poppy leaves and juices totaling roughly 133 pounds (120 pounds of it opium).

In 1839, a new Chinese maritime commissioner, Lin Zexu, arrived to control the trade in Guangzhou. In a letter to Queen Victoria, he bemoaned the wealth taken by "barbarians" and the poison that had spread across the country in exchange for China's "beneficial" exports. Lin forced foreign merchants to turn over more than 20,000 chests of this technically illegal substance, valued at 6 million Spanish dollars, which he burned. Britain responded by starting a war that dragged on until 1842, with intermittent negotiations and British attacks on coastal cities. The 1842 Treaty of Nanjing granted Britain the island of Hong Kong (which Captain Elliott had claimed in 1841) and opened other coastal ports, without legalizing opium or clarifying British (and American) rights in Guangzhou.

China became one of Britain's largest trading partners, but Chinese also began to compete in the opium trade as local growers and intermediaries. Tensions of commerce and nationalism boiled over again in 1856. This Second Opium War coincided with the Great Mutiny and Civil Rebellion in India and the subsequent Government of India Act (1858) that formalized a new British regime in the subcontinent. Britain and China negotiated an initial Treaty of Tianjin in 1858, but the Chinese balked on signing. After further skirmishes, the British and French attacked Beijing, burning the Summer Palace. The 1860 Convention of Peking legalized opium, opened China to missionaries, and ceded Kowloon to the British, among other concessions.

By 1858, the Hong Kong administration had begun to lease its local opium monopoly to a trader or syndicate whose fees constituted a major source of government revenue for decades. In 1883, this local trade was estimated to supply 40,000 to 60,000 addicts (out of a male Chinese population of 160,000). At the same time, emergent transnational connections had also taken on new importance:

> By the 1879s and 1880s, the more important market for the colony's prepared opium was not the local population but the overseas Chinese communities in California, Australia and elsewhere. In 1882, more than 70 percent of the opium prepared in Hong Kong (or five out of seven chests processed each day) went to these destinations. Managed by Hong Kong–based Chinese companies, which made use of European and American steamships and banks, the export of prepared opium from Hong Kong to Chinese communities in the New World intersected neatly with the two great trades that sustained Hong Kong's early economy: the import of opium into China and the export of labor out of China. (Munn 2000:110)

Later, smuggling to the American-ruled Philippines (where opium was banned by 1908) also proved profitable.

Today, opium and its derivatives, morphine and heroin, are seen as public health and moral problems. In the nineteenth century, however, literary experimentation and household use of laudanum was a more common facet of Western life. As Brook and Wakabayashi note, moderate opium use was compared, sometimes favorably, to the impact of alcohol on the British working class, although "the glass-of-sherry argument falls short of adequately describing the actual experience of rum consumption among the European poor or the indigenous peoples in European colonies, many of whom spent their lives inebriated" (2000: 8). An 1893 Royal Commission on Opium reviewed the trade and concluded that it should continue. The British, moreover, did not "officially" trade in opium even though they sponsored its growth in India and preparation in Singapore and took in taxes and revenues from the trade it created. French, Dutch, and Portuguese colonizers in the region used the opium trade as a source of consistent revenues, too; China profited from domestic production as well.

Nonetheless, European protests against opium, often based upon Western religious ideologies, grew louder in the late-nineteenth century. An Anti-Opium Trade Society formed in 1874. Western medicine, initially entranced by opium derivatives like morphine, grew more skeptical as mass addiction beset European and American cities. In the twentieth century, Western protests converged with Chinese government concerns about the drug's impact as an addiction that had captured perhaps one quarter of China's adult male population. Such concerns led to Sino–European treaties to reduce imports and use. For China, Japan's successful suppression of drugs offered a powerful lesson, even though Japanese opium trading would devastate China anew in the twentieth century.

In Hong Kong, opium trading accounted for 29.5 percent of government revenue in 1905; the government itself took over the monopoly in 1914 (Miners 1987: 212). As revolutionaries in the Mainland campaigned against opium, revenues in Hong Kong rose, accounting for nearly half of government revenues in 1918 before falling once again due to international pressure, the failure of Mainland reforms, and increasing criminalization of the trade. By 1935, opium sales accounted for less than

2 percent of the government budget. Britain agreed to end opium monopolies throughout East Asia during World War II (Miners 1987: 232). By this time, Japanese-occupied Shanghai had become a major center for the illicit production and distribution of opium derivatives worldwide.

In 1949, the newly Communist Chinese Mainland finally began to eliminate opium; the drug slowly disappeared from everyday life in Hong Kong as well. Although the 1961 *Hong Kong Report* depicted an ongoing struggle against opium and its derivatives, with 16,663 actions taken under the Dangerous Drug Ordinance, including raids on "clandestine factories, divans and distribution organizations" (1962: 202), Whisson (1968) and Traver (1992) show that heroin was becoming dominant. The 1996 report categorized "drugs" under "Health" rather than "Policing"; the major drugs seized were methamphetamines, heroin, cannabis, and cocaine (1997: 165). While Stanley Kwan's 1987 film *Rouge* romanticized opium smoking in a nostalgic 1930s romance, heroin is the crux of *Chungking Express* (1994), smuggled by South Asians entangled with a blond-wigged Chinese woman in league with a Westerner. The Age of Opium thus has been reprocessed — literally — into another form of illicit global narcotics.

FRONTIER HONG KONG:
THE CREATION OF A COLONIAL CITY, 1840s-1880s

Before the Opium Wars, the British and other merchants had stopped at Hong Kong for fresh water, and had dealt with scattered Chinese villagers there. By 1860, when the colony gained part of the Kowloon peninsula, Hong Kong had lost some of its salience to Shanghai but its permanent settlement had passed 100,000 inhabitants. It also had social institutions and established structures of governance. Nearly 3000 ships brought 1,500,000 tons of merchandise through the port, linking South China with Southeast Asia (Nanyang) and Chinese abroad. Embarkations in Hong Kong (including immigrants) rose from 96,096 in 1860–1869 to 974,360 in 1910–1919, while disembarkations reached 1,288,973 in 1910–1919, a movement that continues in the contemporary city (Tsai 1993: 25).

Hong Kong's growth began even before Great Britain legally controlled the island. With British and Indian troops occupying the island, Elliott built a commercial settlement (separate from existing Chinese villages) by April 1841. Land sales began in June and construction followed before typhoons and fires hit the settlement that summer (to some satisfaction among Chinese observers). The first Governor, Sir Henry Pottinger, established himself in 1842, creating the Hong Kong free port before the final treaty was signed. In 1843, the main city was named Victoria. Pottinger's official appointment came that same year, followed by institutions of colonial rule, including a civil service, judicial system, legislative and executive council, and committees to deal with health and land. As a Crown Colony, Hong Kong had a strong Governor serving at royal pleasure with a strong advisory council (the Executive Council), a weak legislative structure, and an independent albeit appointed judiciary, structures that would shape its life until 1997 and beyond. Governor John Davis, an East India Company veteran, took over in 1844.

The British population of Hong Kong included soldiers, missionaries (Roman Catholic and Protestant), merchants, and others from around the UK and its colonies. Merchants shifted their base from Macau and Guangzhou and began erecting colonial society and the institutions that articulated it, like

St. John's Anglican Cathedral (1849), the Hong Kong General Chamber of Commerce (1861), the Hong Kong Club (1861), and the Hongkong and Shanghai Bank (1865). Lane Crawford, now an elite department store, opened in 1850, and the first game of cricket took place in 1851. Another node of power, the Hong Kong Jockey Club, was established in 1884, the same year the Ladies' Recreation Club opened (Carrell 2005: 100–102).

These pioneers sometimes had powerful links to the Governor and at other times proved antagonists, but together they controlled trade, society, and policy for the emergent colony. They also thought in global terms: the Hongkong and Shanghai Bank opened its Shanghai office a month after its foundation in Central, and by 1900 had established branches in China, Japan, and even Thailand, where it handled the emission of currency.

For such Europeans, urban life was male-oriented, structured around business and governance, and divided by class and service. Hong Kong was a way station to a return home, preferably enriched. It was a colonial/frontier city — a city of easy gains and losses, where an 1875 visitor observed that Europeans "live a very expensive lifestyle; much more expensively, one would think, than they need do" (Thompson: 203).

Colonial society rested on transient foundations of Chinese growth. As the administration and physiognomy of the colonial city took shape, Chinese immigrants joined the thousands who had lived on or around the island. By 1851, the island's population reached 32,983, of whom 31,463 were Chinese (*Hong Kong Report* 1993: 375). Eighty percent of Chinese were laborers, but a few intermediaries with the British would become the foundation of a local Chinese elite. Many also were sojourner males, returning to China when family responsibilities called. Some belonged to secret societies — Triads — political opponents of Manchu and British rule who now have less multiple associations with crime throughout the Chinese world (Tsai 1993).

As more and more Chinese stayed in Hong Kong, diversities of language, history, and housing became apparent. The term Punti (Cant. *Bun de* — "original land") denotes indigenous Cantonese speakers (Faure 1986). The Hoklos and Tanka were seafaring peoples who moved easily to the harbors of the new colony despite government disapproval. The Tanka provided pilots for the colonizers and Tanka women were reputed to consort with *gwei lo* ("foreign devils," Lethbridge 1978). Tankas Loo Aqui and Kwok Acheong grew rich from their collaboration with the British in the Opium Wars (Carroll 2005). Barbara Ward, who worked among Chinese fisherman in the postwar period, when 100,000 people lived on boats, warned that Tanka was also a derogatory term that equated an ethnic boundary with lifeways. At that time, the fleet of 6000 that supplied seafood vital to the Cantonese diet "was probably the largest fishing fleet in the whole of the then British Commonwealth and Empire" (1989: 25). Many Tanka families have now settled in housing estates, although some vessels (no longer sail-powered) are maintained for work and tourists.

The name Hakka literally means "strangers" or "guest people." Again, linguistic definitions and historical origins are often fluid, as anthropologist Nicole Constable has shown (1994, 1996). Hakkas migrated to South China, where conflicts with local landowners (themselves earlier migrants) fomented an increasingly distinctive identity in the nineteenth century. Among the earliest Chinese to arrive in Victoria (Smith 1995: 89), Hakkas spread around the world, from India to England to the

New World. Author Han Suyin (Chou Guang-Ho, born 1917), author of *A Many-Splendoured Thing* (1952, film 1955), was of Hakka/Eurasian descent.

Finally, Chiu Chow people from Swatou and Fukien have formed part of Hong Kong networks at home and abroad, especially in Southeast Asia. Their cuisine remains a valued marker of identity within Hong Kong culture, while prominent figures like billionaire Li Ka-Shing (see chapters 3 and 4) boast Chiu-Chow origins.

Contacts between male Europeans and female Chinese also produced a mixed population of Eurasians. While working class offspring often blended into the larger Chinese population (Lethbridge 1978), others formed the nucleus of a tightly-knit elite network into the next century (Cheng 1976; Hall 1982; Gittins 1982).

Ethnic differences, like regional loyalties and gender differences, collided in a settlement where all Chinese living there were presumed to be displeasing the emperor and "inferior" to the colonizers. Chinese male manual laborers lived in dense settlements known as "Bazaars." Class also emerged as a significant division. The Lower Bazaar on the shore, for poorer laborers, held Chinese brothels, theaters, and gambling houses — institutions of a bachelor society that would be repeated in the Chinese diaspora. A hillside Upper Bazaar (Tai Ping Shan) to the west of the British settlement held shopkeepers and some families. Historian Carl Smith cites an 1844 survey by Rev. Charles Gützlaff that counted only 253 women among 5000 Chinese in the Bazaars and 339 children in the upper, but only 27 in the lowest areas (1995: 40–42; see Cheng 2003).

In this period, a Chinese elite began to take shape. Loo Aqui and Tam Achoy founded Man Mo Temple in 1847. Mercantile associations. Christian missions, the ownership of land, and links to the British all contributed to the formation of this elite. One especially important role was that of the *comprador*, a Chinese middleman for European merchants whose position had emerged in earlier Guangzhou trading. In Hong Kong, compradors for *hongs* such as Jardine Matheson, including Eurasians educated at the Central School, transformed their position as intermediaries in business and culture into new status and power (Hui 1999). By 1858, 65 Chinese Hongs complemented the British elite. A District Watch Force to control crime followed Man Mo Temple as a Chinese organization in 1866. A Chinese Club followed in 1899 and a Chinese Recreation Club in 1912, paralleling segregated British institutions. Chinese merchants also developed regional and family business networks, connecting goods, money, and information among Chinese worldwide.

Meanwhile, British concerns with disease created channels for Chinese influence on government. Osbert Chadwick's 1882 report on sanitary conditions in Hong Kong, for example, noted that Chinese had already adapted their buildings to the dense city, but overcrowding and lack of air and light portended serious problems for all residents. Still, he wrote, "It was unjust to condemn them as a hopelessly filthy race till they had been provided with reasonable means for cleanliness. It was the duty of the Government to see that the means were provided" (quoted in Yau 2003: 18). Dr. Ho Kai (later Sir Kai Ho Kai), trained as both lawyer and doctor in Great Britain, joined the Sanitation Board in 1886, the beginning of a remarkable career in politics and medicine (Choa 2000).

But many Chinese did not trust European medicine even if they had access to it. Tung Wah Hospital, a Chinese hospital offering traditional Chinese medical treatments, opened in 1872 and remains an important Chinese institution today (Lethbridge 1978; Sinn 1988; Smith 1995; Tung Wah Hospital Web site). It soon added educational, social, and political functions and coordinated money and relations with overseas Chinese, such as famine relief contributions to South China. The governing committee of the hospital constituted a visible elite among Chinese who, in turn, could deal with a colonial government that appointed no Chinese to the Legislative Council until 1880. Three compradors held seats on Tung Wah's board until World War II; other spokesmen represented guilds or had been elected by Kaifongs or neighborhood/street committees (Lethbridge 1978: 57–58). The first Chinese appointed to the Legislative Council, the Singapore-born Wu Ting-fang (1880–1882) and Wong Shing (1884–1890) were both founders of Tung Wah. One hundred thirty years later, the Tung Wah board remains a position of prestige. Its fund-raising variety shows are major events of stage and television and rapidly distributed overseas as videos.

As Tsai notes, these elites lived between worlds. Many wealthy Chinese in Hong Kong had family, businesses, and homes in China. At the same time, Mainland popular movements influenced Chinese colonial lives, as in the mass migrations that threatened the colony's livelihood during the Second Opium War (Tsai 1993: 55). While class interests might divide Chinese, they converged around "national" events, like the Sino–French war that erupted in the 1870s over French appropriation of the Chinese protectorate of Vietnam and later attacks on Taiwan (1884). When a French frigate arrived at Hong Kong, dockworkers refused to unload it and residents, presumably including some elite Chinese, asked the British to forbid docking. When Britain refused, a general strike and street riots followed, fueled by propaganda from Guangdong as well as other grievances: Tsai notes that "The crowd attacked British officers and other Westerners in the street because it was obvious to the crowd that they were all sympathetic with the French invaders" (1884: 127). A Sikh policeman killed one coolie, exacerbating the situation. Elites, on the sidelines, jockeyed for influence in counterpoint to British force (1884: 124–145).

Sikh police underscore another characteristic of colonial cities: Those who fall between neat divisions of colonizer and colonized. British imperial connections in India facilitated a flow of people and opium to Hong Kong from its very foundation. Soldiers were followed by merchants, including Parsis (descendants of Persians who followed the prophet Zoroaster), who already had become intermediaries in British business in Bombay and were active in the opium trade. Hormanjee Mody, who arrived in Hong Kong in 1860, soon graduated from opium to stock. With his French-born wife, lavish lifestyle, and public philanthropy (he gave the founding endowment for Hong Kong University in 1911), he rivaled the status of the British themselves.

Sephardic Jews who had settled in India also migrated eastward. The Sassoon family arrived in Hong Kong almost at its foundation, and by 1874 had cornered the opium trade, extending family interests to Shanghai. Hong Kong's Ohel Leah Synagogue, founded in 1902, bears the name of the mother of this prominent family. E. R. Belilos arrived in 1862; by 1881, he was a director of the Hongkong and Shanghai Bank, served in the Legislative Council, and supported the Hong Kong Jewish community. Meanwhile, businessman Paul Chater, an

Armenian Christian from Calcutta, championed land reclamation to extend Central and was knighted in 1902.

Overall, the population identified as Indian by the Hong Kong government rose from 362 (346 men) in 1845 to 1435 (1394 men) in 1870 before dipping again in the late-nineteenth century. Only in early-twentieth-century records do more women appear — 345 out of 1453 in 1901 or 756 out of 4735 in 1931 (Vaid 1972: 20).

Differences of culture and power created conflict. As historian Henry Lethbridge noted for the 1870s and 1880s: "The Chinese, then, were face to face with a population of Europeans whose behavior, from the Chinese point of view, often seemed bizarre, erratic, at times even hostile, aggressive and cruel. In both groups, tensions must have been engendered by the sheer physical propinquity in the crowded urban areas of the central district, by cultural barriers and by the inability of most to speak the other's language (no European Police Inspector could speak good Chinese in 1878)" (1978: 55).

In such a frontier society, tensions could also boil over among the colonizers themselves, as they did during the administration of Sir John Pope Hennessy (1877–1882), an Irish Catholic married to a part Malay woman. After postings in Malaya, West Africa, and the Caribbean, Pope Hennessy entered a city in which racial segregation was the norm, including a 9 p.m. curfew for Chinese. As a European visitor wrote, "You cannot be two minutes in a Hong Kong street without seeing Europeans striking coolies with their canes or umbrellas" (Pope-Hennessy 1967: 193). The Governor seems to have supported "oppressed nationalities" and promoted Chinese interests, creating a general uproar in the colony. He added Portuguese (Macanese), Chinese, and Indian representation to the Legislative Council (Eitel 1983: 529–30) and dealt openly with Tung Wah Hospital. His grandson even claims that "his diminutive size may have helped to endear Hennessy to Orientals, who have often found the normal scale and full-blooded appearance of British residents gross and over-bearing" (Pope-Hennessy 1967: 188). Yet he clearly alienated the colonial British: "On 7 October 1878, the great public meeting of this period was held on the cricket ground to protest his actions" (Eitel 1983: 543). He was removed after popular (European) protest and marital scandal.

Founded as a frontier outpost, then, Hong Kong soon displayed the complex dynamics of Fanon's divided global colonial city. Missionary J. A. Turner left an image of the spatial separation of groups in the city as he passed through on his way to Guangzhou in 1884: "On the slopes of the mountains are cut terraces for the solidly built white-faced houses of the European residents. At the foot of the hill are Chinese shops and dwellings" (1984: 21). In the twentieth century, people, institutions, and reactions would reach new levels of both integration and conflict.

HONG KONG IN THE NEW CENTURY

China's defeat in the Sino–Japanese war (1894–1895) opened the nation to foreign ownership of factories and railroads, but also spurred Chinese entrepreneurs and political reformers, some of whom used Hong Kong as a base. It also changed China's attitude in negotiating the 1898 Second Convention of Peking by which Britain acquired the New Territories. In North China at this time, Britain claimed an indefinite lease on the port of Weihaiwei, but it did not do so for the fields, towns, and islands surrounding Hong Kong, which had a Chinese population of more than one hundred thousand. As

Patricia Atwell suggests in her study of Weihaiwei, both concessions reflected geopolitical issues having more to do with other Europeans than with China (1985; Wesley-Smith 1980). Yet, while Weihaiwei scarcely developed and was returned to China in 1930, the New Territories were incorporated administratively into the Crown Colony and became an integral part of the life and economy of Hong Kong. In fact, various politicians later suggested trading the return of Weihaiwei to China for an unconditional surrender of the southern lands, which might well have changed the future of the colony (Atwell 1985: vii–xiv).

The New Territories provided an agricultural hinterland for Hong Kong, set apart in administration, people, and culture. Its clans also retained strong links to China and Chinese history. In 1931, for example, writing about rice cultivation there, a guidebook and Barker noted that "The rice from the Shatin Valley was reputed to be the finest in China and was sent as part of the annual tribute to the Emperor in Peiping. Now the crop is sent to Hong Kong for export as it fetches a higher price than the Chinese will pay locally. Foreign rice is bought for their own consumption as it is cheaper and rather preferred" (Peplow and Barker 17–18). While roads and railways traversed the mainland and boats connected the islands to Hong Kong, New Territories settlements remained different for decades, whether they be walled villages, fishing villages like Tsuen Wan (Hayes 1994; Hayes and Sinn 1995; Lee and DiStefano 2002), or the people and stilt homes of island settlements like Tai O on Lantau (Wong King Wai 2000).

Meanwhile, the urbanized area on both sides of the harbor thrived, united by the Star Ferry, founded in 1898 by the Parsi Dorabjee Nowrojee. World War I's European battles scarcely affected Hong Kong, although German males were interned and their businesses sold off (Miners 1987). By 1921, Hong Kong's population reached 450,000, with more than 5000 Europeans and Americans, 2600 Portuguese (probably including Macanese and Eurasians), 3500 Indians, and 384,000 Chinese. And, 110,352 Chinese lived in rural areas and 55,000 dwelt on boats (Faure 1997: 49).

New architecture and landscape design suggested an increasingly established city. The neoclassical Supreme Court building formed a varied central cluster with the HKSB, the Hong Kong Club, the General Post Office, and the cricket field. The 1935 Hongkong and Shanghai Bank building became the tallest building in the East. Up the hill to the west, the University of Hong Kong's main building, completed in 1912, marked another nucleus of growth. Schools, barracks, police stations, and homes were also prominent features of colonial architecture. Across the harbor, the Kowloon-Canton Train Station was built in 1915–1916 (it was demolished in 1975). The nearby Peninsula Hotel, opened to the public in 1928 by the Kadoori family, became a center for Hong Kong's elite. A 1924 guide for English-speaking visitors noted that "the European part of the island has the appearance of private grounds — the roads leading from one level to another are lined with palms, ferns and flowers" (*Hong Kong*: 25).

This guidebook scarcely pushed visitors and investors beyond the harbor, Kowloon and Victoria, focusing on the colony as port of trade: "Commercially, Hongkong ranks as the second port in the British Empire; in the matter of vessel-tonnage it is the largest port in the world" (*Hong Kong* 1924: 36). It cites annual entries of 50,000 vessels reaching 35,000,000 tons without accounting for 728,322 local vessels that still defined Hong Kong as a center for the Pearl River Delta. Imports in 1923 reached £61,954,498 (£12,282,398 from the British Empire), while exports stood at £61,372,383 (£6,639,095 to the British Empire; *Hong Kong* 1924).

Chinese businesses had grown as well. Chinese emigrants from Zhongshan and Guangdong used their success in Australia to found the multinational Sincere Department Store (Ma Ying-Piew 1900) and Wing On Department Stores (1907, by the Guo family in Hong Kong and Shanghai; see the Chinese Heritage of Australian Federation Web site). Hong Kong's Chinese Chamber of Commerce emerged in 1896, followed by Chinese-dominated banks such as the Bank of East Asia (Carrell 2005: 85–86; S. Chung 1998). While Hong Kong industrialization is generally read as a post World War II process, the roots of this transformation were evident by the 1930s.

The territory also became a center for film and information for a wider Chinese world. Hong Kong's first film, Li Minwei's *Zuanghzhi Tests his Wife* (1913) was partially financed by Americans and shown in Chinatowns there. Hong Kong produced 117 Cantonese-language films in 1939 (Leung and Chan 1997: 143). While 80 percent of these movies were exported to the Mainland and Macau, they also reached Southeast Asia and North American Chinatowns.

In the twentieth century, the colonial administration increased its limited recognition of Chinese places and people of power (Lethbridge 1978; Sinn 1988). Some Hong Kong Chinese figures like Dr. Ho Kai and Hu Li-Yuan were both spokesmen in Hong Kong politics and visionaries of reform for the new Chinese republic (Tsai 1993: 157–160). Nevertheless, despite some Chinese success. Chow Shou Shon was appointed to the Executive Council in 1926 as its first Chinese member, after a period of stormy local demonstrations (see below). Nevertheless, despite Chinese success, as the city grew, the jostling Lethbridge imagined had given way to segregated spaces where British elites lived apart, except for Chinese servants. These included residential zones, the influential Hong Kong Club, and the Hong Kong Botanical Gardens. Chinese areas were clustered around Tai Ping Shan, Shek Tong Tsui, and the overseas merchant stores, neighborhoods vibrant with business and recreation.

Above all, segregation was mapped out on the Peak, the hill that rose above the harbor and became identified with social height. A 1905 set of satirical letters joked that Hong Kong was divided into "(1) The Peak, a would-be mountain, dotted over with bungalows and villas, wherein live the elect. (2) the lower levels, inhabited by the greater business population. (3) Kowloon, where the soldier folk come from. The Peak looks down on everything and everybody" ("Betty," 7–8). Ordinance No. 1 of 1904, published in the *Hong Kong Government Gazette* of April 29, 1904, made it illegal for any "owner, lessee, tenant or occupier of any land or building within the Hill district to let such land or building or any part thereof for the purpose of residence by any but non-Chinese or to permit any but non-Chinese to reside in such buildings" (50: 752). This did not include servants or chair coolies, hospital patients or visitors, although Matilda Hospital, established on the peak in 1907, accepted only Western patients.

In 1918, a new statement noted that anyone wishing to reside in the Peak District "must make application to the governor in council to do so" (*Hong Kong Government Gazette*, May 31, 1918, 64: 240). Some non-Englishmen lived there

— Paul Chater had maintained a private zoo at his villa. Civil servant and historian Austin Coates depicted a gradation in the Mid-levels: "In the lower part, Portuguese, Jews, Armenians and Parsis; in the upper part — dreadful, but one had to concede it — 'dirty continentals' of whom the French were the most vigorous at nest-building and mountaineering" (in Gillingham 1983: 8). This ordinance was not repealed until after World War II, after the Japanese had turned race and class upside down (*Hong Kong Government Gazette* July 25, 1946, 87: 184).

Paul Gillingham's *On the Peak* captures the caste divisions of Hong Kong society in the 1920s: "Pampered at home by an army of servants, working at a leisurely pace in well-fanned offices . . . catered for by most forms of sport and homegrown entertainment, transported by sedan chair and rickshaw and socialized by membership in a variety of clubs, the expatriate in Hong Kong lived well. It did not matter that some said Hong Kong was a sleepy little backwater lacking the brassy dynamism of Shanghai or the style of Bombay or Calcutta" (1983: 8). Sayer demurs, rather disingenuously, that the 1918 edict opened up what would otherwise have been a European "reservation," an alternative to worse possibilities: "Had this small island been kept as a purely European retreat — on the order of Shameen [the European enclave in the Pearl River next to Guangzhou] — its history, though perhaps curious, would inevitably be trivial" (1975: 129).

Chinese nonetheless challenged divisions of race and place. Robert Ho Tung (1864–1956), a Eurasian who identified strongly with Chinese nationalism, taught his descendants to live in both English and Chinese worlds. Ho Tung and his brothers trained at the English-language Central School and he joined the Chinese Maritime Customs in Guangzhou before working for Jardine Matheson as a comprador. He retired early because of poor health, passing his position to his brother, Ho Fook. Robert Ho Tung had a large family with two Eurasian wives and ten children, including an adopted son. A successful businessman, philanthropist, and community leader, he was knighted in 1915 and became a K. B. E in 1955 (Cheng 1976). He declined to serve in the Legislative Council (although his brother did so) and hosted Sun Yat-Sen for tea in the 1920s. But he also worked with the British to overcome Chinese strikes that crippled the city.

In a 1917 document, Ho Tung foresaw progress for the Hong Kong Chinese:

> It can no longer be said that the Chinese resort to Hong Kong for sordid motives only. If their patient industry and frugality have been the means of amassing for them considerable wealth, it cannot be denied that a large proportion of their accumulated savings is invested in and spent in Hong Kong. So great is their faith in the permanent prosperity of the colony and the safety of domicile under the folds of the British flag that the Chinese are said to own more than three-fifths of the landed property in Hong Kong. (included in Faure 1997: 116)

While colonial expatriates recycled frequently, these Chinese in Hong Kong became increasingly anchored there.

Pleading health issues, Ho Tung sought and gained permission in 1906 to reside in a lavish three-house compound on the Peak; the family also owned town houses, a home in Shanghai and a New Territories farm. Family life on the Peak, nonetheless, could also become isolated — his daughter, Jean Gittins, did not remember being invited to any other homes there, while playmates "on occasion would refuse to play with us because we were Chinese or they might tell us we shouldn't be living on the Peak" (Gittins 1982: 12).

Ho Tung's success remained exceptional, while wider Chinese popular unrest often challenged the colony and its global relations. Protests against the Japanese were a recurrent theme. A boycott of the United States in 1908 denounced Chinese exclusion and ill treatment of even "legitimate visitors" (Ho Kai wrote a reasoned albeit divisive critique of the American position; Tsai 1993: 196–206). Such events and responses became enmeshed with the politics of China, an involvement that intensified with the 1911 revolution on the Mainland (Chung 1998). Civic action by the Hong Kong Chinese became part of a new era, evidenced by a 1912 boycott of trams that refused to accept Chinese coins (Carroll 2005).

In the 1920s, labor movements among Hong Kong Chinese brought the colony to a halt. In a 1922 strike, seamen protested their paltry wages, having learned from successful campaigns in Republican China, although their issues were probably local rather than the mainland conspiracy Governor Reginald Stubbs feared. The Guangzhou government chose not to intervene and intermediaries, including Robert Ho Tung and Tung Wah directors negotiated a successful compromise to end the strike with a raise (Tsang 2004: 88-90).

Three years later, troubles erupted in Shanghai with the May 30th incident, when British Sikh policemen fired into a rioting crowd, killing Chinese protesters. Another killing by foreign police in June in Guangzhou led that city to boycott Hong Kong. Chinese leaders asked their compatriots to leave Hong Kong, and Communists allied with the republican/ conservative Guomindong made inroads among protestors.

Hong Kong students left schools and servants deserted the Peak Hotel; 10,000 female workers joined the strikers, too (Chan 1990: 182). The Hongkong and Shanghai Bank intervened to support Chinese banks facing collapse, while volunteers manned the tram and Star Ferry.

By June 22, 1925, the General Strike had closed 80 percent of businesses in Central Hong Kong. Governor Stubbs declared a state of emergency. Shipping, textiles, the stock market, and land values fell while the governor begged for a loan to keep the colony afloat, and rumors and violence complicated actions on both sides. While the new Governor Sir Cecil Clementi tried to negotiate, the Communist-influenced Guangzhou government supported the strikers. Only the coup that brought the Guomindong's Chiang Kai-Shek to power distracted that authority and helped end the strike.

While Hong Kong Chinese in the 1930s remained divided by class and political allegiance, this was also a potential turning point for the colonizers. Chan concludes that "For the rest of Clementi's term of office in Hong Kong, he acted with the conviction that, for the sake of the colony's well-being, the goodwill of Canton had to be cultivated and maintained at all costs" (1990: 219). Winifred Clift, an acid critic of colonial society, added "A Hong Kong 'strike' is a wonderful eye-opener! I venture to assert that many European women know more about the state of their pantry floors, their sinks, their iceboxes, than they ever did before — and that many European men will in the future look with respect and sympathy upon the market coolie if he ever returns to take up again his essential service" (1927: 39). Such divided urban worlds would change with the intrusion of different global visions that clashed in World War II.

Three

In my lifetime, Hong Kong has had to absorb, house and
find jobs for wave upon wave of hundreds of thousands, nay,
millions of refugees and immigrants from China, my own
family among them. It had to transform itself overnight into
a light manufacturing centre in the wake of the embargo on
trade with China during the Korean War. Then withstand the
shock of disturbances that rocked Hong Kong to its foundations in the upheavals of the mid-sixties. Two decades ago,
it metamorphosed itself overnight into a service economy to
embrace Deng Xiaoping's opening up of the Chinese economy.
And more recently, it trod the often tricky path of transition
from 156 years of British administration to the resumption of
Chinese sovereignty.

Quite a journey. In the space of two generations, Hong Kong
has risen from the ashes of wartime Japanese occupation to
become one of the world's great cities, indeed a great world
city. (Anson Chan, *Hong Kong Report* 1999, 2000: 1)

Former Chief Secretary Anson Chan, whose interpretation of the
origin and future of Hong Kong opened the last chapter, used
family and personal elements to frame the colony's transitions
after World War II. Her narrative juxtaposes local economic
transformation and global shifts, underscoring specific landmarks — the Japanese occupation, postwar transformations,

the 1960s, further economic conversion in the 1970s and 1980s, and reunification with China in 1997. Tactful, perhaps tactical, disconnections are interesting. The China from whom Chan's family fled is the same Communist state that resumed sovereignty in 1997, albeit a state transformed in its outlook under Deng Xiaoping. "Disturbances" of the 1960s also seem to be independent of the upheavals of the Mainland Cultural Revolution. History flows through generations, making memory local, familiar, and Chinese, a synthetic narrative many Hong Kongers would share.

Perhaps most striking, however, are the unspoken questions of agency. Who is Hong Kong? Who are its citizens and what is their identity in these decades of wrenching change? Who is excluded? Are the people of Hong Kong protesting today the same kind of citizens who rebuilt it after World War II or those of 1960s upheavals?

This chapter explores crucial transitions of Hong Kong from the 1930s through the 1960s, as it grew from an entrepôt to a global producer through the crucible of international wars. This story weaves together changing world contexts, new populations, and new government involvement with the human social and cultural transformations of a postwar success story that became a model for the world. It ends with the watershed issues linked to riots in the mid-1960s. The next chapter will follow further economic transformations of Hong Kong, its citizens, and context past 1997.

HONG KONG IN A WORLD AT WAR

In the 1930s, the expansion of another global empire complicated the intersection of China and Britain: the rise of Japan as a world power with broad territorial ambitions and intent on creating a New East Asian Order. Japan's adaptation of Western technology and organization had already proved successful in confrontations with China; it controlled Taiwan and took over treaty port concessions in Tsingtao from Germany in 1914. In 1931, Japan took the Chinese province of Manchuria, later installing the former Qing emperor in a puppet regime. Over the next fifteen years, a new imperialism, blended with an ideology of Asian unity, would challenge European colonial East Asia.

Fighting between Chinese and Japanese broke out in Shanghai in 1932, although these states maintained an uneasy armistice until the Sino–Japanese War broke out in 1937. Taking Shanghai in 1937, the Japanese exploited the separations that already existed (and in which they had participated), exercising increasing control over the International Settlements and the Chinese city over the next four years. Although some Europeans had supported Japan as a counterweight to Chinese sovereignty (Clifford 1991: 273–275), foreigners and some Chinese departed southward, if they could, for nationalist-controlled areas or Hong Kong. In Hong Kong, nevertheless, Fu notes that Shanghainese refugee intellectuals and artists often maintained their distance from the Cantonese population, regarding themselves as a true China displaced in exile, "while in Hong Kong, although everywhere is Chinese . . . it has no Chinese flavor, it lacks a Chinese soul" (2003: 67–69).

The Japanese captured Nanjing in December 1937, massacring tens of thousands of civilians there. In October 1938, the Japanese took Guangzhou, forcing massive waves of refugees into Hong Kong. The *1997 Hong Kong Report* estimates that 100,000 refugees arrived in 1937, 500,000 in 1938, and 150,000 in 1939 — doubling the territory's population to 1.6 million.

The report adds that "at the height of the influx, about 500,000 people were sleeping in the streets" (1998: 408). Some refugees brought capital; others became laborers producing materials for Free China. The Bank of China relocated to Hong Kong and the colony took on new roles as a cultural center. After a Nationalist government ban on Cantonese films was overturned in 1937, Hong Kong produced more than 300 films between 1938 and 1940 (Fu 2003: 63). It was also a center for the distribution of foreign goods, including film, throughout non-Japanese Asia (Fu 2003: 61). Meanwhile the China Defense League mobilized overseas Chinese. Chinese Hong Kong residents thus faced the war in China as a test of local, national, and global identities, whether through active participation in the Chinese war effort or in the exploration of a Chinese identity in Cantonese films (Fu 2003: 76–87). Nonetheless, the British did not include Chinese in plans for defending the colony. A chief censor was appointed in 1939 to eradicate anti-Japanese materials as long as Britain was neutral in the Sino–Japanese conflict (2003: 67).

In early December, the Japanese attacked Western positions on multiple fronts. Hours after the bombing of Pearl Harbor on December 7, 1941, which brought the United States into the war, the Japanese took over the foreign concessions in Shanghai and their army entered Hong Kong from the north. Colonial defenders soon abandoned the New Territories, with British, Indian, and Canadian troops escaping on the final ferries to Hong Kong Island; evidently, local Chinese were not inspired to support the colonizer in large numbers. The Japanese immediately destroyed the airport. They had superior military force (especially since the British were tied down in Europe and elsewhere) and controlled vital food and water from the New Territories. Governor

Mark Young surrendered Hong Kong on Christmas Day, December 25, 1941 (see Snow 2004).

Jean Gittins, the daughter of Robert Ho Tung, chronicled this era from her vantage as an educated upper-class Eurasian, whose Eurasian husband and family fought alongside the British. As she notes, the battle of Hong Kong proved a turning point for Chinese and "people of a mixed Anglo-Chinese ancestry, many of who claimed British nationality while most regarded themselves as Chinese. The tragedy of it all was that until after the Second World War, when so many of the local community died for the Allied cause, racial discrimination was such that they were accepted by neither British nor Chinese" (1982: 8). As she recalled the occupied city and the internment camps, her sympathies are evident: "We were now a Japanese colony — so different from Britain's peaceful occupation exactly one hundred years before." Conversely, she scorned the Japanese: "Under a thin veneer of Western civility their instincts were hostile and savage" (1982: 24).

The Japanese occupiers redivided the city in terms of race and loyalty, interning soldiers and eventually confining most British and other allied civilians in camps at Stanley. Meanwhile, "Chinese and Indians were not to be interned, nor were the sprinkling of Germans who were now allies of Japan. The Eurasians and the Russians, Norwegians and others, although free, were required to carry 'third national' identification passes" (Gittins 1982: 32). Some American Maryknoll Sisters gained this status because of their Irish parentage (Chu 2004: 56). While troops loyal to the British were imprisoned, Japanese sought to recruit Indians to disrupt the South Asian colony and to solidify a new "Asianization" of Hong Kong. South Asian responses varied widely. Still, a Sikh in the Public Works department provided a telling memory. "Working for the Japanese wasn't so very much different. The British didn't really like us. They thought they were better than us. The Japanese also thought they were better. Nobody trusted us. We just tried to stay alive and find enough to eat" (White 1994: 45).

Hong Kong Chinese occupied even more ambivalent positions. Some struggled under Japanization, others fled to neutral Macau, and still others joined the resistance as guerrillas in China or Sha Tin and other sites in the rural New Territories. For all, "Hong Kong was a city of suffering, where hunger, fear, privation, and humiliation became part of everyday life" (Fu 2003: 88).

As the British had done, the Japanese incorporated some Chinese into the façade of administration, while imposing their own superiority. As in colonial Taiwan, Japanese was taught in schools. They renamed streets and monuments to erase British identities, and Japanese movies played in local cinemas. Japanese soldiers brought their families as well, taking over colonial homes on the Peak, occupying the Peninsula Hotel and controlling the Hongkong and Shanghai Bank. Even the Governor's House was rebuilt in a more Japanese style, with elements later maintained by British regimes.

Controls and shortages became widespread, but life for the former colonizers in Stanley proved grim, as 3000 people — who often had lived in luxurious separation from crowded Chinese quarters — crammed into a school, barracks, hospital fortress, prison, and the former Indian Quarters. While some escaped, for most others, overcrowding, disease, and lack of food, especially the imported goods of colonial life, made life difficult. In addition, "Some of the British felt that if it were not for the many Europeans in the camp there would be sufficient food for them" (Gittins 1982: 66). Nevertheless, internees organized schools, churches, social clubs, and even gardens while trying to follow news of family, friends, and the war itself (Gittins 1982; Chu 2004; Snow 2004).

As Japan began to lose the war, life in Hong Kong became harsher, especially with regard to food. The occupiers forced emigration to the Mainland; by August 1945, Hong Kong's population had dropped to about 600,000 — equivalent to its population in the 1920s and smaller than refugee-swollen Macau.

After the Japanese surrender in 1945, Britain reestablished sovereignty; Governor Mark Young resumed his office on May 1, 1946. Japanese goods and companies would not regain popularity for decades. Yet, the culturally constructed continuities of colonial power had been interrupted across Asia and the world, raising questions for Hong Kong and its future (Snow 2004).

FROM A COLONIAL ENTREPÔT TO A
NONDECOLONIZED PRODUCER, 1945–1966

As participants in a 1996 conference at Oxford reiterated, Hong Kong's decolonization differed significantly from that of other units of the British Empire (Brown and Foot 1997). First, its path did not run from colonial status through development of political institutions to fledgling (sometimes precarious) independence. Instead, Hong Kong was reunited with an existing sovereign state. Second, no particular local group emerged to claim rights of governance — China and Britain decided issues of Hong Kong rule in negotiations leading to the 1984 Joint Declaration. Finally, postwar issues on a global stage transformed Hong Kong and the Chinese state, producing a sociocultural anomaly among decolonizing nations. When Hong Kong "returned" to China, it was a global territory of great wealth and connections, a node in world capital flows beyond Britain or China. As John Darwin said, "Hong Kong's political history makes nonsense of the decolonizing process as it is usually imagined" (1997: 16).

Such expansion must have seemed unimaginable in the aftermath of World War II. Jean Gittins confirms Anson Chan's image of a postwar city of ashes. Released from her internment, she saw that "Misery and chaos characterized the former carefree city. Streets were dirty and deserted. There was a total absence of public transport — in fact, hardly a single public utility functioned. . . . An odd shop was open but shoppers looked drab and confused. Pale, sad faces peered from behind upstairs windows" (1982: 156).

Rebuilding Hong Kong, however, immediately posed questions of sovereignty — who would rebuild the city and how? Britain itself faced postwar expenses that shaped discussions about how much it might commit to reconstructing a distant colony (Sweeting 1990). Treaty port concessions elsewhere in China had been eliminated as a wartime alliance strategy in 1943. India had gained its independence in 1947, starting a march toward decolonization that would transform other British colonies and the other East Asian nations the Japanese had occupied. Britain held the New Territories by lease for fifty years more, but China refused to acknowledge the legitimacy of colonial occupation.

Even before World War II ended, Winston Churchill, Franklin Roosevelt, and Chiang Kai-Shek had explored formulae to shift control of Hong Kong, perhaps making it a free port (Hook 1997). No agreement was reached because of strong

British opposition and the complicated nature of the wartime alliance. Britain reinstated colonial rule with the support of President Harry Truman (Yu and Cheng 2004: 30), while Chiang Kai-Shek avoided confrontation, needing his best troops (and at least tacit Western support) in his increasing struggles with the Communists in the north. Despite renewed colonial control, Hong Kong needed the Mainland for food, and Chinese crossed the border easily, soon reconstituting the population of the war-torn city.

Once the Communist People's Republic of China (PRC) was proclaimed in 1949, resolution of Hong Kong's status stalled for decades. Mao Zedong, engaged in massive transformations of the Mainland, expressed little public interest in Hong Kong. China, in turn, could find Hong Kong useful as a limited gateway to evade international boycotts. Whether through social programs or censorship, Britain sought to avoid internal disorder so serious as to invite Chinese intervention, especially during the turmoil of the Cultural Revolution in the late 1960s. Only in 1972 did the PRC, having replaced Taiwan in its United Nations (UN) Security Council seat, ask the UN to remove Hong Kong and Macau from the category of colonies awaiting decolonization (Lam 1985).

China's 1950 Friendship Treaty with the Soviet Union and its subsequent involvement in conflict in Korea meant that the West identified Hong Kong as an outpost against communism — like Nationalist outposts in the "neutralized" Straits of Taiwan. Border closures cut formal trade and limited movement back and forth, although streams of refugees reshaped the city. The *1951 Hong Kong Report* observed grimly that "industries, which had developed and expanded with extraordinary rapidity since 1945 were early in December 1950 faced with the most serious crisis they had yet run into in their short history when in view of the active Chinese intervention in the Korean hostilities the United States government placed a strictly enforced and virtually complete embargo on all shipments of goods to China" (1952: 7–8). Despite opulent shops and rebuilding, "Unemployment began to assume serious proportions as more and more of its inhabitants were reduced to bare subsistence level" (1952: 9).

As this report suggests, the postwar U.S. presence in East Asia had grown beyond early American roles in the opium trade, the treaty ports, and the Spanish–American war, after which the U.S. had occupied the Philippines. While the Philippines had become a commonwealth in 1935 and gained independence in 1946, the U.S. retained a strong military and economic presence there. After World War II, U.S. forces had also occupied Okinawa and Japan, helping to rebuild the foundations of renewed East Asian industrialization. Soon, the U.S. also became involved in Korea and later in Southeast Asia. U.S. investments and interests in Hong Kong would grow as well during this period; in 1955, the United States ranked well below Britain, the Commonwealth, and Asian destinations for Hong Kong trade, yet by 1960, it became the foremost destination for trade, surpassing Britain and Japan combined (*Hong Kong Report* 1956; 1962).

Declassified documents from the National Security Council of the Eisenhower administration from 1957 and 1960 show that the U.S. administration saw Hong Kong as an ideological battleground where "Free World" rather than British values and prosperity itself could be showcased and exported to fight Communism. The Unites States sought to encourage capitalist development in Hong Kong. It also wanted to use Hong Kong

Chinese media to influence overseas Chinese. And Hong Kong became a place to gather intelligence about Communist China (Yu and Cheng 2004: 37–39).

American interest in Hong Kong shaped images of the city that would underpin the growth of tourism and even R & R leaves in a militarized East Asia. American television shows like ABC's *Hong Kong* and Hollywood films like *Love Is a Many-Splendored Thing* (1955) and *The World of Suzy Wong* (1960) showcased beautiful Hong Kong "Chinese" women saved by American white knights. In the first movie, William Holden's journalist character dies in Korea. In the second, based on a novel by British author Richard Mason, the artistic Holden saves a young Chinese prostitute. The myth of Suzie Wong remains present in Hong Kong tourism materials despite local disdain and reinterpretation in films like Peter Chan's *Comrades, Almost a Love Story* (1996; see Marchetti 1993; McDonogh and Wong 2001).

These Technicolor images remind us that a visitor to Hong Kong in the 50s and 60s still saw a colonial cityscape. The same institutions of government and finance dominated Central, while the pitch of the Hong Kong Cricket Club (see Web site), emblematic of colonial spaces and rhythms, occupied a central symbolic space for 124 years, from 1851 to 1975. Predominantly Chinese settlements spread westward and eastward beside the harbor, and included densely packed tenements along with bustling shops, factories, and street markets. Refugee settlements sprawled on hills and unclaimed land (and in the Walled City). Meanwhile, the islands and farmlands of the New Territories remained bucolic, their calm sometimes interrupted by refugees and increasing colonial control. Amid the concurrent regional shifts, however, postwar Hong Kong underwent fundamental economic changes, transforming place, society, cultural imagery, and the nature of citizenship.

ECONOMIC DEVELOPMENT

The Communist triumph in the Mainland in 1949 made capitalist cities such as Shanghai seem increasingly precarious for foreign businesses. While one historian's judgment that "revolution meant that Shanghai transferred itself bodily" to Hong Kong (cited in Bickers 1997: 54) is extreme in that it identifies Shanghai with Westerners and wealthy capitalists able to leave, Communism constrained Hong Kong's major coastal competitor and spurred a transfer of capital into Hong Kong textiles, shipping, media, and other sectors of the colonial economy, expanding prewar production.

Shanghainese investments, in particular, were associated with the textile industry, which hired about 42 percent of the local labor force by 1962 (*1962 Hong Kong Report* 1963: 72–75). Yet, the impact of the Shanghainese should not overshadow the work of tiny factories created by Cantonese owner-manager-entrepreneurs in Hong Kong, adapting rapidly to a cutthroat export market without any safety net (Lei 1999). That 1962 *Hong Kong Report* listed 7305 registered factories employing 297,897 people (in the census, twice that many claimed to work in factories and building trades; p. 67). Despite possessing limited raw materials, water, and even land for construction, "low taxation, plentiful productive labor, the advantage of a free port, excellent shipping and commercial facilities and freedom from locally imposed trade restrictions"(1963: 68) all worked to facilitate production. All of these, in turn, reflected Britain's relatively noninterventionist colonial development policy.

As the 1988 "Made in Hong Kong" exhibit showed, both Shanghainese and locals had already invested in manufactures for the Southeast Asian market by the 1930s, fostering innovations in Hong Kong–based design. When production and marketing boomed after 1949, Hong Kong's new global connections led to interdependencies in production, distribution, and design:

> American foreign policy was to stimulate industrial and commercial development linked to the U.S. economy in Japan, South Korea, Taiwan, and Vietnam. Hong Kong suddenly became favored by American importers. . . . . [including] leading companies armed with detailed specifications of designs to be manufactured at low cost by Hong Kong firms. Second, the Federation [of Hong Kong industries] assisted six American specialist designers to set up in Hong Kong in 1961, who were soon to dominate the local design scene. Third, Chinese traditional crafts, now no longer available to America or Europe, began to be produced, with suitable modifications, to fill the vacuum. (1988: 14)

The plastics sector and the self-made billionaire Li Ka-Shing exemplify these changes. Plastics have long been identified with inexpensive Hong Kong goods (although they were later eclipsed by cheap electronics). In the early 1960s, the government lauded "the manufacture of plastics, one of the largest sources of employment which, from simple beginnings, today produces a wide variety of products including the eminently successful plastic flowers" (*1962 Hong Kong Report*: 72). Li, a 1940 Chiu Chow immigrant from Swatou, became an orphan during the war, and at seventeen began to work in menial positions. After the war, Shanghai capitalists stimulated the colony's plastics industry, leading to firms like the China Plastics Company and the Kader Industrial Company. Li steadily built knowledge and connections as a salesman in plastics goods before launching his own company, Cheung Kong, in 1950 at the age of twenty-two. Despite the Korean War's negative impact on trade and the movement of supplies, plastics production boomed for local and global markets, taking over the traditional forms of production of household goods, such as furniture, pens, and toothbrushes. By the late 1950s, Li found a niche in creating plastic flowers, with global exports reaching HK$10,870,669 in 1958 (Chan 1996: 49–61; Ching 1999). His factory and land purchases in North Point and his increasing number of global contracts also allowed him to speculate on the "next" Hong Kong economic resource — real estate.

An interesting contrast emerges in another export product of the 1950s and 1960s: film, where Shanghai and Southeast Asia intersected in Hong Kong. After 1949, Hong Kong became a major destination for Shanghai producers, stars, and others in the film industry. The markets for Hong Kong film, never locally sufficient, also shifted. With China closed, the city's new talent and capital cultivated markets in Southeast Asia.

Three elements explained the success of the film industries in the following two decades. First was the development of two major movie studios, Shaw Brothers, and MP & GI (Motion Picture and General Investment Film Company). Second was the growth of small-scale Cantonese production, creating a massive output of cheaper Cantonese films. Third was the shift of content, from dialects to subject matters that helped explain how Hong Kong saw itself in relation to its region and the

West. Global politics played their part, too: Shaw Brothers and MP & GI were relatively politically neutral, while two lesser companies, the Great Wall Studio and Asia Studio, made films that were more blatantly ideological, with pro-communist and pro-nationalistic sentiments, respectively.

The two types of Hong Kong cinemas, Cantonese and Mandarin, echo divisions of industrial production that we have already highlighted. Cantonese films were local products, tending to be traditional and conservative, whether period swordfight films or melodramas imbued with Confucian values. Mandarin films, on the other hand, descended from Shanghai, and provided more sophisticated products for a large national market. In the 1950s, however, Cantonese films underwent stylistic changes, adopting a more realist aesthetics and a social consciousness. Many small production companies also were making Mandarin films, but the quality was uneven and markets small; the Nationalist government in Taiwan imposed heavy duties on imported Mandarin films from Hong Kong, again favoring Amoy and Chiu Chow films for Southeast Asia.

Film companies were multinational. The Shaw Brothers had come from Shanghai, but had established the Nan Yang Film Company in Hong Kong to make Cantonese films for Southeast Asia; this became Shaw and Sons after the war. Besides production, the Shaw Brothers established the major distribution and exhibition chain in Southeast Asia in the 1930s. In 1957, Run Run Shaw moved to Hong Kong, erected a massive studio in Clear Water Bay, and restructured the company as Shaw Brothers.

MP & GI found its capital among Southeast Asian Chinese, primarily in Malaya. Its head, Lok Wan Tho, owned another major distribution and exhibition chain. In 1951, he established a distribution subsidiary in Hong Kong, buying Western and Chinese films to be shown in its theaters in Southeast Asia. He formed MP & GI in 1956.

These studios competed intensely from the late 1950s to the early 1970s. Shaw Brothers produced both period dramas and musicals through the early 1960s; its other successful genre was the Kung Fu film, which broke away from a more restrictive Confucius ethos and celebrated male heroes. MP & GI were particularly strong in contemporary drama, featuring very "modern" female stars in roles like air hostesses and nightclub singers. Its forte was women's movies: not the long-suffering Confucian women of Cantonese melodrama, but carefree, wise women with the material trappings of the West.

These companies thus replicated the model and the success of Hollywood studios, with vertical integration of production, distribution, and exhibition; at the same time, they functioned very much like Chinese families, a recurrent theme in Chinese globalization. Shaw Brothers always was a family movie empire; MP & GI, originally a family's side business, became a passion for the European-educated Lok, who sought to modernize Southeast Asia and imbue it with a more individualistic, capitalist lifestyle.

While plastic flowers and cinemas represent vastly different worlds of production, both underscore the creative transformation of Hong Kong in the 1950s and 1960s. In both cases, capital and workers from China — experts and newcomers — became involved in industries that drew on techniques and ideas from existing production while creating new demands and markets. In neither case (as in Hong Kong's work in textiles, shipbuilding, or the incipient production of electronic goods) was the local market the dominant feature — nor were

China or Britain. Networks formed and reformed by regional connections and diaspora provided a foundation for continuing growth and reinvention, as we see in subsequent chapters. Yet, in order to more fully understand the transformation of the colony, we must turn from production to public policy and sociocultural changes.

SUBJECTS AND CITIZENS

Postwar development of Hong Kong as a production center is inseparable from the story of refugees. The spread of war across China into Hong Kong had produced rapid oscillations in population. After the war, however, returning exiles were joined by throngs fleeing further war in China. Between 1946 and 1950, the colony's population rose from 1,600,000 to 2,360,000, straining housing, infrastructure, and resources. The refugees faced an increasingly impermeable border. After 1953, constraints on movement into China would bond Hong Kong peoples to the territory in new ways.

Chinese residents also reevaluated colonial domination through the prism of British defeat, a view administrators called the "1946 outlook." Steve Tsang writes:

As time went by, the local people put things in better perspective and remembered the pre-war conditions as they actually were. There had been too much privilege, snobbery, discrimination, racial prejudice, corruption and absentee exploitation against the local Chinese. They began to see the pre-war government as having failed to give due regard to their interests. This change in public attitude became an important factor in the socio-political scene of the immediate post-war period. (2004: 142)

Hong Kong Chinese found a new "partner," Governor Mark Young, who increased Chinese presence in the Executive Council and government service, and instituted an income tax to create a new financial independence for the colony. He also favored increasing local participation in political processes. Limited functional constituencies were allowed to elect representatives to the Urban Council in 1953. His successors, however, chose a less interventionist approach (Tsang 2004).

Civic development took place during a period of extreme uncertainty and struggle for many citizens. The tenements where Japanese had confined British prisoners as punishment reverted to housing for Chinese. The *1951 Hong Kong Report* lamented the "row upon row of 4-storey buildings, the ground floors of which are usually shops, while the upper floors are dwellings, each floor consisting of one room subdivided into cubicles of approximately 64 square feet in which an entire family may live, using a communal kitchen and latrine shared by three or four families. In many of the older buildings of this kind, there are no washing facilities and the inhabitants are dependent upon public conveniences and bath-houses" (1952: 77). These tenements raised concerns about respiratory illnesses and the population's general welfare; their crowded settings permeate Hong Kong melodramas of the period. Lee Tit's *In the Face of Demolition* (1953), a Cantonese realist melodrama set in a decrepit Tong Lau, is representative of the films of its time. The ensemble cast displayed an array of tenants whose everyday struggles defined the harsh existence many working people faced in Hong Kong.

Equally preoccupying to the British were squatter settlements that climbed unstable hills and sprawled over "unoccupied" lands, housing 200,000 or more refugees in makeshift houses: "Since many of these are built of wood, packing cases, corrugated iron and sacking and are constructed extremely close to one another, the dangers of fire and disease are great" (1952: 78). Underscoring the seriousness of the housing crisis, the 1951 report adds that "while most squatters are poor, extremely few are destitute and some are quite well-to-do. . . . There are few squatter families without at least one wage-earner with a comparatively steady income . . . and that the squatters can by no means all be described as refugees since many are old-established Hong Kong families who have been forced to become squatters by the housing shortage" (1952: 83). Moreover, these self-constructed settlements took land that would soon be needed for industrial expansion.

Housing policy reform was spurred on by a catastrophic conflagration on Christmas Eve 1953, when a fire in the Kowloon squatter area of Shep Kip Mei left 50,000 people homeless. While some victims crowded existing houses, others moved to the street (Drakakis-Smith 1979; Smart 1986, 1992). In 1954, the government acted through both a Resettlement Authority and a semipublic/commercial Housing Authority. This was not simply an effort at social welfare, as the Commissioner for Resettlement noted: "Squatters are not resettled simply because they need . . . or deserve, hygienic and fireproof homes; they are resettled because the community can no longer afford to carry the fire risk, health risk and threat to public order and prestige which the squatter areas represent and because the community needs the land" (cited in Drakakis-Smith 1979: 44). Colonial order and prestige, fire, and health concerns and the need for land for building factories and offices underscore the top-down vision of this effort that situated class and opportunity in contested spaces. This was evident before the fire; the 1951 *Hong Kong Report*, for example, noted that "efforts to keep the center of the city free from squatter's huts have been successful" (1952: 79). In other areas, factories, commerce, and residences converged. Even Li Ka-Shing combined his factory in North Point with apartments as he expanded from manufacturing into real estate.

The initial government housing betrayed limited goals. Mark I Resettlement housing (visible in Alan Fong's 1980 film *Fathers and Sons*) were six to seven-story buildings, often H-shaped, without elevators, or private kitchen and sanitary facilities. Authorities allocated 2.2 square meters per adult and half that for a child — 11-square-meter flats (100 square feet) were to hold five people in a family. Other facilities were equally sparse, with one toilet for every eighteen residents with little forethought given to garbage or schools. But rents — $14 per month in the late 1950s — were less than some people had paid in squatter settlements. By the end of the 1950s, this public housing held 250,000 people. The housing authority offered better and roomier housing at higher rents, but did little for the poor left behind in tenements.

By the 1960s, the government moved toward registration and containment of squatters, recognizing the rights of those in illegal housing to resettlement while trying to prevent others from making the same claims as it attacked slums. A new Housing Board began to advise the government in 1965, and by 1973 the number living in various forms of public-assisted housing, improved over their initial designs in many cases, rose from 800,000 to 2.2 million (Drakakis-Smith 1979: 97; Smart 1992).

In addition, the government encouraged private housing at this time through redevelopment and higher building ratios for lots. The government would not constrain this growth until the mid-1960s (Richardson 1977), which allowed profits for owners but permitted problems in construction that continue to plague Hong Kong. This market, in which Li Ka-Shing participated, offered upwardly mobile families a reward for the deprivations of government-assisted housing, just as inexpensive housing facilitated cheap labor and potentially pacified working classes.

A growing Chinese middle class had other goals. In 1965, Mobil Oil funded the comprehensive development of high density "suburbanized" housing at Mei Foo Sun Tuen in Kowloon. The plan called for 100 twenty-story blocks with apartments ranging from one to four bedrooms that would house 90,000 people by 1976. In addition, it offered commercial facilities (market and mall), schools, churches, cinemas, and public transportation to work in Kowloon and Hong Kong. This development was clearly aimed at "families for whom the so-called 'European style' or 'luxury-class' apartment commonly required by the colony's temporary residents has become their standard as well" (Rosen 1976: 2). This image of parity with Westerners is telling, although Mei Foo, like other private housing, faced a declining market that only revived in the 1970s.

Public education expanded at this time as well, again serving multiple goals of civic improvement, pacification, and meeting the needs of a changing economy. In prewar education, expatriate children were sent abroad, while a stratified system of religious and other schools served a fraction of local children. The Seven-Year Plan of 1954 marked a government commitment to wider educational responsibility (Sweeting 1993). Primary school enrollment soared from 171,536 to 484,536 in this period, although not yet reaching all children of the swelling population. While the government raced to build schools, generally oriented to Cantonese language students, the *1961 Hong Kong Report* still noted that "as fast as some children leave after the morning session, others swarm in for instruction in the afternoon. In the evening many of the same schools cater for further children in an early evening session, or are used for evening classes or an adult recreation and training center" (1962: 112). Fifty-three thousand students enrolled in Anglo–Chinese grammar schools and 31,000 in Chinese middle schools. Confucian values of education and family met opportunity as the local population adapted to global changes.

For many, the limits of state welfare were overshadowed by economic opportunity. New factories offered possibilities for old and new families to achieve a steady income, as per capita GDP rose from $14 in 1948 to $500 in 1966 (Salaff 1995: 23). As Janet Salaff has pointed out in long-term work on Hong Kong, this opportunity structure must be seen through the prism of gender and family as well as class and migration. Women took on roughly half the manufacturing jobs in the colony, usually low-skilled and low-paid positions that demanded little beyond primary education (although there were limited opportunities for both higher education and career placement in the civil service and professions). As her vivid case studies in *Working Daughters of Hong Kong* show, family obligations and the workplace continued to dominate the lives of many women through the 1970s (1993). Meanwhile, family provided a safety net in the private sphere that supplanted a weak public one (see B.K. Leung 1996; Wong, White, and Gui 2004).

In the end, it would be wrong to see squatters and elites, workers and capitalists, fathers and daughters as if they lived separate histories: their lives meshed in factories, in competitions for space, and in dreams of growth and improvement. Together, they changed Hong Kong in relation to China, Britain, and — to a lesser extent — the U.S. Despite many obstacles, local observers noted the speed and depth of transformation. The *1962 Hong Kong Report* was upbeat about the recent history of the colony, noting "unprecedented development"; "the steadily increasing part which the Government has played, directly or indirectly, in the provision of housing and other forms of social services"; "the spectacular growth of new factories and workshops"; "private building on a wide scale"; and "an increased and ever increasing tempo . . . in every aspect of Hong Kong's daily life" (1963: 345). Local success meshed with new global ties, including trade and tourism, with a record 253,016 visitors, 35 percent of them from the United States.

Hong Kong was not independent of China, though. It remained a center for reexport of materials from Asia to China, which accounted for HK$77 million in 1962 (*1962 Hong Kong Report*, 1963: 77). In 1960, the growing but water-starved territory began to import water from China, although this did not allow the city to escape regional droughts when water service ran for only hours. After 1967 though, water extraction from the East River became a permanent lifeline to Hong Kong from China, paving the way for dependencies in fresh food supply and sewage disposal (Lam and Chan 1997).

Infrastructural connections echoed human ones, evident in the continuing flows of refugees and those who tried, with great difficulty, to maintain ties with families in the Mainland. In 1962, the official government report noted an increase in illegal immigration, with over 50,000 people crossing the border in May: 5620 were arrested on May 23rd alone, when 5112

83 Transformations of Hong Kong, 1930—1970

were returned to China. Family reunification was an important theme — as it has remained since the Handover. The immigration department also complained about the work created by shifting American attitudes toward Chinese migration, which would eventually create a new outflow as well (1962: 214).

Economic and social developments in Hong Kong and China spurred questions about Chinese rights and governance for middle and working classes outside the colonial system that relied on a Chinese elite and increasing numbers of trained Chinese civil servants who, nonetheless, rarely held top positions. While the bitter insults of prewar colonialism were distant, various issues came to the fore in political incidents in the mid-1960s despite economic growth and British propaganda asking Hong Kong people to become good citizens (Robertson 1996).

HONG KONG REVOLTS: THE CRISES OF THE MIDDLE 1960S

In April 1966, a five cent increase in the first class fare of the Star Ferry across the harbor sparked two days of riots, primarily by young working class males. Petitions had circulated against such an increase the year before and newspapers had criticized them, but the level of reaction surprised authorities. Most events were relatively localized and damage limited, despite the arrest of nearly 1000 people after demonstrations at the port and in Central. The Report of the Commission of Inquiry noted that "there is little doubt that the public had some sympathy for people who, in spite of normal Chinese reticence, felt strongly enough to demonstrate in public" (Commission of Inquiry 1967: 111). It concluded that "social workers gave evidence of a sense of insecurity among young people in Hong Kong arising from a feeling of impermanence and not-belonging. They held that the former arose partly from the traditional view of Hong Kong being an entrepôt (for people as well as goods), a place where one worked for a time and hoped to move on" — whether one was Chinese or expatriate (Report 1967: 125).

A year later, more serious urban disturbances erupted from the tinder of a labor dispute at Li Ka-Shing's artificial flower works, which became the focus of activities by Hong Kong communists linked to — but not under direct control of — the Maoist forces of the Cultural Revolution. The Cultural Revolution brought together internecine power struggles and divisions of young and old, "revolutionary" and "bourgeoisie," that would tear China apart for a decade. While Mao Zedong generally had left Hong Kong alone, its symbolism as a badge of shame and center of capitalism were powerful in China and overseas (as became clear in Macau's tumultuous protests in the same period).

Strikes resonated with the frustration of the working classes, but many elements were at play in this tumultuous year. Leftists in Hong Kong were inspired by the Cultural Revolution, but their visions were mediated with ideas of anticolonialism and class struggles. Many in Hong Kong sought a specific brand of localism and nationalism. Since the Communist Revolution of 1949, a Hong Kong brand of nationalism also had been struggling with ideas of Chineseness. Some on the Left, such as the Joint Labour Union, equated nationalism with Chinese socialism (Chow 2000) and its global context. A contemporary propaganda volume, for example, argued that "The present large-scale national persecution of the Chinese in Hong Kong launched by British imperialism has been a deliberate move . . . part of an anti-China plot conceived by the British Government in conspiracy with US imperialism" (*The May Upheaval in Hong Kong* 11–12). Some on the Right, including the Chinese Student Weeklies, suggested that to be Chinese was to be anti-Communist, because the Communist Party was stifling the economic progress of China. However, in 1974, a student activist of the day recalled that "after the 'May Storm' of Hong Kong in 1967, the deep contradiction of society, the contradiction of capitalist and labor, the contradictions of colonial government and the oppressed masses, were all exposed. One could no longer hide the faces of colonialism and capitalism" (in Chow 1997: 105). Another fraction promoted the concept of peace and prosperity, successfully convincing the majority of the Hong Kong population that any disturbance would hurt the welfare of both workers and elites.

When the British responded calmly, albeit forcefully (reading China as being unwilling to intervene), Hong Kong Maoists escalated the conflict in a summer bombing campaign that alienated wide swaths of the Hong Kong population, who grew more wary of the violence of these local communists and the implications of Chinese turmoil than of the actions of the British administration. Residents recalled bodies of victims of the Cultural Revolution literally floating down the Pearl River (Chow 2004), which only increased concerns. By December, the colonial administration brought the riots under control with the tacit support of the Chinese government.

In contemporary Hong Kong, the riots have become an uneasy subject for many. Before Deng's capitalist revolution, the official Chinese view of the riots was still one of "anti-British resistance." It failed because its cultural revolutionary tactics were too extreme, but not because of its objective as a labor uprising. Some Democrats, by contrast, read it as an indictment of the

Mainland government. No matter how the history of these disturbances has been rewritten by different interested groups, they marked an important turning point for Hong Kong. As Ian Scott concluded:

> The 1996–7 disturbances represented a major crisis of legitimacy for the regime. They posed questions about the stability of the political arrangements which had remained virtually unchanged since Lockhart's incorporation of economic and traditional elites into the government system of the 1890s. By the 1960s, the gap between those elites and the rest of the population, characterized by the absence of channels for political communication, poor working conditions and very little income re-distribution, had grown to the point where unrest was almost inevitable. The alienated youth of Hong Kong's industrial revolution made their comment on the system in the anomic violence of the 1966 riots. Their discontent might well have been exploited by communist organizers in 1967 had the party planned its strategy more carefully. (1994: 124; see Wong Cheuk Yin 2004 for a reinterpretation of the crisis of legitimacy)

After 1967, the colonial government became more responsive to the needs of the Hong Kong people. Social and political discontent in the 1960s led to a series of colonial reforms, ranging from further training for police to civil service reform to adoption of Cantonese as an official government language in 1974. Private employers offered slightly more equitable wages and more humane working conditions. Was it decolonization, or was it pacification created around the promise of "Peace and Prosperity" that allowed the colonial government and economic elites to continue their rule and to consolidate their power? In any event, the colonial government was able to marginalize the Left in Hong Kong, setting the stage for the further development of Hong Kong as a "modern" and "materialistic" metropolis of the twentieth century. Yet the events and changes also prefigured the coming of age of a new Hong Kong with citizens born and educated there, a Hong Kong Chinese population created in a different place and milieu. Chow Wing Sum, for example, claims that prior to 1967, many Hong Kong people were only living in a displaced China. The geographical features were different, but Hong Kong was still conservative, in the Confucian sense of the word. However, after 1967, Chow sees Hong Kong people as more open; by the 70s and 80s, divorce and premarital sex were more acceptable, and people were more opportunistic and open to material pursuits (2000: 53–62). While Chow has made value judgments here, his underlying thought is that Hong Kong became more Westernized and global after 1967. Hong Kong struggles, then, can never be divorced from the conflicts among traditional Confucian patriarchy, Chinese modernisms, and the West, whether they were manifested in politics, economics, or everyday culture and practices.

Yet the colonial administration's increasing wariness of China after 1967 was also an important new factor. Tellingly, Governor David Trench, whose 1966 Dickinson report had studied the possibility of a wider political franchise, bemoaned the influence of China. "If Hong Kong could be towed 100 miles out to sea it would be quite different and not necessarily a better place. But, since it can't be, every single policy — social, political or economic — is coloured by China's nearness, China's attitudes and the consequent difficulty of being certain of an assured future" (in Flowerdew 1997: 24).

Toward the Twenty-First Century:
Speed and Paradox
Four

As the strategies that represent Hong Kong and constitute its visibility move along flowing lines of speed and change, the experiences we have traced are still ongoing, still a work in progress. (Gutierrez, Portefaix, Manzini 2002: 42)

The 1967 Hong Kong riots and its aftermath signaled changing relationships among the British/colonial governments, the people of Hong Kong, and Mainland China, laying the foundation for further transformations, both local and global. This "work in progress," however, faced a continuing paradox that sociologist Keith Hopkins observed in the 1971. That is, "Hong Kong is one of the few poor countries in the world where people are rapidly growing richer," yet "it seems strange that Hong Kong is still, in spite of this economic advance, a British colony, one of the few left in the world" (1971: xi).

Development and colonialism converged in interesting ways within shifting global/local connections. Economic restructuring from the 1970s onward diminished the importance of manufacturing in Hong Kong, especially as cheaper factories grew in China (often with Hong Kong connections). Hong Kong became a tertiary center where tourism, finance, trade, real estate, and information all expanded, including managerial and intermediary roles vis-à-vis China, reinforcing to some extent the "Westernness" of the colony. Growth brought increased class and income inequality as well, although large-scale social reforms, carried out by the colonial administration in a time of prosperity, mitigated some of this. While the rich fueled increasing consumption and one of the most expensive property markets in the world, half the population lived in publicly sponsored housing. While older, less skilled workers suffered, some could still envision opportunities for their educated children or grandchildren, opportunities that also attracted immigrants from the People's Republic of China. One hundred seventy-eight thousand immigrants arrived in 1979 (Ma 2004: 683). In 1997, 50,000 legal residents arrived (mainly wives and children), while 50 illegals were arrested each day (*Hong Kong — A New Era* 1998: 381).

At the same time, local development faced the looming uncertainty of 1997. By the early 1970s, the People's Republic of China took on a new global status and Britain and China reinaugurated discussion of Hong Kong's future that crystallized in the 1980s. British insistence on an extension of "democracy" and the events of Tiananmen Square in 1989 heightened political and economic tensions thereafter, amid what commentators referred to as an "end-game syndrome." Nonetheless, after 1997, Hong Kong and its way of life survived in the new albeit vague status of a Special Administrative Region (SAR).

Amid these processes, which received increasing global attention in the 1990s, new generations grew up amidst unprecedented prosperity. As more immigrants from China continued to arrive, the experiences, aspirations, and fears of a critical mass of *Heung Geung Yan* (Hong Kongers) sparked debates about Hong Kong identity that continue globally to the present (Lau and Kuan 1988; Faure 1992; Turner 1996; Lee and Leung

1995; Abbas 1997; Chow 1997; Lau 1997; Matthews 2001; Lee 2003; Callahan 2004; Tsang 2004 and others).

This chapter begins with general economic transformations of the 1970s and 1980s (which are treated in greater detail by Meyer [2001] and studies published by the City University of Hong Kong Press [for example, Lui 1997; Kwong 1997], among other sources). The chapter then turns to political changes of the period, linking local policy reforms and Sino–British negotiations — again the focus of many detailed studies (see Tsang 2004). These streams are integrated into a discussion of transitions from Tiananmen to the present, including post-Handover crises. Within this framework, questions about global/local identity in Hong Kong culture, language, and action may be posed. The chapter concludes by rereading the cityscape introduced in chapter 1 for continuities and for processes that are remaking Hong Kong.

RESTRUCTURING HONG KONG'S ECONOMY, 1970–

Steve Tsang assessed the new maturity of Hong Kong as an economic unit at the end of the 1960s — another point of take-off — in somewhat rosy terms:

> As the 1970s dawned, Hong Kong had a solid industrial base, excellent trade networks, modern international banking, insurance and other business servicing facilities, an increasingly educated workforce, and efficient public services to support and sustain a modern economy. It has also seen the transformation of its workforce from one made up of desperate immigrants or refugees struggling for survival into a modern labour force who were themselves consumers and a positive factor in further economic development. (2004: 174)

Hong Kong was a place of full and expanding employment and growing GDP — as it would be for decades. The Hong Kong GDP grew from HK$7.4 billion in 1961 to HK$23.0 billion in 1970, before doubling (49.3 billion) in 1975 and nearly tripling by 1980 (141.8 billion; US$18 billion). Per capita income rose in this time from HK$2,300 to HK$28,000 (US$295 to US$3,590). By 1995, the same measures would reach $1011.6 billion (US$130 billion) and HK$ 179,500 (US$23,000, Lui 1997: 18). As of 2004, GDP passed US$200 billion, while per capita income passed US$28,000.

Prosperity differed across sectors. Manufacturing positions fell from 47 percent (1971) to 41 percent (1981) and 28 percent (1991). Jobs in finance, insurance, and real estate increased from 1.6 percent in 1961 to 10.6 in 1991; the work force in retail, wholesale, hotels, and restaurants rose from 171,000 to 611,000. By the 1990s, 60 percent of the Hong Kong labor force worked in the service sector (Lui Hon-Kwang 1997).

This growth involved multiple transformations. Tourism, for example, was spurred by increasing American interest in Asia and growing wealth in other Asian countries, for whose elites Hong Kong became a destination; these short-haul trips still dominate the market (Kwong 1997). Visitors, in turn, helped re-create Hong Kong as a global shopping center. A consumption-driven economy transformed land and property, eventuating the now-ubiquitous malling of Hong Kong (Chung et al. 2001; Gutierrez, Portefaix, and Manzini 2002). Tai-Lok Lui has underscored the multiple meanings of Hong Kong's first mall, the Ocean Terminal, which opened on May 23, 1966: "Despite its image of being a big shopping mall serving the local leisure class and overseas tourists, it was perceived as more than just another venue of high consumption.

It was a place for modern and Western ways of life. Its modern atmosphere was found liberating — it was a rendezvous for the young white-collar and factory workers . . . and also a salon for young intellectuals" (2001: 37).

Even if tailors still cajole passersby with suits made overnight and gaudy cheung-sams, Hong Kong became an entrepôt for elite goods. By the time the Landmark shopping complex opened in Central in 1980, designer European brand names such as Chanel, Gucci, and Louis Vuitton offered exclusive shopping there, in Pacific Place or the arcades and shops surrounding the Peninsula Hotel. These stores attract local shoppers, Asian, European, and American visitors, and, increasingly, Mainland Chinese. Joyce Ma, of the Wing On Department Store family, even created the elegant boutique Joyce, which spread across Asia before it was taken over by Wheelock and Company in 2000 as a result of the regional financial crisis.

Still, global elite commerce has amplified rather than replaced older forms of exchange. While malls and shopping districts from Central to the new transportation, entertainment, and commercial centers of New Towns vary in clientele and stores, Mong Kok, where the famous Woman's Street is located, continues to attract shoppers from all over the SAR because of its trendy and cheap goods. More supermarkets, with a work force that includes more women, have opened to compete with traditional wet markets. Meanwhile, many wet markets have been moved into the lower floors of government high-rises that represent multifunctional district centers with libraries, performing spaces, and other Urban Council offices. Street hawking still provides some employment for those with limited education and skills, offering cheap goods and food to different strata of Hong Kong society and a regular trade for recent immigrants, both legal and illegal (J. Smart 1989; Cheng and Chow 1997). While many residents feel that traditional trades and crafts are disappearing, a nostalgia underscored by a 1995 Hong Kong Museum of History exhibition (called *"Of Hearts and Hands"*), Hong Kong has become a vibrant consumer society with goods and services for very different segments of the population.

Banking development in this era has followed a somewhat different logic. The government had restricted banking licenses in the 1960s, easing limits later as international banks sought to establish themselves in the city. In addition to Hong Kong's transportation and communication networks and proximity to China, Meyer argues that the networks of specialized finance it had built for a century provided a continuing platform for consolidation and growth: "Hong Kong's social network of capital" (2000: 199). Banks attracted other financial services — lawyers, accountants, and consultants — creating an invaluable center of regional headquarters for global firms. Hong Kong's centurial hongs have provided continuity and management resources.

Other longstanding economic institutions such as the gold exchange and the Stock Exchange have reformed as well. The Hong Kong Stock Exchange, for example, had been run as a small-scale operation since 1880. By the 1970s, entrepreneurs challenged it with alternative exchanges before consolidating them in 1986. While the stock market modernized, its unregulated environment led to startling fluctuations in the early 1970s, including a one-day drop in the Hang Seng index from around 1700 to 450 in 1973. In 1974, amid worldwide financial woes, the index fell to 150 points; the market closed for four days in 1987 during another crisis. However, this speculation seemed to fit laissez-faire capitalist Hong Kong culture (if not also its love of gambling). With no capital gains tax, many citizens speculated on the stock market, from the very rich to the working class. When an Initial Public Offering was announced, people lined up overnight to apply for them, money in hand. When the market was robust in the early 1970s, these stocks seemed to double or even triple the initial price. However, when the market crashed, small investors, some of whom had gambled their life savings, suffered while institutional investors, local and foreign, had the flexibility to rebound.

The legitimacy of the stock market was guaranteed by the colonial government, which had faced many complaints about corruption, especially in its police force. Governor Murray MacLehose's establishment of the ICAC (Independent Commission against Corruption) in 1974 again promoted Hong Kong as a global business center "of world standards." (The films *Lee Rock I and II* (1991–1992) recall the rise and fall of a famous crooked policeman in this era and the impact of the ICAC.)

Economic development transcended the limits of the colony in the 1980s, as Hong Kong expertise and connections became newly valuable in cross-border investment. Investment in China allowed Hong Kong to move production across the border, with management, investment, and commerce filtered through Hong Kong. Local connections changed as well.

Governor MacLehose modernized the colony's transportation infrastructure through the subway system, on which construction began in 1974, unifying the island and Kowloon with rapid transport and cross-harbor car tunnels. Such projects spurred new building, which spilled out of Central and into development of new shopping, hotel, entertainment, and office complexes in Causeway Bay, Wan Chai, and Tsim Sha Tsui.

Yet while some grew rich, it also became more difficult for working Hong Kong people to find substitute employment, which sometimes paid less and proved more unstable (Smart and Smart 1998; see chapter 5). The housing sector encapsulates these concerns with opportunity and inequality. Real estate speculation took off in this era of global–local restructuring. The general explanation for the high housing prices in Hong Kong has always been its vast population and limited buildable land. Jean Jaulin and Jean-Francois Huchet, however, assert that "the rise in real estate prices is above all the result of a deliberate policy pursued by the British Administration since 1983 with the approval of Peking. The signing of the Joint Declaration in 1984 set a ceiling on land sales of fifty hectares a year from 1985" (2004: 263). With an artificially limited supply of land, land prices rose much faster than income. From 1970 to the mid-1980s, land prices increased 15.5 percent annually, while wages increased 11.9 percent. From 1984 to early 1993, land prices doubled the rate of wage increases. By 1993, the price of a four-hundred-square-foot flat in the city would equal fifteen years of income for a college graduate (Hui 2004: 282). Speculation shaped the tumultuous reconstruction of the landscape itself.

Developers profited handsomely, creating an oligopoly led by Li Ka-shing's Cheung Kong corporation (Jaulin and Huchet 2004: 264). Nearly 30 percent of government revenue came from property and land until after the Handover, while upper classes also profited from the real estate bubble. Developers, in turn, obtained loans from foreign banks. In 1998, Japanese banks held one-third of the loans extended to real estate development, followed by Germany (11.4 percent), the United States (7.3 percent), and France (6.8 percent);

Hong Kong banks only wrote 12.7 percent of these loans (Hui 2004: 285). In this ambience of speculation and movement, "stir-frying" property and stocks reached a fevered pitch before the 1997 Handover and subsequent waves of Asian recession, even among those only aspiring to middle-class status. This rampant capitalist environment obviously leaves those with no initial capital behind; home ownership was not possible for most lower income families.

We can recapitulate the structural transformations of this period once again through Li Ka-Shing, who, with further capital from his marriage, expanded his interests in property, turning the factory over to executives. In the 1970s, he mounted a takeover attack on a hong, one of the British corporations that embodied colonial rule in Hong Kong for more than a century. Aided by Pao Yue Kong, a shipping magnate who in 1972 had become the first Chinese on the board of the Hongkong and Shanghai Bank, Li controlled Hutchison Whampoa by 1978. Li also linked his plans to China through his involvement in Citic corporation and other connections, giving him leverage with pre- and post-Handover governments. He also became a philanthropist, creating his own foundation and donating a university to his native Shantou (Chan 1997; Ching 1999).

SOCIAL POLICIES AND CIVIC TRANSFORMATION

In 1976, journalist John Hughes noted that "if Hong Kong, incredibly, is allowed to live out its legal term of colonialism, the world of that twenty-year-distant era will be so transformed that Hong Kong's fate and influence will be of even less importance than it is today. The Chinese, in their terribly patient way, will have remoulded Communism" (1976: 189). In the 1970s, changes in China and its Communism clearly shaped the fate of the colony as Governor Murray MacLehose guided Hong Kong into a new international context while developing new local policies. In particular, a 9 percent annual growth in GNP over the decade allowed him to foster programs in education, welfare, and housing that went beyond the reactive measures of the 1950s and 1960s.

Housing intervention began with a Ten-Year Housing Program in 1972 aimed at providing housing for nearly two million people. Squatter clearance continued throughout this period as well (Smart 1992). Such clearance often entailed the disruption of families and communities that had grown around the makeshift streets and businesses of enduring settlements. As various sections were cleared in the early 1980s, complaints were heard from small industrialists and shopkeepers who had combined residence and business in ways they could not do in public housing. In many squatter settlements, others had profited from renting space to later arrivals. The social complexity of squatter areas preceded political action and organization that would resist development for decades. The Walled City was only cleared in the 1990s. Squatter housing survived in Diamond Hill as of 2000, beside the elegant Hollywood Plaza — a social disjunction chronicled in Fruit Chan's *Hollywood Hong Kong* (2002).

Where could people move? The year 1973 saw the reorganization of the Housing Authority and initial construction of New Towns, which adapted British garden–city ideals to a deconcentration of population through the New Territories. A preliminary town plan by Sir Patrick Abercrombie to develop inclusive residential and workplace settlements as alternatives to the crowded urban districts was in place by 1948. Given the government's ownership of all land, such planning was potentially quite powerful. These new urban residential complexes, built around transportation hubs and commercial centers, including traditional village cores, eventually set the pace for subsequent development of New Territories centers such as Sha Tin and New Towns such as Tsuen Wan, Tuen Mun, and Yuen Long (Bristow 1989; Hayes 1993). This planned development, which incorporated cultural facilities, schools, and health and welfare services, also set the model for subsequent extensive upscale private development around commercial podia. In any event, squatter clearance and New Towns, while offering better living conditions, sometimes challenged working conditions because new settlements did not have enough jobs to offer their residents, and many had to travel long distances to their workplaces, or settle for part-time jobs (Smart 1986).

Still, even if many citizens felt better off, others could not participate in the speculative markets discussed above. Lui notes that not only did the Gini coefficient of income inequality rise from 0.377 in 1976 to 0.421 in 1999, but also "the gender-earnings gap was significant and pervasive during 1976–1991" (1997: 15). In an anthology of the lives of working-class women, Choi Pao King (2002) interviewed women who went to evening schools when factory work took them away from regular schooling in the1970s. For them, educational, residential, and employment opportunities were limited, despite the growth of the Hong Kong economy (see Salaff 1993). They lived in cramped boats, squatter estates, private apartments, and public housing in Shau Kei Wan. Boats and squatter dwellings lacked proper plumbing and hygiene, and faced the threat of fire and typhoons; nearly all the residents shared bathrooms and kitchens. In 1976, a fire swept Oi Dit Chui Wan (Aldrich Bay), a boat and squatter area, forcing residents into public housing. Today, landfills and high-rise residential buildings have replaced their coastal dwelling sites.

John Myers, working in the resettlement estate of Kwun Tong in the 1970s, also discovered generational divisions in these Hong Kongers' outlooks for the future. Parents had become satisfied with resettlement and were open to further government programs to improve housing. Among youth, however, "for the more upwardly mobile and better educated the primary reaction tends to be embarrassment. . . . Among the poorly educated whose future is perceived as bleak there is an increasing tendency toward involvement in petty and organized crime" (1976: 31). As middle-class youths consumed more and more, they sought to leave these developments behind. Meanwhile, an urban perception of outlying public housing towers scarred by youth gangs — not unfamiliar from Europe and the United States — established images of space and class played out in the Handover year in the wildly successful teen films *Young and Dangerous* (I–IV, 1996–1997). This saga of gang buddies begins in a nondescript housing development in the 1970s with confrontations of Triads and schoolboys. The stories develop alongside the restructuring of the colony, incorporating images of metropolitan glamour, sexual magnetism, and bloody gang fights to the Hong Kong story.

Housing developments were also transformed by Governor MacLehose's 1977 Home Ownership Scheme. This promoted the sale of public flats to private ownership, foreshadowing subsequent privatization schemes that increasingly vested Hong Kong citizens in place and property through the 1990s (Lau, Lee, and Zhong 2004).

New education policies also buttressed opportunities and economic progress. Compulsory primary education was introduced in 1971; in 1978, it was extended to age fifteen (completion of secondary school). By 1990, Hong Kong had 785 kindergartens and 668 primary schools — 50 government, 78 private, and the rest managed by voluntary agencies with government assistance, including many religious institutions. The same division occurred in 434 secondary schools (Cheng 1991; Chu 2004). Over time, more technical schools also appeared.

The growth of tertiary institutions especially enhanced Hong Kong's work force. Hong Kong Polytechnic opened in 1984, and Hong Kong University of Science and Technology opened in 1988 (Sweeting 1992). Students whose parents had fled China with little now gained university degrees. Indeed, forecasters soon worried about a surplus of college-educated employees, although cross-border management and emigration would offer new opportunities in the decade ahead.

Some local social policy issues were clearly global. On May 4, 1975, about 3743 Vietnamese refugees, among them many ethnic Chinese, landed in Hong Kong, which shared this human flow after the Vietnam War with other Southeast Asian countries until refugees could resettle in the West. Eventually, 214,555 Vietnamese passed through Hong Kong; 140,000 were granted asylum in the West and 67,000 repatriated (see Immigration, Hong Kong Web site). During three decades, these boat people were kept in detention centers and refugee camps where many complained of substandard living arrangements, despite Hong Kong's HK$2.6 billion in expenditures (Torgrimson 1991). Human rights groups, including international celebrities, accused the Hong Kong government of inhumanity. Yet, some citizens in Hong Kong felt that the West itself was at fault because its nations should have accepted refugees more rapidly.

The Joint Declaration demanded that all Vietnamese refugees be resettled before the Handover. Unconditional temporary asylum was replaced in 1988 by a screening to determine whether Vietnamese were political refugees or economic migrants. The forced repatriation that followed angered many; riots broke out in the camps. The last refugee camp, Pillar Point, closed in 2000, and the remaining 1408 refugees gained Hong Kong residency. Essentially, Hong Kong citizens were trapped in international events beyond local control with multiple interests and players. Moreover, before assuming sovereignty, the Chinese government already had exerted its power to determine rights of abode. Ann Hui's *The Story of Woo Viet* (1981) and *Boat People* (1982) attempted to address many of these issues: Vietnamese refugees, ethnic Chinese Vietnamese, the Vietnamese Communist government, and the treatment of Vietnamese Boat People in Hong Kong. At the same time, some critics in Hong Kong read these films as allegories of the territory's changing relation to China.

FROM COLONIAL RULE TO THE HKSAR

Alongside social policy initiatives from the government, the dominant political narrative of the 1980s was the end of colonialism. China replaced Taiwan in the UN Security Council in 1972; U.S. President Richard Nixon's visit to Beijing followed. These diplomatic openings challenged Cold War barriers that had isolated Hong Kong. Increasing openness in trade and communication accompanied fear about the future, especially with regard to the Cultural Revolution, whose impact and image had already crossed the border in the 1960s. New struggles for leadership became evident in the 1970s, as Mao reinstated his former deputy Deng Xiaoping to power. But the pragmatic

Deng still had enemies among the radical Gang of Four and was purged again in 1976 after the death of Premier Zhou Enlai. Only with the death of Mao and the subsequent purge of the Gang of Four did Deng begin his rise to power once again, a trajectory that would take China in a different direction in the decades ahead. By the late 1970s, after years of suspicion, hostility, occasional agreements, and mutual transformations in cross-border relations, Governor MacLehose raised the future of the colony and the possible extension of British sovereignty during a 1979 visit to Beijing. He also participated in the initial negotiations, although most discussion involved his successors and British Prime Minister Margaret Thatcher herself.

By 1981, China took a firm position, comparing Hong Kong to Taiwan (still under the rule of the Nationalists, who had abandoned the Mainland in 1949), but promoting the model of "One Country, Two Systems" to allow for a relative degree of autonomy and difference for Hong Kong within the context of a larger Chinese state. When the newly elected Thatcher arrived in Beijing in 1982, she hoped to maintain British claims, but found the Chinese unyielding on a 1997 return. On leaving a meeting with Premier Zhao Ziyang, in fact, Thatcher slipped on the stairs of the Great Hall of the People, an event taken as ominous by Hong Kong residents excluded from these conversations. Indeed, throughout the talks, Hong Kong's economy quickly registered local and global public fears in response to the tiniest clues. Flowerdew, for example, notes that the value of the Hong Kong dollar fell 10 percent in three hours on September 23 when talks adjourned without the designation "useful and constructive" or a concrete future meeting date (1998: 35). By 1983, Britain had surrendered sovereignty, working with China's plan to create a SAR whose social and economic system would remain unchanged for 50 years, with a Basic Law codifying and preserving Hong Kong rights and practices. Nevertheless, that same year, Urban Council elections were opened to Hong Kongers over the age of twenty-one, foreshadowing debates ahead over democratic reform.

In December 1984, leaders of the two sovereign nations signed the Sino–British Joint Declaration, agreeing on a transfer of sovereignty from Britain to the People's Republic on July 1, 1997. Annexes to this agreement set forth China's guarantees of continuity for Hong Kong's social and economic systems and its rights and freedoms, including speech, travel, religion, and the press. Yet these rights would be guaranteed under Chinese law, clearly demarcating Hong Kong's subordinate position and raising issues about Hong Kong's identity and way of life.

In 1985, China appointed a consultant committee, including Hong Kong residents but under PRC control, to draft the Basic Law for the SAR. This hybrid process created anxieties in Hong Kong before the law was finally promulgated in 1990. As we see today (chapter 1), its provisions remain an area of contestation between the Chinese government and many Hong Kong people facing "One Country, Two Systems."

The years leading up to the Handover represented a curious political and economic amalgam, where visions of reunification produced real uncertainties in Hong Kong's population amid growing wealth and opportunity. While some fled or threatened to flee to Australia, Britain, Canada, or the United States, even those who established residency elsewhere often returned to Hong Kong for the opportunities it offered (see chapter 7). By 1996, Wong Yue-Tim estimated that 60 of every 100 Hong Kongers who left returned, sometimes after establishing dual residency (1997). But this decade also had witnessed further dramatic changes in Hong Kong *and* China.

While Britain and China negotiated the future *for* Hong Kong, Britain explored plans to expand electoral participation in local governance in Hong Kong that challenged Chinese understandings of the change of sovereignty and led to renewed conflict. Through the late 1980s, government surveys and publications hinted at the possibilities of limited direct elections to the Legislative Council as early as 1988, while Chinese and Hong Kong delegates were still drafting the Basic Law that might or might not recognize this process. The two powers diverged over strategies of incorporation: China brought Chinese Hong Kong elites into consultation in drafting the Basic Law, while Britain talked of moving slowly toward democracy, recognizing functional constituencies and individual voters. Some Hong Kong proponents of democracy, notably Martin Lee and Szeto Wah, dissented publicly from Chinese deliberations and even burned copies of the Basic Law once it had been drafted in 1989.

Beginning with the 1991 Legislative Council elections, Britain belatedly offered direct election of some representatives of the Hong Kong people. After arriving in 1992, Chris Patten, the final Governor, also became a strong advocate of more participatory rule, a position strengthened by his Conservative Party connections in Britain (Dimbley 1997; Flowerdew 1998; Patten 1998). More direct elections to the LegCo followed in 1995, when Patten increased direct voting and separated Legislative and Executive branches more clearly. China, however, grew increasingly irritated with British innovations. The erstwhile metaphor of the transition as a "through train," which ensured continuity gave way to China's more family-based image of constructing a "separate kitchen" (political framework). China marginalized British electoral changes, in fact, by appointing its own provisional Legislative Council (Tsang 2004). Nevertheless, even limited experiences of participation laid the foundation for those in Hong Kong who continue to demand more democracy from Beijing.

Global and local perceptions of Hong Kong's evolution were transformed in the summer of 1989 by popular protests in Beijing's Tiananmen Square, in front of what had been the Forbidden City. Hundreds of thousands of students and workers there and across China sought reforms pleading their case on a global screen through television coverage, faxes, and telecommunications. Many people in Hong Kong were in contact with these protestors and rallied in their support. This made it all the more shocking when tanks and soldiers moved brutally against the protestors on June 4th. One million people took to the streets of Hong Kong in protest as confidence in the Joint Declaration evaporated. There was a new exodus from the colony. Britain was asked to extend citizenship to 3.25 million subjects, but refused to do so. Meanwhile, 50 to 100 illegal Chinese immigrants crossed the border each day, despite border enforcement, tempted by the same dreams (Yep, Ngok, and Zhu 2004).

Hong Kong proved resilient; within eighteen months, real estate prices had regained their pre-Tiananmen levels and people prepared for partial elections to the Legislative Council. The introduction to the skeptical *Other Hong Kong Report 1991* noted that

During the Sino–British negotiations over the future of Hong Kong in 1982 and 1983, and also during the one-year period after the Tiananmen incident, the mood in Hong Kong was one of doom and gloom. However, during 1986 to 1988, and also in the first half of 1991, real estate prices spiraled upward, and the mood of the market was one of exhilaration. The seasoned observer knows that Hong Kong people are prone to overreact, and the Hong Kong economy is prone to cycles of boom and bust. The cynic may even characterize the Hong Kong community as manic depressive. (Sung 1991: xxi)

The boom recognized the success of Hong Kong's ongoing economic transformations. In the early 1990s, Yueng Yue-Man noted the geographic centrality of Hong Kong and its multiple systems of connection — air, telecommunications, and shipping — which made it a world city not only for Asia (especially China), but also as a chronological placeholder for 24-hour banking between London and New York. Hong Kong ranked "sixth in the world in foreign exchange markets, seventh in stock market capitalization, fourth in loan syndication, fourth in the number of foreign banks, and eleventh in terms of external assets of banks" (1996: 155). By 1995, ten million visitors arrived each year, 22 percent from the PRC (Kwong 1997: 10, 27–32). Locally, the "success" of the property market made Hong Kong one of the most expensive cities in the world to live in, a great market for foreign investors and businessmen. This success also puts property ownership out of reach of the majority of its population, but who instead find space in public/subsidized housing. Still, as Helen Cheng observed in 2001: "Their own experiences make the people I interviewed deeply believe that upward mobility to an eventual high-class life in Hong Kong is indeed achievable. Home and the consumption of home as a physical form, seem more flexible as class boundaries than the cultural capital of music or art" (2001: 225).

During this period, Hong Kong's presence abroad has developed in new ways, betraying colonial and postcolonial uncertainty. The Hongkong and Shanghai Bank, for example, embarked on its own aggressive globalization, purchasing foreign banks and opening branches. Its acquisition of Marine Midland Bank in the United Kingdom and United States led to a new headquarters for the Hongkong Shanghai Banking Corporation (HSBC) in London in 1992. The bank also expanded in Europe, Australia, and Asia. Meanwhile, Jardine Matheson moved its headquarters to the Caribbean in 1984.

The approach of 1997 raised other questions about the diverse residents of Hong Kong. The population of South Asians also increased after World War II, reaching twenty thousand by the 1960s. By 1997, this multigenerational population included Hindus, South Asian Muslims, Sikhs, and Nepalis (retired Gurkhas). Their status was challenged by Chinese sovereignty, which led some to petition the British government for citizenship (Vaid 1972; White 1994). Filipinas, mainly fixed-term contract domestics, were a mainstay of dual-career families and had replaced Chinese amahs, who were part of Wong's world growing up in the 1960s and 1970s. Yet even they wondered about future employment and Mainland competition. Finally, Hong Kong was at least a temporary home to other Western expatriates — British, Americans, Canadians, and Australians — and elite Chinese with dual passports, which raised questions of loyalty (at least for those taking Hong Kong Special Administrative Region offices). The major issue of people and movement that continued after the Handover, however, was that of the Mainland immigration, a longtime demographic feature of Hong Kong's formation that now seemed to threaten an overwhelming flood of new co-citizens (Callahan 2004).

Amid these lingering issues, then, Hong Kong seemed to move inevitably toward the Handover. In early 1997, the new chief executive, Shanghai-born businessman Tung Chee-hwa, was elected in a televised vote by 400 PRC-selected delegates. Tens of thousands packed Victoria Park on June 4, 1997, for what some feared might be the last commemoration of Tiananmen (it has not been). Finally, on the night of June 30th, PRC President Jiang Zemin and Charles, Prince of Wales, partici-pated in the televised ceremony at the new Convention Center jutting into the harbor below Wan Chai. For many hours after midnight, people thronged the streets, going to Handover ("Hangover") parties, watching fireworks over the harbor, glancing at new guards from the People's Liberation Army or trying to catch a glimpse of the departing royal yacht. As Tsang observed, at this crucial point, "Whether Governor Patten, or for that matter anyone, represented the people of Hong Kong at the transfer of power was a moot point. The people of Hong Kong had been specifically excluded from the negotiations for their future in accordance with PRC policy. . . . Hong Kong was handed over with its people reduced to spectators and provid-ers of entertainment for the day's celebration" (2004: 271).

Chris Patten's memoirs later noted that "Hong Kong is where the story of Empire ended, but it is a footnote to a tale already largely told" (1998: 3). Jiang Zemin celebrated the "return of Hong Kong to the motherland" through a different prism; as the *Guangzhou Daily* proclaimed more effusively, "It is time for the

Chinese nation to wash away 100 years of shame and feel proud and elated" (Knight and Nakano 1999: 90, 197; Callahan 2004). The Handover as global spectacle (Knight and Nakano 1999; Lee, Chan, Pan and So 2002) evoked more apocalyptic visions elsewhere, often tinged with anti-Chinese sentiments (Cayrol 1998). The Hong Kong–based Japanese journalist Ichiro Yoshida recalled queries from his homeland, like "What's going to happen to brand-name goods?" and "Will the Democrats get arrested when Hong Kong returns to China?" (in Knight and Nakano 1999: 25). Even Jan Morris, after decades of reporting on the colony, chose the Handover as her final reportage, subtitling her revised text "Epilogue to an Empire" (1997; 2003: 438–441).

Western popular fiction also played with this foreboding. John McClean's *Tartan Dragon*, retelling the history of the colony through a fictional Scottish *taipan*, ended with its protagonist sailing away in the wake of the royal yacht (1996; see Siu 1997; New 2000). Fictional post-Handover Hong Kong sometimes retains these overtones as a battleground of communism and the West in the work of Steven Coonts (*Hong Kong*, 2002) and James Thayer (*The White Swan*, 2004). Even Hong Kong–born filmmaker Wayne Wang created protest suicides amid the moral decay of empire (and echoes of Suzie Wong) that permeate his Handover opus, *The Chinese Box* (1999). By contrast, Wong Kar-Wai has evoked a future haunting date in his 2004 movie *2046*, an evocative allusion to the end of the SAR woven into another intimate story of time, people, place, and memory in Hong Kong. Evans Chan has also explored Handover issues in a broader frame in his 1998 film *Journey to Beijing*.

The Hong Kong way of life did not end in 1997. As one Hong Kong friend remarked to us a few days before the event,

"The best thing is that the British are leaving Hong Kong. The worst part is that the Chinese are coming." In the days after the Handover, the "horses still ran and the people kept dancing," as one popular phrase put it (*ma jiu pao mo jiu tiu*). While the new government had replaced the British Legislative Council, new elections were held in 1998, 2000, and 2004. But a major challenge for the HKSAR was economic rather than political. The Asian financial crisis of 1997–1998 affected every country in Asia. While Hong Kong had healthier foundations than Thailand, Malaysia, or the Philippines, it too fell into recession. Unemployment rose from 2.2 percent in 1997 to 8.3 percent in 2003, the highest figure since 1981. Stories of eligible applicants lining up for scant openings peppered the news alongside reports of suicides of those whose businesses had failed. Property prices fell by 30 to 50 percent, leaving some flats worth less than their mortgage; middle class Hong Kong property owners found themselves with "negatively valued" properties (Callick 1998). The rate of economic growth slipped from 10.5 percent in 2000 to 0.1 percent in 2001, although it has rebounded since.

In addition to economic problems, avian flu and Severe Acute Respiratory Syndrome (SARS) have also beset the territory. Issues of Mainland immigration and political rights reached a critical point in 1999, when China overruled the Hong Kong judiciary, but continued to erupt around many issues, as we have seen. Despite Tung Chee-Hwa's 2004 reelection, his popularity plummeted, stimulating protests even after the economy rebounded. In the 2004 LegCo elections, meanwhile, 140,000 people voted for 30 functional constituencies, defined by profession or industry, while 2.8 million decided the other 20 geographic representatives.

A new transition arose on May 5, 2005 when Chief Executive Tung resigned, citing health problems. He was replaced by Chief Secretary (Sir) Donald Tsang Yam Kuen, who had served for decades in the colonial Civil Service and holds an M.A. in Public Administration from Harvard; he had been active in pursuit of the Hong Kong Disneyland project as well. The resignation also raised questions about the term of a new replacement and the extent of voting. In the end, China ruled that this would only be a replacement term of two years, decided by the 800 votes of the Election Committee. Tsang resigned temporarily to run for this office and was replaced by HKSAR Financial Secretary Henry Tang Ying-Yem. On June 16th, Tsang was declared Chief Executive in the absence of any other valid nominations, and plans began for him to move to the refurbished and renamed Government House.

Despite these complex problems and developments, those who forecasted the collapse or disappearance of Hong Kong and its people were wrong. While in his 2005 address, Tung apologized for problems in government, and in meeting the needs of the poor, he could still speak of the need to build a beautiful future for the country (*Ming Bao* January 12, 2005; Bradsher 2005b). Years of prosperity followed by challenges have generated a stronger voice and identity in the Hong Kong people themselves, as we have seen in chapter 1, in response to SARS and Article 23. Yet, the construction of a Hong Kong identity within shifting global relations evokes many issues.

WHO IS HONG KONG?

Despite the fanfare of the Handover as a transformative moment, a Hong Kong identity has emerged more slowly over many decades through people: families reproducing themselves in the city, making use of its places and reflecting on its opportunities, constituting a growing, educated Chinese middle class whose economic and political interests came into focus in the 1990s, alongside a struggling working class whose achievements have always been less visible. In the decade before the Handover, questions of identity attracted many scholars and observers. Lau Siu-Kai and Kuan Hsin-Chi, examining the "ethos" of the Hong Kong Chinese, found that it encompassed "a constellation of elements with different origins: Chinese tradition, Western modernizing influences, and local developments. . . . [that] have not been undergirded by supportive institutional changes, but are largely the product of changing conventions or practices" (1988: 190). When introducing the 1996 exhibit "Hong Kong Sixties: Designing Identity" at the Hong Kong Arts Centre, Director Oscar Ho asked, "If our father is British and mother Chinese, who are we?" (1996: xiii). In the volume accompanying this exhibit, Matthew Turner used the landscape of Hong Kong — especially the International Style performance space that is known as City Hall — and the documents of the Handover to frame questions of identity.

> From the standpoint of International Law, it is clear that the Hong Kong people are "people." But an identity that can be possessed can also be taken away, just as the Hong Kong people have been "divided," constituted as a "community," only to be dissolved, reconstituted and dissolved again with the ebb and flow of politics. In the end, cultural identity, like democracy, cannot be given by lawyers, politicians or professors — it must be made. (1996: 31)

Turner's answer, at least within the context of this exhibit, linked identity to a less politicized idea of *lifestyle*, "for life-style can be expressed, but it cannot easily be censored" (1996; see Mathews and Lui 2001).

Lau and Kuan, like Turner, see differentiation from the Mainland as part of the process of identity creation. Hong Kongers coming of age in the 1970s had less direct affiliation or experience of China either through migration or political ties, and their colonial education stressed the utility of English while ignoring China after 1949. "New" Chinese immigrants also became a foil for Hong Kong "difference." Ma Kit-Wai, for example, has highlighted the 1970s television drama of Ah-Chan, a mainland immigrant and "shallow country bumpkin" who represents "stupidity, low analytical skills, backwardness and poverty." Ah-Chan became a Hong Kong label for Chinese from the PRC. Conversely, Hong Kong people are "smart, capable, educated and modern" (2002: 686). Even though these Hong Kongers are descendants of immigrants, they embody the ambivalence of separating themselves from China while grappling with their own Chineseness, sorting out modernization and tradition, ideology and materialism. On the eve of the Handover, Siu Fung Han, a columnist in *Ming Pao Monthly*, explained the elite who had matured in the 70s: "This generation of Hong Kong people . . . would not see themselves as having unquestioned emotional ties with China. However, they want to understand China from an enlightened perspective, to help China progress, making China part of the world. . . . If this generation were given the necessary space, they would bring the world through Hong Kong to China, helping China enter the twenty-first century with pride" (2002: 713; Mathews and Lui 2001; Lee 2003; Callahan 2004; Carroll 2005).

Hong Kong people are Chinese, but not China's Chinese. This view of Mainland China and its people is a product of political processes that created boundaries between two Chinese spaces, exacerbated by differential political and economic development. At the same time, issues of who may *be* in Hong Kong (right of abode) remains a thorny issue that pits Hong Kong people against potential immigrants (see Callahan 2004).

Others have looked for Hong Kong identity in cultural practices. Ackbar Abbas, writing about the "aesthetics of disappearance" of Hong Kong, has posed culture and identity as a challenge to a city based on transience, borrowings, and speed as well as the displacements of colonialism: "Historical imagination, the citizens' belief that they might have a hand in shaping their own history, gets replaced by speculation on the property or stock market, or by obsessions with fashion or consumerism" (1997: 5). This sense of speed and image has led many to turn to film as a key to a changing city and society. Some, for example, have read the science fiction film *Wicked City* (1992), in which mutants pit an animated Bank of China building against a jumbo jet, as an allegory of fears before the Handover. Since Michael Mak and Tsui Hark remade a Japanese anime film, one must be careful about reading into the text. Other films dealt with emigration and citizenship, including Clara Law's *Floating Life* and the 1997 Golden Horse winner, *Comrades, Almost a Love Story* (see chapters 5 and 7). Yet another Handover film, *Bodyguard of the Last Governor* (1996), satirized all Hong Kong political players in a vulgar slapstick comedy. In this film, the last white British governor is abruptly replaced by the London owner of a Chinese takeaway who purportedly represents the only Chinese friend of a new British Prime Minister. Chinese political figures of Hong

Kong and the Mainland were also targets of satire in a tale held together by the "romances" of Anson Chan.

Yet, any selection of film as data is dangerous. More than 3000 films were produced in Hong Kong from 1989 to the Handover, and the many writings on film (including Abbas [1997], Teo [1997], Yau [1999], Fu and Desser [2000], Bordwell [2001], and the publications of the Hong Kong International Film Festival) underscore multiple elements of cinematic and civic identity. Hong Kong film production in the 1980s and 1990s included teen romances, swordsman and martial arts epics, gangster films, and melodramas in search of a shrinking audience, while Hong Kong viewers also patronized Hollywood, European, and Japanese films. Urban cinematic identity also includes the experiences of *going to the cinema* in neighborhood houses and malls and exploring film via television and pirated Video Compact Discs (Wong and McDonogh 2001a).

Rather than providing simple answers, these films allow us to explore the cultural production of identity on multiple screens. While questions of time, place, and identity became a context and problem for filmmakers like Wong Kar-Wai, whose art films have been taken as icons of Hong Kong's fragmented worlds (Abbas 1997; Fu and Desser 2002), works by Wong are not necessarily the films Hong Kong people went to see — or where they saw themselves. A more popular and representative film would be Ann Hui's *Summer Snow* (1995), with a marvelous performance by longtime Hong Kong actress Josephine Hsiao. The film shows a working woman struggling to deal with competition in the office and demands of her family, as her father-in-law faces Alzheimer's. The settings — market, mah jong, small business, and bureaucracies — are everyday features of life for many people in Hong Kong. Romances and comedies, staples of commercial production, also localize a cinematic identity and a language, including Cantonese puns and vulgarity, that define Hong Kong products scarcely screened abroad beyond Chinatown rentals (Lai 1997).

Meanwhile, in the 1980s, Hong Kong filmmakers like Tsui Hark, John Woo, and Ringo Lam spread images of Hong Kong abroad through their innovative action films, epitomized in the coolness of Chow Yun-Fat in genre films like *The Killer* (1989). Martial arts stars like Bruce Lee and Jackie Chan had already tested the waters beyond their pan-Asian (and African) followings, but these new works combined martial arts and film noir with questions of character, loyalty, and morality that resonated with earlier Cantonese melodramas.

After exploring film, architecture, and literature to evoke this critical project of cultural identities, Abbas notes the dangers when

Almost every film made since the mid-eighties, regardless of quality or seriousness of intention, seems constrained to make some mandatory reference to 1997. . . . It is not the appearance of "Hong Kong themes," then, that is significant in the new Hong Kong cinema, but rather, what I call a problematic of disappearance: that is to say a sense of the elusiveness, the slipperiness, the ambivalences of Hong Kong's cultural space that some Hong Kong filmmakers have caught in the use of the film medium, in their explorations of history and memory, in their excavation of the evocative detail — *regardless of subject matter.*" (1997: 24)

Thus, the lack of a fixed historical and cultural identity is also a part of Hong Kong life.

Turning from cultural production to social practice, we might also ask how Hong Kongers can hear "themselves" in media and other spheres. As a colony, Hong Kong has always lived with at least two languages. English has been the official language since the colony was established and the medium of law, official journalism, and international relations. However, Chinese (primarily Cantonese, see chapter 5), is the language spoken by the majority of the people, with its own literature, journalism, and musical/operatic culture. Other peoples speak other Chinese dialects, whether Chiu Chow or Shanghainese.

Before 1967, Chinese Urban Council representatives and postgraduate students had demanded recognition of Chinese as an official language, rather than a mere tool of education and communication. After 1967, different student unions formed a "Chinese Language Joint Committee" to demand the adoption of Chinese as a official language, collecting 300,000 signatures. Since the colonial government had promised to be more responsive, it lacked the moral legitimacy to oppose such change even though expatriates were more likely to be monolinguals. The colonial administration finally passed the Official Language Act in 1974 (Kwock 1992; Scott 1994).

This was one of the first successful joint reform movements in Hong Kong. It meant that laws in Hong Kong would be translated into Chinese; nonetheless, where there were discrepancies, the English text would prevail. The act also aimed to raise the status and standard of the Chinese language, even though most high schools used English as a medium of teaching. More importantly, this movement blended different global and larger regional political trends, including decolonization, localism, and Chinese nationalism. Its organizers saw it as a grassroots human rights movement.

Mandarin, the official language of China, entered schools slowly despite opportunities in the 1970s and 1980s. After 1997, it became the official language of the state now present in Hong Kong. Many immigrants had some exposure to it from Mainland education; it represents the correct form of written Chinese even in Hong Kong journalism, academic, and literary texts (Pierson 1992). It has also joined Cantonese and English on television. At the same time, the aural culture of Cantonese in film, opera, theater, Canto-pop, television dramas, and other genres has grown with Hong Kong prosperity, creating passing fads among citizens of the PRC in the 1990s and audiences abroad.

The distinguishing feature of language for Hong Kong people may be the flexibility and repertoire that emerge from their education and that facilitate success. The ability to use three languages correctly and strategically, in fact, has produced a fourth option, Hong Kong "Chinglish," primarily Cantonese with English terms or phrases inserted where necessary. This intimate creole continues to bind diasporic families and populations. Movies like *Comrades* (1996) or the teen action film *Gen-X Cops* (1999) also celebrate this linguistic flexibility as central features of global/local life.

Finally, as we suggested in chapter 1, Hong Kong identity also encompasses creative political action and responsibility, exemplified by environmental activism. Under the early colonial regime, exploitation of the land triumphed over stewardship. The few interventions by the British government in Hong Kong's first century generally dealt with factors that might cause disease among Chinese inhabitants, especially if problems could spread to the British (Choi 1993). As the colony grew and industrial and residential waste increased, plans and procedure to control pollution were discussed, but organizations like the Town Planning Office lacked implementation or enforcement powers within a noninterventionist government.

Reactive offices and policies took shape in the 1970s and 1980s. An Environmental Protection Agency appeared in 1981 and became a policy-oriented Environmental Protection Department in 1986 (Choi 1993; 32–33). Governor David Wilson made an increased commitment to this cause in the 1980s and a White Paper was published on June 5, 1989, the day after Tiananmen events (Siddall 1991). Still, a 1993 review in *The Other Hong Kong Report* bemoaned years of bureaucratic negligence with regard to air pollution, water contamination, and other environmental damage under a vague strategy of government "command and control" (Man 1993). Cecilia Chan and Peter Hills also painted a grim yet detailed portrait of the increasingly wealthy colony:

> Each day, Hong Kong produces more than 12,500 tons of solid waste, 16 tons of floating refuse and 2 million tonnes of sewage and industrial waste water. In addition, the territory produces 100,000 tons of chemical wastes each year (EPD 1990: 21, 25). . . . Floating refuse in Victoria Harbour is an eyesore. . . . Sulphur dioxide and oxides of nitrogen emitted by power stations and factories are another major problem. Chronic respiratory tract infections and asthma are common among the population. (1993: 1)

Grassroots responses to environmental issues have crossed language and ethnic barriers. Both local groups and large nongovernmental organizations (NGOs) such as Friends of the Earth and Greenpeace have focused on local polluters and more specific issues and global concerns (Man 1993: 336–37; Ng 1993). For instance, Hong Kongers have expressed concern about Victoria Harbor reclamation that has trimmed the channel to the width of a river and has made any cleansing more difficult. Others have focused on saving specific resources such as the Mai-Po marshes and traditional farmlands from development. Pink dolphins, a symbol of Hong Kong, have become icons of the dangers of pollution. Debates over sustainability (Hills 1996) also point to the problems of density and development, forcing creative responses in planning and design (Chan and Hills 1994; Wong 1996; Yeh 1996; Cody 2002).

Civic consciousness and action about the environment in Hong Kong use terms and educational models of Western environmentalism to construct a new stewardship of place. They also have posed questions for China, both before and after the Handover. Plans by China Power and Light to construct twin nuclear reactors 30 miles north of Hong Kong at Daya Bay, Guangdong, spurred one million Hong Kongers to sign protest petitions to the Chinese government in 1986. Hung Wing Tat concludes that "calls for genuine consultation and democracy emerged as the main objective of the opposition campaign. The environmental event turned out to be very political indeed" (1993: 44). Subsequent concerns have grown around shared regional issues emerging from South China development, which we discuss in the next chapter.

Who are the 7 million people of Hong Kong and what is their identity? Obviously, such a question seems simplistic as we review the data and experiences of this variegated place. Yet, within the framework of transformations we have shown in this chapter, even more than in earlier historical episodes, it is important to realize the challenges of becoming Hong Kong that became evident at the moment of its seeming disappearance, to which we can see responses in culture, consumption, language, political activities, and other realms. Such identities also have been created around changing places and memories, both local and global.

THE CREATIVE DESTRUCTION OF HONG KONG

Having traced the political and economic changes of the last four decades, it is important to read Hong Kong as continuous and changing, embodied in both people and the cityscape itself — the building and rebuilding of Hong Kong and its surroundings throughout its history. Transformations of the cityscape in the last six decades have reconstituted the life, speed, and image of Hong Kong (Magnago Lapugnani 1996; Gutierrez, Portefaix, and Manzini 2002; Cheung et al. 2004). Architectural historian Chung Wah Nan retells the history of Hong Kong in terms of its built environment:

> The prosperous economic development of Hong Kong could be epitomized by its building development. The prewar scene consisted of low rise building on both sides of the harbour, with Victoria Peak rising above the city below, the post-war scene comprised more four- to five- story buildings pushing up the hill, and ten- to fifteen-story commercial buildings on both sides of the harbour, as more land had been reclaimed at the expense of the harbour. The third phase, the present phase, has 40–60-story commercial buildings creeping towards the narrow harbour while more high-rise residential buildings squeeze up Victoria Peak. The last phase, the future phase,

might have the Fragrant Harbour narrowed down to a gutter and the Peak hidden completely, dwarfed by buildings!" (1989: 15)

In *The Creative Destruction of Manhattan, 1900–1940*, historian Max Page adapts Joseph Schumpeter's term to define the "vibrant and often chaotic process of destruction and rebuilding" that reshaped the form and social life of that city in those crucial decades (1999: 2–3). Reading Page's thoughtful work, "creative destruction" also seems applicable to both the postwar physical transformation of Hong Kong and other East Asian cities and the social and cultural changes we have highlighted. Skyscraper cities housing millions of new citizens and linked by highways and rail have erased farms. Land has been reshaped — tunneled for highways, leveled for housing, and filled in to create more land itself. Chinese commercial and residential buildings and even postwar skyscrapers give way almost overnight to buildings that are newer, bigger, and brighter. In the New Territories, family compounds like Sam Dai Ok are now museums dwarfed by surrounding high-rises, while "traditional" villages manipulate height and density to add new flats. Shantytowns compete with elegant high-rises, a physical tension that Fruit Chan exploits in his 2002 *Hollywood Hong Kong*. Older buildings that survive, Chinese and colonial, become invested with new meanings of a fragmentary past (Abbas 1997; Cody 2002), where threats even to the International Style Wan Chai Market evoke worries of preservation memory and identity (Bradsher 2004b; see Discover Hong Kong Web site).

Some changes are not lamented. Tenements, squatter housing, and even the first public housing blocks built after the war were cramped and unhealthy. Multi-use skyscrapers of the 1960s boom that housed factories and families have been plagued by fire and decay. Colonial symbols also had dual meanings in a divided city. When the Hong Kong Club, a taipan palace that had only admitted Chinese as servants for decades, was torn down and replaced by a new building, even some who regretted the demolition of the historic edifice were not sorry to see the destruction of what it had stood for. Debates filled Chinese and English newspapers (Chugani 1978, 1979) but did not stop the club, which now hosts many Chinese elite members in its new building in Central.

To explore changes and continuities of Hong Kong sites of identity, we focus on two institutions whose buildings were transformed at the end of the colonial period — Sir Norman Foster's Hongkong and Shanghai Bank headquarters (1986) and I.M. Pei's nearby Bank of China (1990). Both elite landmarks dominate views of the harbor in postcards, currency, Web sites, and cinema, representing political–economic power and conveying layers of cultural meaning (see Figure 4.1; they stand at the far left). The first (now part of the HSBC) knit together colonial capital throughout the British enclaves on the China coast, while anchoring colonial rule. The Bank of China, chartered in 1912 in Shanghai under Sun Yat-sen as a transformation of the Imperial Da-Qing Bank, arrived in Hong Kong in 1917 and moved its headquarters there temporarily during World War II. It remains both distinctive and symbolic in the cityscape, as we noted with regard to the movie *Wicked City* (1992).

A pamphlet prepared for the 1985 inauguration of the Hongkong and Shanghai Bank spoke of ongoing destruction and renewal at 1 Queen's Road:

Each of the three headquarters built by the Bank has been recognized as an outstanding example of the architecture of its time. Each has been designed and built to meet the needs of the time and, as far as possible, to anticipate change in the future. Each has set new standards of building and introduced new technology to the territory.

Together the four buildings chronicle the emergence of a worldwide banking group, and the development of banking and financial community around it. It is a story central to the rise of Hong Kong itself and one which now points clearly into the twenty-first century.

Founded in 1865, the bank's offices, storeroom, and housing for European employees were first lodged in Wardley House among other mercantile buildings on the waterfront. Later, a renaissance-style building reminiscent of Macau was commissioned with separate counters for English and Chinese transactions. Local British architects Palmer and Turner built the third building in 1935 to outshine the bank's Shanghai branch; its construction offered an important stimulus in the Depression as the Sino–Japanese conflict edged closer. Acquiring the site of Hong Kong's City Hall (a recreational and cultural rather than governmental edifice), directors asked Palmer and Turner to "please build us the best bank in the world" (Lambot and Chambers 1986: 60). This Art Deco edifice became the tallest tower between Cairo and San Francisco, with technological innovations like high-speed elevators and central air-conditioning. It was the first building in the world to use high-tensile steel throughout. The *Morning Post* of

October 17, 1934, proclaimed: "The Bank is an institution which must instill pride in the breast of every Hongkong native, whether he be foreign or Chinese. . . . The new bank symbolizes also Britain's friendly contribution to China's modernization — great walls of China, though erected under British flag" (in Lambot and Chambers 1986: 77), although this symbolism would be tested under Japanese occupation (Snow 2004).

After the war, a similar Palmer and Turner edifice for the Bank of China (1950) rose nearby. At the HKSB centennial, the square in front of the venerable HKSB headquarters was relandscaped and inaugurated as a garden under the aegis of the government and the bank; this valuable open space also makes the building clearly visible from the harbor.

By the late 1970s, this third building became inadequate in Hong Kong's expanding role as a global banking center. Norman Foster Associates won the contract for a new building in 1979, although construction was complicated by demands to build the new building without disrupting the old one on the same site. Foster built it above the existing bank, using its side girders to build up and down from the middle. At the same time, he played with light, air, and technology, creating new forms of sheathing. In the end, the building was not only inventive, but also extremely expensive (Williams 1988).

Such architectural claims meant that the building was featured in a monograph, architectural reviews, and textbooks. It was also reproduced: Foster himself accepted a commission for a smaller-scale version in Tokyo. The building appears, like the Bank of China, on Hong Kong currency. Souvenir banks available for sale echo those of the 1935 building distributed to previous generations of Hong Kong schoolchildren. Its triangular (bow tie) frame even resonates with the HSBC logo worldwide.

The building has other meanings in everyday life. People might not remember the architect's name (or that of the Bank of China), but they know the institutions and buildings. Filipinos use the plaza below Foster's building as a meeting place on Sundays, which changes the meaning of the spaces of Central. *Feng shui* (geomancy) was evoked as well as an important local facet in the bank's construction. Local legends held that the old bank buildings kept gold from sliding down the Peak, so the new construction could not alter that relation. Foster consulted experts to harmonize the building with dragons and forces of traditional Chinese thought that mediated his own strong linear elements.

Not all Chinese interpretation was so positive, however. A graduate student in 1997 told us, in some seriousness, that cooling tunnels to the harbor had been built for submarines to move gold out of the bank at the Chinese takeover. Another repeated urban legend explained that its unique external framing meant that workers could dismantle it overnight if necessary, Handover-related interpretation as well.

When the Bank of China decided to replace its building with a new symbol of both the state and the bank, they went to a Chinese architect, the expatriate I.M. Pei. Working on a smaller budget than Foster, he produced a design that could be interpreted as classically Chinese, seeking inspiration "from bamboo" and incorporating barrel arches in the main lobbies. Its interlocking triangles soar above the harbor, shifting like a prism, striking for both its height and in its difference from the rest of the skyline.

Geographically, surrounding roads make the building less accessible than Foster's tower: "If one wants to go to the Bank of China Building, one may experience something like a mutation in built space" (Cheng 1997: 107). Its glass spires are also angular and disturbing — as one acquaintance said, "The building is cutting like a knife. I would not live in the direction it cut." While the HSBC touts good *feng shui*, the Bank of China was interpreted as attacking the Governor's home, causing the death of Governor Wilson.

Again, it is difficult to separate architectural interpretation from politics: "The Bank's prismatic tower dominates almost every view of Hong Kong harbour and is symbolic of the power of the People's Republic of China" (Cheng 1997: 106). Christina Cheng Miu Bing also shows how this statement of power resonated in the construction of another Bank of China tower to dominate Macau across the Pearl River before its Handover. The Bank of China left behind older Chinese modes and the borrowings of its earlier building to embrace technology and postmodern form. It would be as notable as Foster's more expensive work among professional architects worldwide. In the end, this work inscribing their rivalry into the landscape of the city and its global image.

Development in Central has continued since the Handover; Cesar Pelli's new tower not only became the highest building in the city, but also, for the first time, has partially blocked the Peak from Kowloon side. Other buildings prove less memorable despite exuberant multistory foyers, postmodern detailing, and public spaces fitted with giant televisions. While these buildings are emblematic, the transformations of modern Hong Kong have been more far-ranging — and development has spread more widely, as will be seen in chapter 6. To understand both the human and built environment, however, it is necessary to look beyond local history, society, and culture to Hong Kong's changing participation in its wider regional economic, social, and cultural milieu, South China.

Five

The Western view conceives of changes in China as responses to a Western impact. The Han view conceives of changes in south China as the integration of local societies into a unified fold. There has never quite been a south China view. Guangdong was never the center of any history. It is ironic how much happened in Guangdong that was of crucial importance to the overall political development of China even as Guangdong remained on the periphery. (David Faure 1996: 10)

In Peter Chan's award-winning 1996 *Comrades, Almost a Love Story*, the Northern-born Chinese hero Xiaojin (played by Leon Lai Ming) moves to Hong Kong in the mid-1980s to make his fortune. Celebrating his newfound opportunities in a McDonald's, he encounters Li Qiao (Maggie Cheung) behind the counter. She impresses him with her many business schemes, fluent Cantonese, and incipient English. Later, they lose money on a New Year's scheme to sell records of Taiwan-born star Teresa Teng (Deng Lijun), and Li Qiao admits she comes from nearby Guangdong. The movie follows other romances and migration to the United States, where these intermittent lovers reunite in Manhattan in 1995. Only in a concluding flashback does the audience learn that Li Qiao arrived in Hong Kong on the same train as Xiaojin.

This movie offers a positive image of a cross-border immigrant, challenging the boorish Ah-Chan Mainlander stereotype of earlier years. At the same time, the movie reinforces stereotypes of wily, active Southerners, always scheming to get ahead — a view known widely throughout China. It also reminds us not to confuse overlapping identities of city, region, nation, and state. When reading Hong Kong at the intersection of peoples and trajectories of two global empires, China figures as both state and nation. Yet Hong Kong's people, culture, language, cuisine, and history remain more intimately connected to the people and culture of South China. The province of Guangdong and its capital, Guangzhou (Canton), dominate the watershed and delta of the Pearl (Zhujiang) River that flows into the South China Sea past Hong Kong and Macau. Hong Kong forms part of this ecological, political, linguistic, and sociocultural region — Lingnan or South China — that has taken shape over millennia of human action that transcend mere centuries of colonial incursion (Marks 1998). The South differs in history, culture, and image from the heartlands of Imperial Chinese to the north, although, at least since the Ming Dynasty, its connections to this nation-state have strengthened (Faure 1996; Siu and Faure 1995; Hook 1996; Marks 1998). Nonetheless, even when the South sets the pace for Chinese development, it has evoked suspicion.

Today, plans for the Pearl River Delta tout its united potential, whether through the schemes of tourism offices (Kwong 1997), new networks of business and transport (Smart 2002, Lok 2003), or architect Rem Koolhaas' visionary plans (Chung et al 2001). Guangdong's population grew 37.5 percent between 1990 and 2000, from 62.83 million to 86.42 million; its GDP, buoyed by expansion in the 1990s, may have increased 13 percent in the year 2003 alone. New airports, new institutions, and new interests ranging from

Chinese overseas investors to famous architects have made Guangdong newly global; in the twenty-first century, some envision it as the core of an even larger consortium of nine Southern provinces and 456 million people (Cheung and Chow 2004).

While Hong Kong represents a lynchpin for this growth through investment, trade, and global connections, the changes in cross-border zones mean that Guangzhou and satellite industrial cities may shape the future of the HKSAR, which has depended on the area for food and water since the 1960s. Growth and integration have also brought problems: SARS, pollution, crime, floating populations, and controversies with northern China and the state. Thus, South China (Lingnan) provides a critical context for reading Hong Kong, the state, and the world.

The continual cultural interconnectedness of the area is personified by Sun Yat-Sen (Sun Zhongshan/Sun Yixian, 1866–1925), claimed by many to be the father of modern China. Generally speaking, Sun's visions for China evoked the South's openness and development (Sun 1994), as did his life. Born to a peasant family in Cuiheng, forty miles north of Macau, Sun followed his emigrant older brother to Hawai'i, where he enrolled in English language missionary schools. Hawai'i, an important destination for emigrant Chinese, was still an independent kingdom, although U.S. missionaries and entrepreneurs exercised considerable influence there. Disagreeing with his brother over Christianity, Sun returned to China in 1883. Moving through Hong Kong, his village, and Guangzhou, Sun converted to Christianity and underwent an arranged marriage in his village before enrolling in the colony's College of Medicine for Chinese. He began his career as a revolutionary, too, building on support from his family and local networks, émigrés abroad, global Protestant missionaries, and Anglicized Hong Kong Chinese elites — all outside the traditional leadership of Imperial China (Bergère 1998: 28–33). His first efforts at reform/revolution failed, however, which led to his exile in Japan in 1895.

Globalism through personal networks defined Sun's influence on China through the 1911 Revolution (which found him traveling in the United States until called back to assume the presidency of the Republic). Sun's ability to work with (and to alienate) Southern intellectuals, radicals, missionaries, and diverse foreign agents — Japanese, Russian, and American — both supported and constrained him until his death in 1925.

Global ties also shaped Sun's second marriage in 1914 to Song Qingling, a Shanghainese Christian educated at Wesleyan College in Georgia. Her father, Charlie Soong (Song Jiashu) had become a millionaire through American evangelical patronage; her brother Song Ziwen (T. V. Soong), sister Song Ailing, and brother-in-law Kong Xiangxi all played roles in finances of the new Chinese Republic. Her other sister, Song Meiling, married Sun's sometime ally in the Guomindong party, Chiang Kai-Shek. An epic film about this family hit Hong Kong cinemas shortly before the Handover (*The Soong Sisters*, 1997).

Today, both Communists and Nationalists invoke Sun as an ancestor. There are pilgrimage sites at his birthplace and his monumental tomb (in Nanjing) and a mausoleum in Taipei. Macau maintains his house and garden. Hong Kong memorializes him at Hong Kong University and plans a museum. Yet, beyond this, the Four Modernizations adopted by Deng Xiaoping after 1978 have brought Sun's vision back into the Special Economic Zones (SEZ) of the South, the region where he was born.

Sun Yat-Sen was hardly typical of the South — or any other part of China or the world — but his life, career, and thought all embody the traits that Hong Kong shares with its region — a China linked to traditions but open to opportunities and influences; a China of regional movement and global connections. To put Hong Kong in this context, we begin with the meanings of Guangdong and South China in contrast to Northern centers and viewpoints. We then focus on three key cities that triangulate especially clearly with Hong Kong — Macau, the initial European colony; Guangzhou, the capital and reemergent center; and Shenzhen, the transborder Special Economic Area created to better connect Hong Kong and China. The chapter closes by contrasting South China with Shanghai, the northerly Chinese capital of growth and global contact.

DEFINING THE SOUTH

A well-known proverb throughout China defines regional differences by urging "Suzhou to wed, Guangzhou to eat; Hangzhou to live and Laozhou to die." While the culinary fame of Guangdong derives from its rich coastal environment and long growing season, not all images are so positive. For other Chinese, Guangdong peoples were "willing to trade with barbarians and other Han-speakers alike, and for this reason [were] susceptible to influences coming from other parts of as well as from outside China. However, because of their distance from the center, they were tolerably unorthodox. These southerners were ill-cultured rather than hard to govern, unusual enough to adapt readily to change but were settled far enough from the center not to upset stability" (Faure 1996: 1).

Given China's stress on unity from empire to Communism, provincial identities and differences are both everyday issues

— insofar as each Chinese is grounded in local family, language, and culture — and far-reaching problems. Even at a crucial juncture like the transition from Empire to Republic after 1911, Bergère notes:

> This whole debate brought back to the surface the old problem of the relations, at once contradictory and complementary, between the China of the South, looking out to the sea and dominated by forces of change and the China of the North, open to the steppes, symbol and refuge of the imperial ideology of hegemony and centralization. However attached they were to the republican idea, the democrats of the South were, in 1919, reluctant to attack "the strongman of the North," the embodiment of the continuity and unity of the nation. Faced with the Peking regime, the only other solution was independence for the provinces or possibly a separatist Southern Republic — either way, division for the country. How could patriots possibly countenance this? (1998: 241)

What does this South mean? We find different answers in features of environment, people, history, culture, and future.

In fact, the referent of the term "South" shifts depending upon the speaker, project, and orientation. To Hong Kong residents, Shanghai is northern; to those in Beijing, it is southerly or central. For some initiatives, the South may be stretched to include provinces from Fujian/Fukien to Guanxi and Hainan, and even Taiwan. We refer primarily to Guangdong as one of China's 27 administrative districts, while noting links to Guanxi and other Southern provinces. In English, the people, predominant language, and culture of this area are commonly referred to as Cantonese; Faure has argued, however, this term has no exact Chinese equivalent and simplifies peoples and debates over time (1996: 38).

Guangdong Province covers 177,901 square kilometers, less than 2 percent of China's total landmass (Hainan Island became a new province/Special Economic Zone in 1988). Geography and human action have shaped this land and its society over centuries (Marks 1998). Guangdong centers on lands drained by the Pearl River system, China's second largest river in terms of discharge, and lands built up out of its delta over centuries. The major tributaries of the Pearl — the East, West, and North rivers — lack the alluvial plains that have shaped life along the northern Yellow and Yangtze Rivers (Neller and Lam: 436–441). In the mid-1990s, in fact, 63 percent of the population actually lived in inland mountainous districts that lagged behind boom cities of the delta (Edmonds 1996: 111–112). Guangdong's climate is warm and wet — a subtropical area where monsoons blow off the Pacific Ocean each summer. This makes it a fertile area where some areas produce three crops of rice in a single year and contributes to the abundance of fresh vegetables and greens in Cantonese cuisine. Guangdong's 3368 kilometers of coastline (10.52 percent of China's total) are also distant from imperial capitals and have linked Southern peoples to others beyond China. Before Europeans arrived, Arab and Indian traders planted Muslim as well as Buddhist populations in the Delta, while Guangdong's traders circulated through China and Southeast Asia. For centuries, therefore, Guangzhou (as Macau and Hong Kong would later be) was a "frontier town where civilizations met" (Faure 1996: 2).

Guangdong was populated by Han peoples from the North who mixed with native Yue peoples in the first millennium BCE.

The area came under imperial power in the Qin (221–207 BC) and Han dynasties (206 BCE–220 CE). Chinese rule and identity there consolidated in the Ming dynasty (1368–1644) through the effects of changing imperial policies and through new inland passes that expanded sea and land connections to the north (Faure 1996ab). Trade with northern China commodified staples like rice and expanded the local silk and cotton trades (Marks 1998).

Helen Siu and David Faure have noted how stories of migration, told through lineages, became important elements in the history of many Southerners, especially as Guangzhou became more than an outpost of empire, increasingly integrating its provincial hinterland into the economy and cultures of China: "Once the lineage was given a pivotal position in territorial organization, being able to trace one's ancestors from the centre and having the written documents to prove that became the means by which ethnic identities were ascertained" (1996: 44; Freedman 1966; Faure 1989).

Despite this increasing integration, May-bo Ching has argued that Guangzhou intellectuals and politicians in the Qing period also grappled with the term *Wenham* (Cantonese *manta*, glossed as "culture"):

> First, it implied that Guangdong as a place of culture counted within the Chinese high culture, which was acceptable to the literati in other parts of China. Secondly, it implied that a unique Guangdong culture, identified with the literature of Cantonese vernacular, had Chinese roots. Thirdly, towards the early Republic, the term also included Hakka and Chiuchow traditions within Guangdong culture, challenging the traditional centrality of the Cantonese within Guangdong. The interplay

of these three notions of "culture' was closely related to Guangdong's position within national politics as well as the evolution of politics within Guangdong. (1996: 51)

As Ching's careful analysis shows, Guangzhou scholars explored local identity *within* their incorporation into China. This entailed participation in pan-Chinese study of the classics as well as recognition of the language of Guangdong (based on the speech of Guangzhou). Intellectuals also attempted to write in Cantonese in schools and newspapers, echoing the florescence of vernacular forms like Cantonese opera. All of this helped differentiate the peoples of the South from those of the North, even as lineages and culture linked region and nation.

Lau suggests that Guangdong's population has represented between 3 and 9 percent of China's population since the fourteenth century CE. It reached a highpoint in 1877 (1998: 472), when cycles of population growth and decrease had given way to steady growth that strained land and resources, especially in the four southwestern counties known as See Yap — sources of continuing Cantonese migration to the United States. In the eighteenth and nineteenth century, for example, Taishan (Toisan) county faced increasing demands on its hilly and difficult agricultural land, exacerbated by struggles between Han migrants and local Hakka peoples and widespread social movements like the Taiping Rebellion. Thousands of young men left, passing through Hong Kong, their node of communication and sometimes reconnection with strong family networks in Taishan and around the world. Their dialect of Cantonese became a standard of American Chinatowns. Taishan in 1988 had a population of 963,364, while an estimated 1.1 million of its descendants lived abroad in 78 countries (Hsu 2000: 16).

The people of the South are not homogenous either, as we have seen from Hong Kong. Distinct linguistic and cultural groups include the dominant Cantonese (gongdonghua) speaking group along the Pearl River as well as the Hakkas and the Chiu Chows of northern Guangdong, who have diffused across Southeast Asia. From the nineteenth century onward, Hakka and Chiu Chow speakers argued for recognition as Chinese of different but related language groups. Others pushed aside by migrations from the North, however — the Yao, Zuang, and Dan — became marginalized as non-Chinese minorities.

The use of language to define cultural groups is problematic, of course, as we have seen in Hong Kong. In South China, individuals and families may be multilingual (in addition to speaking Mandarin), while Gongdonghua includes dialects not readily shared among speakers. In fact, students of Chinese language vary on whether Southern speech or even the Yue family most closely identified with "Cantonese" is a language, dialect, or group of dialects intermingled across spaces and speakers (Norman 1988). While all Chinese languages share an ideographic writing system that unites the state and extends it, Cantonese speech diverges from written forms in terms of word order, word selection, and vocabulary.

Southern groups also are distinguished by foodways within general characteristics that set Cantonese food apart from other Chinese cuisines (Anderson 1988). Cantonese cuisine relies on freshness and diversity, is based on seafood and fresh vegetables, and is cooked quickly. Long-grain rice is the staple accompaniment, rather than the wheat of the North. Equally characteristic of Cantonese cuisine is the context of eating, especially *yam cha* (drinking tea) or *dim sum* (little bit of heart) — the custom of sharing small servings of delicacies with tea as a morning or midday meal. This cuisine, like the languages of the region, has also shaped Chinese cuisine abroad. At the same time, Southern cities have also developed *sai chan* — interpretations of Western food that are comfort food for Hong Kongers and symbols of hybrid identity in Hong Kong films.

Among other Chinese, Cantonese cuisine also has a some-times negative image based on Southerner's appetites for eating exotic foods, such as snake or various wild cats and rodents. As Charlotte Ikels notes, "Cantonese are aware that outsiders, even within China, do not eagerly embrace every item of Cantonese food. They mock the more timid eating habits of other Chinese by asserting that while 'Shandong people do anything and Beijing people endure anything, Cantonese people eat anything!'" (1997: 9). Some outsiders linked this prodigious appetite to the mysterious origins of SARS.

Yet, neither geography, production, language, or food are fixed characteristics of difference in the South so much as features that evolve over history that, while distinct from that of other regions of China, remain clearly interwoven into the changes of the modern Chinese state and empire. From the mid-eighteenth century until 1842, Guangzhou was the sole port of entry for foreign trade, creating a wealthy and innovative urban setting that became a crucible of Chinese–European relations. In the early twentieth century, reformers used Hong Kong and Guangzhou as a base to rethink the state. At the end of the century and into the twenty-first, the paths toward Chinese capitalism and even political change have again been tested there, among diverse cities and citizens.

Visitors to contemporary Guangzhou encounter building activity that seems to surpass even Hong Kong — in part because the city is catching up in both infrastructure and consumption. A sleek new subway line (without HKSAR crowding), a new airport, skyscrapers, hotels, and malls are all creating a new sprawl across previously independent towns and new suburbs. Throughout the city, offices and stores spring up rapidly, while restaurants flourish whether they are the historic tea houses serving dim sum to hundreds each day or McDonald's. Within this activity, nonetheless, monuments of Southern history also remain. The tombs of the Southern Yue kings of the Western Han, for example, recall local sovereignty in a divided China (100 BCE). The Tomb of the Islamic Ancestor represents a Tang dynasty legacy of cosmopolitan populations. Across from the Qingping market (reaffirming stereotypes of Cantonese cuisine in its variegated goods), Shamian Island, once the center for Western traders, retains richly hued buildings with white trim and balconies amid gardens and quiet streets, a coastal style echoed in some downtown developments today. At Shamian's tip, the White Swan Hotel caters to global businessmen and stocks supplies in its gift shop for parents of newly adopted Chinese girls.

Despite Guangzhou's initial monopoly on foreign trade, Hong Kong and later treaty ports weakened this position, fomenting crises and emigration after the 1840s. Guangzhou remained a political, economic, and cultural center, possessing both the academies and the media through which Guangdong identity crystallized (Ching 1996). Its citizens defined cultured Cantonese as an accent/dialect and, despite the official role of Mandarin in public fora, media, and schools, the language remains strong today. Production, exchange, and information flowed through the city, which in the 1930s still was one of the three major ports of China (along with Shanghai and Shantou; Woo 1998: 371).

After the 1949 revolution, Guangzhou occupied a more peripheral role within a circumscribed China, with continuing outside leadership imposed on the city and a lack of investment in basic infrastructure. But its physical (and social) distance from Beijing ironically facilitated economic experimentation in late 1970s as part of Deng Xiaoping's modernization projects. Guangdong agreed to pay a lump sum payment to the central government in 1979, keeping any surplus that its locally governed development generated (Cheung 1998: 31). In the next five years, Guangdong registered an average annual growth rate of 11 percent; foreign investment reached US$1.29 billion, 42 percent of the national total (1998: 38). While conservative Communists grumbled, Deng Xiaoping endorsed this project on his 1984 tour.

Through the 1980s, a state central apparatus controlled provincial economic changes. But, at the same time, there was a gradual localization of Communist leadership and, eventually, an increasing Guangdong presence in the central government in the 1990s. This tension of local development and national controls has marked Southern Chinese development to the present, while the success of nationwide initiatives in the Special Economic Zones, discussed below, and connections to global capital have changed the civic form of the capital since the 1980s, as well as its everyday life. Guangzhou's population has risen to seven million, equaling Hong Kong, while the city spreads over more than two hundred square kilometers within a network of other intermediate market and industrial cities. Increasing immigration, traffic, and pollution have necessitated more planning and construction (Woo 1998).

Physical changes correspond to the social developments observed in Charlotte Ikels' *Return of the God of Wealth* (1996). Ikels and her husband Ezra Vogel, the eminent Western historian of Guangdong (1969, 1989), have observed the city over decades. The speed of contemporary change is a recurrent theme in their work. As Ikels writes, "The economic reforms have their most visible impact, not surprisingly on the material circumstances of daily life. . . . There is simply more of everything around — more food, more clothes, more shelter, more transport, more and better service personnel — and also greater diversity" (1996: 54). At the same time, these observers have highlighted cracks in the system, from gaps in social safety nets and education and strains on family to obesity and problems of waste disposal.

Within Guangdong, other fast-growing areas have challenged the capital. Shenzhen (below) exceeds Guangzhou's per capita income and its production of goods like calculators and televisions and boasts the province's only stock exchange. Even as Guangzhou's production, trade, and growth have rivaled Shanghai, Beijing, and Tianjin since the mid-1990s, other regional industrial cities like Dongguan, Foshan, Jiangmen, and Zhongshan have surpassed it in individual sectors and overall growth rates, reducing the capital's proportion of provincial production and income (Cheung 1999: 29–30). And any increase in economic reforms means more competition from other areas.

The most compelling question about Guangzhou's future is its definition in a region including Hong Kong. Hong Kong companies dominate foreign investment in the city and province

(Smart 1998; Cheung 2003b), and tempers have flared when Guangzhou leaders propose a competing container port or the new airport. As one of the deans of Chinese urban–regional studies, G. William Skinner, has written about these twin metropoles:

> If anything, because of its technological edge and international orientation, not to mention its superiority in shipping, banking and insurance, Hong Kong is likely to prove the dominant metropolis. In contrast with a century ago, Hong Kong now provides regional-city-level urban functions for a hinterland that incorporates the very areas from which its population largely originated. And in even sharper contrast with a century ago, Hong Kong today *is* the cultural center of Lingnan. (1999: 77)

Yet, in 2003, Guangzhou's mayor, Li Shushen, summed up the situation at the Guangzhou–Hong Kong Joint Cooperation Conference in different terms: "We are not asking Hong Kong not to develop. In the same vein, there are some projects that we need to develop and we hope Hong Kong will not expect us not to" (Leu and Cheung 2003). To understand these hopes in a wider context, we turn to two other regional centers, Macau and Shenzhen.

MACAU: THE OTHER COLONY

Centuries before the British claimed Hong Kong, another empire, Portugal, already had established its enclave on the Pearl River, whose colonial status would endure until 1999. Macau, a peninsula connected to two smaller islands, Taipa and Coloane (all expanded dramatically by land reclamation), was a staging ground for the opium trade and a source of intermediaries for the British colony. Today, at 435,000 inhabitants (a 20 percent increase in the last decade), this small, highly urban Hong Kong Special Administrative Region (HKSAR) will soon be dwarfed by the contiguous Special Economic Zone of Zhuhai, whose population may pass one million by 2010.

History and culture have created a distinctive cityscape in Macau. Soaring new hotels on landfill around the hydrofoil port evoke hypermodern Hong Kong (one building copies the triangles of the Hongkong and Shanghai Bank). Yet, one walks through the central city, the shaded arcades and balconies of narrow streets recall Lisbon, filtered through warmer, wetter climates in Portuguese colonies that had taught settlers the value of shade and air circulation. Stately churches and colonial buildings like the Leal Senado demarcate colonial legacies amidst Chinese temples and Chinese and global commerce: traditional Macau specializations like cookies and beef jerky mixed with youth-oriented goods from chains like G2000 and Giordano that have spread throughout Asia (see Figure 5.1). Elite residential areas offer rainbows of vividly colored houses with white trim and luxuriant gardens. While the colors on older buildings may have faded from pollution and the elements, neon signs, laundry hanging from balconies, shops, and street markets contribute to a jumble of lights, colors, and signs (*Património Arquitectónico Macau* 1988; *Bun Fun Dik O-Mun* 1999). Churches and squares on Taipa and Coloane may seem lost in a sleepy colonial history, yet their colors and ornaments recur in new and expensive housing and resorts. Signs and people remind us, though, that the colonial legacy lives within a strongly Chinese local population (Piña-Cabral 2003).

Macau's culture emerged from different imperial strategies, connections, peoples, and products chronicled in the collections and Web site of the Museu de Macau (see the tour on the

Figure 5.1
Central Macau, 1997 (photograph by the authors).

Web site). Officially established in 1557 after decades of coastal encounters between the Portuguese and the Chinese, Macau became a wealthy juncture in a diadem of colonial ports from Portugal to Japan. Portuguese trade ships followed the coast of Africa to Angola, around the Cape to Mozambique, across the Indian Ocean to Goa on the Indian subcontinent, then to Malacca (in modern Malaysia), up the coast, and finally to Nagasaki. Silk from China brought silver from Japan, which was in turn used to purchase Chinese trade goods like porcelain and silk. Spices and slaves joined the flow on the return to Europe and on to Brazil. When Spain and Portugal unified (1582–1640), Macau became a node of Iberian global exchange, connected to Manila and the Spanish galleons of the New World.

Knowledge and belief traveled along these routes, too. Roman Catholic missionaries followed the Portuguese flag;

Jesuits arrived in Macau in the 1560s, creating foundations for missions in China and Japan and their college (founded 1594). The façade of their church of São Paulo (built 1603; destroyed 1835), remains a key symbol of the city.

The Golden Age of Macau ended in the mid-seventeenth century, when Japan closed its doors to foreign trade and religion, and the Dutch and other Europeans challenged the trade routes of a newly independent Portugal. Macau did not disappear so much as survive in isolation — next to China, but not part of it. The city/colony regained importance when Guangzhou became the center for trade between the Chinese and the West. Portuguese merchants gave way to the British East India Company and American traders, who established homes in Macau for the months they could not remain in the factories (barracks) in Guangzhou; Macau's Protestant Cemetery bears witness to their life and death there.

Hong Kong, with its deepwater harbor, quickly replaced Macau as a global port. As its opium trading narrowed to local monopolies, Macau assumed a less savory role, dominating the coolie trade in unfree Chinese labor with the New World until it became illegal in the 1870s. Over the next century, many Hong Kong residents associated Macau, outpost of a fading colonial empire, with vice. Gambling became legalized in 1847, and was a major source of government revenue. As historian Jonathan Porter writes, "By the 1920s and 1930s, Macau had become one of the world's notorious 'cities of sin,' where gambling, prostitution, and opium houses flourished. . . . Macau never lost its notoriety as a seedy, disreputable, and sometimes dangerous place, a refuge for down-and-out and a haven for smugglers, spies, and other malevolent characters" (1996: 94). Meanwhile,

Chinese swelled the population from 63,991 in 1899 to 150,000 in 1930 (Shipp 1996: 78).

As a Portuguese colony, Macau remained neutral in World War II, making it a haven for Pearl River Delta refugees (its population reached 600,000 by 1945); Japanese may also have been wary of hurting Japanese settlers in Brazil (Snow 2004). In 1946, Macau became one of the few places in the world that permitted legal trade in gold, again contributing to its dubious and unsavory reputation. After the 1951 United Nations (UN) embargo on China, smuggling became profitable as well. By the 1960s, Macau had a weak colonial administration, powerful gangsters, and tense relations with Chinese. The result was a constant state of "unstable equilibrium" that characterized social and cultural life there (Piña-Cabral and Lourenço 1991: 114). Riots between students, workers, and police in the winter of 1966, spilling over from the Mainland's Cultural Revolution, resulted in Chinese deaths and the destruction of historical monuments. British and Americans also became targets of protest and boycotts, while pro-Communist Chinese attempted to introduce Mao into even Catholic classrooms (Shipp 1996: 91). Indeed, the unrest that transformed Hong Kong society in the 1960s convinced Portuguese authorities to cooperate with China by secret agreement in 1967 and 1979, when Portugal effectively acknowledged that it was administering a Chinese territory, paving the way for reunification (Shipp 1996: 94). As Portugal underwent its own revolution, brought on in part by the exigencies of its African colonies, it even discussed returning Macau to China in the mid-1970s, although China was not then especially interested (Shipp 1996: 95).

Macau's eventual return to China in 1999 received less global attention than the Hong Kong Handover. By then, Portugal had lost its colonial possessions and became more integrated into the European Union; migration from its colonies has led to a new diversity of food, colors, and peoples in Lisbon. Unlike Britain, which limited Hong Kong claims on citizenship, Portugal offered more acceptance to those born in Macau.

Today, while Macau's citizens have left behind opium for handicrafts, foodstuffs, and tourism, gambling remains important. Hong Kong tolerates gambling through the Hong Kong Jockey Club's off-track betting offices and the incessant games of mah jong, whose clacking tiles resonate in restaurants and from apartment windows along small streets. But in Macau, gaudy casinos like the Lisboa Hotel are urban landmarks, and central streets boast jewelry stores and pawn shops for a rapid, irregular flow of cash. Until the Macau Handover, gaming concessions were held for decades by a syndicate controlled by Hong Kong millionaire Stanley Ho Hung-Sun; in the 1990s, this syndicate provided half the government revenues.

Images of lawlessness still haunt the city. Hollywood movies like *Macao* (1952) used this seedy and mysterious air, as do potboiler novels like David Carney's 1996 *Macau*, with characters like the crime syndicate boss Crystal Lily and Nicholas the Russian. In Hong Kong cinema, Macau also appears as a site for gang violence and betrayal (*Young and Dangerous I*, 1996), while other films highlight its flashy casinos (*Casino Tycoon* 1992). Such imagery pervades the culture of Hong Kong off-screen as well; when we went there in spring 1997, Hong Kong friends asked how we could take our child into such a dangerous setting. For an American family, occasional targeted killings in a gang war were scarcely imposing; for Hong Kongers, it was the "frontier."

Macau differs from Hong Kong in other ways as well. A significant Macanese (Eurasian) population emerged by the eighteenth century, when few Portuguese women ventured to this distant colony. Porter estimates "perhaps 800 Portuguese and Macanese and almost 161,000 Chinese" in 1960 (1997: 95); researchers put the number closer to 4000 in 1991 (Piña-Cabral and Lourenço 1999; see Teixera 2000, Piña-Cabral 2003). Whatever their numbers, their ability to negotiate European and Chinese worlds made them important in the early Hong Kong colonial administration; "Portuguese" became a popular label for mixed-race people rather than "Europeans" in the newer colony. The Macanese dialect had nearly disappeared by the late-twentieth century but the characteristic food of Macau synthesizes more than simply Iberian and Cantonese influences, retracing the routes of Portuguese expansion. Portuguese Chicken, for example, mixes potatoes and tomatoes from the New World with curries and coconut milk from South/Southeast Asia.

Before 1999, Macau changed the emphasis of propaganda and urban projects to contrast its history and culture with Hong Kong's creative destruction. A renovated History Museum, in the fortress dominating Macau, a new Museum of Art, and a Museum of Wine underscore this heritage. Beach resorts and luxury hotels promote an image of fun and relaxation, again contrasting with the driving energy of Hong Kong. Tourism and gambling converged anew in 2004 with the opening of the $240 million Sands casino, forerunner of new Las Vegas interests in the SAR as an East Asian regional gambling and entertainment center that will include a new $1 billion imitation of Venice as well as additional casinos, restaurants, and luxury suites. Stanley Ho, also has plans for additional casinos and a waterfront amusement park, which will increase attractions for newly-wealthy Mainland Chinese (Shuman 2004). Residents have told us that speculative construction of seaside villas and new high-rise apartments had been planned with mainland Chinese investors in mind as well. Meanwhile, a new border-crossing links the former colony to a new Special Economic Zone, whose pollution sometimes darkens skies over Macau. Nonetheless, Macau's connections to and contrasts with Hong Kong remain significant. Discussion of a potential 40-kilometer bridge across the Pearl River promotes an even closer bond: Would this make Macau a suburb of Hong Kong like Stanley or Lantau?

As Jonathan Porter writes in his rich portrait of Macau as "the imaginary city," it long has been "a threshold between two worlds, which some Europeans and Chinese succeeded in crossing and others did not. Even when they did not, they encountered people from across the threshold" (Porter 1996: 186). Today, it seems a nostalgic backwater by comparison to Hong Kong and Guangzhou, but the new Special Economic Zones across the border from Macau (Zhuhai) and Hong Kong (Shenzhen) have created another vision of place — global cities without form and history.

SHENZHEN: WORLD CITIES FROM SCRATCH

Since 1978, the once agricultural landscape north of Hong Kong has developed rapidly into a center of global manufacturing and commerce as well as services for the metropolis. Its population has exploded from 23,000 to estimates of 6 million for the municipality in 2003 (with perhaps 4 million temporary residents). The Shenzhen cityscape mixes modernity, reconstructed tradition, and chaos in ways that recall the former "frontier town" descriptions of Guangzhou, Macau and Hong Kong (see Guangzhou News Web site; see Figure 5.2). Green space and civic monuments are lacking amid sprawling factories, offices, a

Figure 5.2
Shenzhen, 1999 (photograph by the authors).

stock exchange, and housing. For the cross-border visitor, shops offer imitation Prada and Gucci, various amusements, and pirate DVDs (although the World Trade Organization has imposed new restrictions on piracy); for those in poorer regions of China, Shenzhen represents an opportunity that has spurred substantial legal or illegal migration (O'Donnell 1999, 2001).

The possibility of making money and consuming drive the city. Wal-Mart and Sam's Club, for example, have opened successful branches there, combining U.S. and Chinese goods. "In the food section, white bread, U.S. style birthday cakes, sliced pizza and breaded fried chicken are lined up next to eel, chicken feet, pork meatballs and frozen dim sum" (Marshall 2003: F13). Indeed, as a *Los Angeles Times* reporter notes, "Many customers here treat Wal-Mart in much the same way an American might venture into Harrods in London. Families dress up and go there for the day. Young people visit on dates. The store is a must-see for out-of-town visitors" (2003: F13). The behavior suggests a rapid evolution from village to city toward Hong Kong–style global consumption.

Shenzhen was created by the 1978 initiative of the Chinese Communist Central Committee under Deng Xiaoping to develop the Four Modernizations in Industry, Agriculture, the Military, and Science. In the South, Deng specifically promoted openness to foreign investment with tax concessions, tariff-free imports of raw materials, and exports of finished goods from a designated zone. Other reforms reduced administrative delays, along with improved transportation, centralized development, and labor services. The 327-square-kilometer Shenzhen SEZ, created in 1980, offered space, efficiency, cheap labor, and a receptive government. It attracted $218 million in investments in its first year (1980) and ten times that by 1994 (Chu 1998: 492).

Over the past fifteen years, foreign investments — often from Hong Kong or channeled through it — have created large subsidiary units and small factories with flexible workforces. Shenzhen was supposed to promote international investment, but as Josephine and Alan Smart have shown, this development has also solidified Hong Kong's position. Often using family connections, Hong Kong firms invested in and moved operations from the SAR to the new lands to take advantage of cheaper labor in Shenzhen (1998; see Kueh and Ash 1996; Cheung 2003b). Hong Kong has become the conduit as well as the guarantee of future development.

Yet, Hong Kong is also a competitor. Ching Kwan Lee (1998) provides a Shenzhen update on Janet Salaff's classic work (1993) on gender and industrialization in Hong Kong by contrasting the women and regimes of labor that characterize both places. She looks at a typical laborer in Hong Kong: Yuk-Ling, a forty-three-year-old line manager assembling audio equipment for Liton industries while managing a double-employment household. After two decades of work, however, she was able to call on fellow workers and company flexibility for support. By contrast, Chi-Ying, at Liton's plant in Shenzhen, was a twenty-two-year-old child of peasants from Hubei, recently arrived in the city. Her monthly paycheck was a fraction of Yuk-Ling's, but she managed to send some home and spend the rest for herself, finding independence despite the authoritarian workplace (1998: 1–10). Still, as Lee notes, it was the Liton factory in Hong Kong that closed during her fieldwork, leaving Yuk-ling with an uncertain future (1998: 170–177).

Despite cross-border opportunities that have changed both places, crossing remains easier when one goes North, whether to shop, reside, play golf, or invest and move jobs (although Hong Kongers are wary of crime in Shenzhen). Goods and profits move southward, and Mainland tourism has become an increasing feature of the Hong Kong economy. Defining the border remains a constant concern. Points of crossing have expanded their hours to provide uninterrupted service, while plans for a new rail line will increase transport options. In fall 2003, Li Luoli, secretary general of the China Development Institute, even followed up on a suggestion of Li Ka-Shing to propose that the tariff border separating Shenzhen and Hong Kong be moved to the Shenzhen-Guangdong frontier, creating a large free-trade zone and integrating the two areas even further (Cheung 2003).

SUMMING UP THE SOUTH

As these brief urban portraits suggest, Hong Kong, Guangzhou, Macau, and Shenzhen have become increasingly connected, partly as a result of global politics. In recent decades, it has become much more common to talk about a zone of development and envision plans for the Pearl River Delta or some other configuration of Southern and coastal regions. While these discourses build on shared traits of culture, social structure, language, and history, they also involve transformations that alter features of Chinese life, whether through the earning power of working women or the questions raised by mass media. Still, growth and economic development remain the framework through which the Chinese publicly discuss the Pearl River Delta's future. A 2003 plan by the Guangdong Development Planning Commission, for example, envisioned six new cities of one million inhabitants each by 2010, coupled with a doubling of highways and constant increases in GDP and exports.

As Xinhua News Agency has noted, "The ambitious development includes programs on infrastructure, environmental protection, wide application of information technology, and growth of the high tech sector in the region" that "accounts for one third of China's exports" (June 22, 2003). Other ambitious infrastructure projects include the Guangzhou airport and the possible bridge between Hong Kong and Macau. The new South China Mall in Dongguan, at 7.1 million square feet, is four times the size of the largest mall in the United States and includes a theme park as well as "cityscapes" of Paris, Hollywood, and Venice (Barboza 2005).

Even more striking is a 2004 discussion among nine southeastern provinces (including Hong Kong and Macau) to create a planning unit whose population would rival the EU. This group, which included Yunnan, Sichuan, Guizhou, Guanxi, Hunan, Jiangxi, and Fujian, also sent a political message to Hong Kong, according to observers: "With Hong Kong residents demanding greater rights to elect their leaders despite strong opposition from Beijing, a succession of senior officials made a point of underlining the extent to which Hong Kong's economy now depends on the mainland" (Bradsher 2004: 7). Moreover, Hong Kong was not included in the original proposal floated by Guangdong Politburo member Zhang Dejian; SAR Chief Executive Tung Chee-Hwa was forced to scramble to host the first Pan-Delta Forum and insure a position within this new framework (Joanilho 2004; Cheung and Chow 2004). In 2005, a working meeting of the Guangdong–Hong Kong Joint Cooperation Conference in Guangzhou has supported this framework of structural connections and investment.

Guangdong, at least for the next few decades, will contain multiple administrations in its SARs, SEZ', and other regions.

These units apply the policies of the nation-state but also seek their own distinctive paths. Many political issues are intensely local, as Hong Kong's *South China Morning Post* has observed in Shenzhen. Here, rather than reducing the impact of the Communist Party, reform meant increasing government efficiency to avoid local protest: "Mr. Yu [Shenzhen's mayor], like Richard Daley, has to make sure the city works. If it does not, people will not hesitate to protest. Surprising as it may seem to some, mainland residents can wage small-scale protests against the poor provision of urban services, property disputes, and other relatively mundane matters without fear of retribution. Labour strikes, Falun Gong protests, and the like are, of course, a different matter" (Mitchell 2003). Political change thus meets economic changes in ways that recall the problems of an earlier Hong Kong. Others go beyond small protest: the critical *Southern Metropolis News*, a Guangzhou-based newspaper whose group reports on social inequality and environmental issues, has faced repeated government crackdowns and raids, yet remains among the "freest" media of the People's Republic of China (Kahn 2004).

Moreover, urbanization and globalization have created new regional problems. Migrants without jobs account for a "floating" population that may represent 25 percent of the regions' total population. This flexible labor pool, whose presence keeps down wages and can be immediately tapped to fill needs, is also associated with rising crime and housing problems (Cheung 2003b). Run-off into the Pearl River and the air pollution from China's factories now contribute to problems in Hong Kong and Macau, which had been seeking to bring such issues under control. Diseases also cross borders, as bird flu and SARS have shown. Meanwhile, older dependencies can create new dilemmas. Hong Kong now competes with Shenzhen for (polluted) water but cannot use China as a dumping ground for plastic wastes as it did in the past (Ng and Ng 1997).

The expansion of the Pearl River Delta economy also raises questions with regard to the rest of China. Floating workers, for example, contribute to Southern Chinese growth, but will their home provinces be able to provide social services if they return to retire? Inequality also sparks competition — yet as other provinces take advantage of economic reforms, the national position of Guangdong may appear weaker. In fact, debates over "freedom" question the meanings of modernization, whether the contest is waged in the streets of Hong Kong or the offices of the *Southern Metropolis News.*

The once-isolated Asian dragon of Hong Kong now has a family, forcing its citizens and neighbors to rethink relations on a local and global stage. In the twenty-first century, regional integration is advanced, but also complex. Hong Kong is no longer a global city without a hinterland, but neither does it have a clear role in a region or a nation-state. South China provides a cultural and social framework to understand the past and future and mediates the global and the local in ways that will continue to change in decades ahead. Another Chinese global city, Shanghai, provides an appropriate closing comparison of regionalism, localism, and the nation-state in a global perspective.

SHANGHAI AND CHINESE GLOBALISM

The Hongkong and Shanghai Bank linked entrepreneurs in the British colony to what would become the most cosmopolitan city of China, Shanghai. When the Shanghai office on the Bund overshadowed the bank's Hong Kong headquarters in the 1930s, Hong Kong erected a taller one. But Shanghai was already the dominant city — one of the largest cities in the world, home to a large Western community and hundreds of thousands of Chinese: elites, workers, intellectuals, and political activists. Sixty years ago, Professor W. J. Hinton, formerly of the University of Hong Kong, saw Shanghai as a model for the colony: "If I am right, in fifty years or so from now, Hong Kong will be rather like Shanghai, the Colony corresponding to the Settlement, a little bit of British territory adjoining a wealthy, prosperous and happy Chinese city" (1941: 261). By the 1980s, however, the situation was somewhat reversed, as Shanghainese envied Hong Kong's globalism, cosmopolitan cultures, and wealth. Today, the power and image of Shanghai as a global metropolis of 30 million people that dominates the economy of contemporary China underscores its profound transformations and showcases the intersection of China with ideas, goods, and people from the West.

Shanghai, on the banks of the Yangtze River (which drains north-central China), is an old settlement, but through most of its history lacked such a dominant position. While it became a county in 1288, nearby cities like Suzhou and Hangzhou took on more political importance and played key roles within China. As historian Betty Wei reminds us, it is wrong to let the image of a later cosmopolitan Shanghai ignore a longer history of urban and regional development (1987).

When the Treaty of Nanjing opened new ports, Shanghai was transformed. Its administration was divided among British and French concessions and the Chinese county — the foundation for future power struggles. Foreign firms and settlers invested in trade and industries like textiles in which Chinese entrepreneurs and compradors became active and wealthy agents. Shanghai became a center for production long before Hong Kong. After 1895, Japan gained the right to build and own factories there, and both Japanese and American interests grew within this complex urban system. As Nicholas Clifford explains:

> Companies established their headquarters in Shanghai, and although Westerners retained managerial control, they depended largely on a network of Chinese traders and bankers — starting with the Chinese compradors in their own firms— to handle the financing and marketing of goods in the interior. Thus, the goods they imported were sold to Chinese merchants in the ports, who then handled their distribution in the interior. So too, exporters depended upon Chinese merchants to bring their goods to the waterfront, where the foreign houses bought them and shipped them abroad. (1991: 44)

Workers, women as well as men, manned the factories and explored opportunities unknown in rural China (Honig 1986).

Chinese outnumbered foreigners even in the British and French concessions. In the 1850s and 1860s, Wei cites only a few hundred foreigners there, while the Chinese census showed over 100,000 Chinese in these enclaves alone. By 1900, the population of all foreigners had reached 100,000, while Chinese *in the foreign settlements* had topped 500,000, with millions in other areas (1987: 64–72). By the 1930s, Shanghai rivaled London, Tokyo, and New York in size.

As Xiong Yuezhi has argued, this foreign extraterritorial presence in Chinese territory allowed an image of "Shanghainess" to emerge, in which migration, exposure to Western technology and ideas, and a society based on wealth rather than background all underpinned an emergent Chinese modernity (1996: 100–105). Another modern observer of a renewed Shanghai reminds us: "Shanghai was the city of firsts for China: the first electric trams, the first stock market, the first night clubs, the first movie industry. It was also the city of superlatives, possessing the tallest buildings, the most banks, the cleverest entrepreneurs, the best products, the freest press, the fullest cultural life, the fiercest gangsters and the grandest gambling dens" (Yatsko 2001: 13). This sense of cosmopolitan modernity, whether romanticized or suspect, shapes a mediated image of Shanghai pervading its own historic film industry as well as modern films from China (Zhang Yimou's 1995 *Shanghai Triad*), Taiwan (Hou Hsiao-Hsien's *Flowers of Shanghai* 1998), and Hong Kong (Tsui Hark's 1984 *Shanghai Blues*). This imagery also attracted Hollywood, from Josef Von Sternberg's *Shanghai Express* (1932) to *Indiana Jones and the Temple of Doom* (1984).

Romantic cosmopolitan images should not blind us to conflicts in the city. For masses of female workers in the textile industry, Shanghai offered opportunities they might not have in their impoverished home provinces, but at the cost of hard and lonely lives (Honig 1986). Leo Ou-Fan Lee, who has examined the distinctive modernity of Shanghai popular literature, underscores the ambivalence of a divided city, where a Chinese guidebook might praise Western goods but write of its elegant hotels: "These places have no deep relationship to us Chinese . . . and besides, the upper class atmosphere in these Western hotels is very solemn, every move and gesture seems completely regulated. So if you don't know Western etiquette, even it you have enough money to make a fool of yourself, it's not worthwhile" (1999: 13). In this complex setting, nonetheless, a distinctive

Chinese intellectual exploration of the future emerged that was neither borrowing nor imitation so much as it was a reaction and a critique of both China and the West. It also translated into political action, fed in part by powerful visions from the Chinese Communist Party. New visions of China also faced the wounds of foreign imperialism, apparent in incidents like that of May 30, 1925, when foreign soldiers in the foreign concessions shot into a crowd, killing Chinese protestors.

As we have seen, Shanghai was an early target for Japanese expansion through investment and then via occupation. After World War II, with foreign concessions eliminated, Shanghai's cosmopolitan people and economy faced uncertainty compounded by China's civil war. Companies retreated to Hong Kong, and were soon followed after 1949 by capitalists, filmmakers, and other refugees fleeing the Communist regime.

Shanghai's development over the next 50 years diverges sharply from Hong Kong because it was part of the Chinese Communist state. It remained the largest economic producer for that state — with 13 percent of China's total industrial output and one-fourth of its exports as late as 1980. Nevertheless, for decades, Shanghai occupied a subordinate political position, with leaders appointed from other areas. It became the launching point of the Cultural Revolution, in part because Mao's wife Jiang Qing, Gang of Four leader had been an actress in Shanghai cinema. Yet this radical movement devastated the city because of its suspect foreign associations and cosmopolitan cultural identity. By the 1980s, exports from Guangdong exceeded those from Shanghai for the first time since the Treaty of Nanjing (Yatsko 2001:15). Shanghai residents even turned to Canto-pop (Hong Kong popular music) and Guangzhou fashions as markers of modernity.

Reforms by Deng Xiaoping that changed the South also smoothed Shanghai's return to its position as a Chinese world capital. The revitalization of production and finance in the city has gone hand-in-hand with foreign investment, with the city reshaped by new skyscraper headquarters and residential complexes. Transportation headaches have resulted as cars overwhelm bicycles and mass transport. Now, moreover, Hong Kong people travel to Shanghai for its excitement and energy as well as its opportunities.

Shanghai now has passed Hong Kong in many measures of growth from population (the city alone may pass twenty million by 2010) to vertically increases in GDP, double digit annually since 1992. Shanghai has 2800 skyscrapers, constructed since 1992. Perhaps an equal number are on the drawing board as the city prepares to host a 2010 World's Fair. Given the amount of buildable land and the attraction it holds for people across China, the city faces choices between upward densification and concomitant congestion in multiple Central Business districts along the Yangtze on the one hand and vast suburban sprawl on the other. Issues of affordability versus luxury development, as well as corruption in the stock market, point to capitalist issues that Hong Kong has already grappled with (see Shanghai's Information Resource Network Web site)

Other differences between the cities remain significant. While we have contrasted Shanghai and Hong Kong cinema in the past, this competition has not redeveloped in the same way. Shanghai is now the center for Chinese television, with filmmaking centered in Beijing. Shanghai holds many international headquarters and handles distribution to and from North and Central China, but South China has developed an independent system centered on Guangzhou and Hong Kong, with continuing Southeast Asian links as well. Geographer David Meyer argues that the difference between the two cities stem from a divergence in the meanings of globalization itself:

> Continued economic growth and development of China will catapult Shanghai to the upper tier of the world's metropolises because its trade, finance and corporate management firms dominate exchange networks in Central and North China, an economy with a population of about 800 million or more. Foreign intermediary firms dealing with those regions will require a major operation in Shanghai. Nevertheless, Hong Kong will continue as the pivot of intermediaries who control and coordinate exchange with South China, an economy that includes perhaps 400 million or more people; Hong Kong's regional economy, therefore, surpasses most nations. In contrast to Shanghai, however, Hong Kong intermediaries represent the highest-capitalized, most-specialized bridges between the global economy outside Asia and the economies of Nanyang, China and Northeast Asia. Mainland Chinese and foreign intermediaries, therefore, that need access to those wider global capital markets will base their premier office in Hong Kong, not Shanghai. (2000: 235)

This trajectory may not be so clear, since growth in both cities depends on the changing Chinese state as well as local, regional, and global features of politics, culture, and society. Hong Kong and Shanghai both recreated themselves in the contest of new globalization in the nineteenth century. They nonetheless remain united and divided by reforms that defined them during that era: One a Chinese city shaped by foreign concessions, the other a foreign colony. To understand these differences on yet a larger scale, we move beyond China to compare Hong Kong to other East Asian cities — and meanings of a Greater China — related and competing with those we have seen so far, but re-created through different landscapes, histories, and meanings.

Hong Kong and Cities of East Asia
Six

What does it take to be Asia's financial centre? Can vertically challenged Singapore win the race? The race is on. New skyscrapers will be dotting the skyline of Asian cities such as Taipei, Shanghai and Seoul within the next five years. Apart from forcing planes to alter flight patterns and acting as backdrops for Hollywood stunts, these skyscrapers play a more serious role — as flagship business and financial centers for cities where they are located. (Chow 2003)

In journalism, academic works of political economics, and city sloganeering, images of dragons, tigers, lions, and other beasts often symbolize East Asia's rapid postwar socioeconomic transformations and differentiate these processes from Western development. Ezra Vogel, for example, moves from the millennial symbolism of dragons and power in China to postwar Japan and "four nearby little dragons — Taiwan, South Korea, Hong Kong and Singapore — [that] modernized even more quickly" (1991: 1). These dragons differ: postwar Japan set the pace for a new Asia as it rebuilt production, fostered private investment and dynamic innovations, created a burgeoning domestic market, and sustained export triumphs. As others followed these paths, Japan faced competitors among Asian NIEs (Newly Industrializing Economies), as "Made in Hong Kong" and "Made in Taiwan" challenged "Made in Japan" in stores around the world. Manufacturers in and from these "little dragons," in turn, looked for cheaper production in the 1970s, 1980s, and 1990s, allowing Guangdong to become a Fifth Dragon rather than a sleeping one (Kueh and Ash 1999) or creating the expectations that Thailand would emerge as an "Asian Tiger" (Askew 2002: 1; see Rock 2001). Yet, during the recent Asian recession, Korean sociologist Eun Mee Kim asked if such economies were, in fact, "Four Asian Tigers or Kittens?" (2000: viii).

While less Orientalist imagery also exists in the discussion of this global economic shift — references to Asian "Miracle" economies, "emerging world cities" (Lo and Yeung 1996), or the Pacific Century — this collective menagerie brings together place, time, production, policies (careful government intervention and encouragement of foreign investment), people, and culture. Other features, both local and global, may be more or less explicit in the analysis, including the variable role of Confucian values, the historical presence of Chinese populations and of family and trade networks in these areas, the relations of ports and hinterlands, the decline of European colonialism, and the rise of American intervention (both military and financial) since the Cold War. And these economies are constantly increasing cross-border connections through cooperative associations like the Association of Southeast Asian Nations (ASEAN), shared investments, mobile managers (but rarely labor), flows of knowledge, and cutthroat competition. Within this framework, Hong Kong is a model city for Asia and a competitor within a complex macroregion.

Shared features, however, should not obscure differences among East Asian cities, nations, and peoples. Just as Hong Kong shares much with South China and reemerging Shanghai but remains distinct from much of China, so the stories of "dragon development" differ in scale, context, and cultural history. Japan, the prototype for modernization in Asia both before and after World War II, already has appeared in our discussion because of Hong Kong's many ties of commerce, politics, finance, and knowledge with that state, yet it is difficult to compare a city–region with a nation–state of 130,000,000 people that also has a profoundly different experience of imperialism, defeat, and dramatic renewal in this century. Taiwan shares with Hong Kong a position inside and outside of China, although the political, ethnic, and economic history of that island and its capital differ from those of Hong Kong — as do local debates over the future. In Korea, American intervention and divided national politics have raised issues far beyond the Hong Kong case. Finally, Southeast Asia, with the exception of the highly successful neo-Confucian state of Singapore, has figured primarily in this book as a market. Thailand, Vietnam, Malaysia, Indonesia, and the Philippines are all in later phases of sometimes-uneven economic development complicated by internal struggles (see regional map in Figure 6.1).

East Asian cities and states include global powerhouses, those still "developing," and "problem states" such as Burma under brutal dictatorial rule. There are states ruled by monarchs, dictators, and elected governments; multicultural states and those that have or seek an ethno-national identity; states defined by Confucian heritages; and others whose dominant populations are Buddhist, Muslim, Christian, secular, or multireligious. Within these states and their cities, as in Hong Kong, people construct global bonds through labor, hope, strategy, and protest.

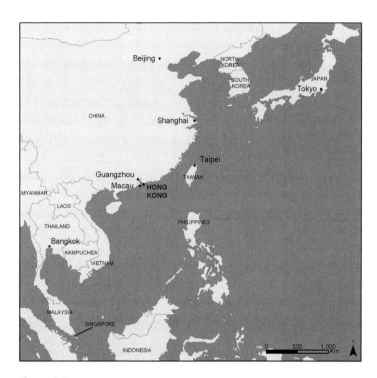

Figure 6.1
Hong Kong in East Asia. (Courtesy of Cartographic Modeling Laboratory of the University of Pennsylvania.)

This chapter cannot delineate all the meanings or experiences of globalization in East Asia. Instead, it explores three cases that cast special light on global Hong Kong before returning to more general notions of Asian world cities and their changing landscapes. Within this broad panorama, selected examples not only illuminate the economics of the Pacific Century, but also relate to either Hong Kong or the global Chinese connections that are explored in this book.

Thus, the first case study is Taipei, Taiwan, which has grown from a backwater Chinese outpost to the capital of a Japanese colony to an ostensible capital for the Republic of China (ROC) as a whole to one of the original global/national dragons now "on its own." With a population of nearly 3 million, Taipei anchors an economic dynamo with a GDP of US$282 billion (2001) and, to some extent, offers an alternative model of a democratic global China (Callahan 2004: 179–208). Taipei is especially relevant to Hong Kong because the Mainland so strongly influences each place, including how they relate to each other. Singapore, the "Lion City," shares urban scale and political and cultural postcolonial "Chineseness" with Hong Kong, but is also an independent city-state, posing questions of identity and action for Hong Kong. The last case study is Bangkok, Thailand, where recent growth has created a new tiger despite the recent recession and the impact of the 2004 tsunami on coastal resorts. While the capital and cosmological center of the Buddhist Thai kingdom, Bangkok has deep connections with China and Chinese migration. While Tokyo, Seoul, Kuala Lumpur, Manila, or Ho Chi Minh City might also provide significant comparisons, this limited selection provides the opportunity to highlight global connections and differences that frame Hong Kong in its macroregional context.

This chapter ends with the battle of dueling skyscrapers, tourist projects, and economic infrastructures for the twenty-first century now raging across the regions. Here, the discussion complements an analysis of the historic landmarks of Central Hong Kong (see chapters 1 and 4) with the new Hong Kong International Airport, the Cyberport, and Disneyland as gateways, literally and figuratively, to regional and global futures.

ANOTHER CHINA: TAIWAN AND TAIPEI

The social and cultural history of Formosa/Taiwan intersects with Hong Kong frequently, from early contacts between China and the West to colonial forays by the Spanish, Portuguese, and Dutch that promoted Taiwan's intermittent autonomy (see Taipei Web site). Moreover, Taiwan's role has been complicated by the history of interactions between the island's aboriginal populations and Chinese migrants. Taiwan became a pirate center in the late Ming and early Qing dynasties. Despite China's reincorporation of the island in the eighteenth century, Japan claimed it after the Sino-Japanese war (1894–1895), once again separating it from domination by Imperial China. After the war, it took on a new role as a site of an alternative China, diverging from the Mainland of the People's Republic.

As a colonizer, Japan combined domination and assimilative strategies with modernization, including improvements in transportation, hydroelectric energy, industrial development, agriculture, and education. Under the Japanese, Taipei, which only had been recognized as a capital in 1875, became a more ordered colonial city, with monuments like the European-style University and Presidential Office Building. After World War II, China reclaimed Taiwan, suspicious of its people's cultural differences, economic advancement, and links to Japan. In February and March 1947, protests flared against Chinese rule, but a savage military repression left tens of thousands of Taiwanese dead. Successive governments suppressed memories of the events of February 28th; only after years of democraticization was a monument to this tragedy unveiled in Taipei in 1995. In 1997, February 28th was declared a national holiday.

Such repression was part of Taipei's transformation from a middling provincial capital into a national one after the defeat of Guomindong forces in China's civil war. While some capitalists fled to Hong Kong, other elites — most importantly, military officers and politicians led by Chiang Kai-Shek — moved to Taiwan, although the population there resisted this new regime and its martial rule. With Chiang's government came imperial treasures and artworks that symbolized the history and authority of the Chinese state, now proudly displayed in the National Palace Museum in Taipei. This quest for legitimacy altered the landscape of the provincial city. New symbols were introduced, including a massive memorial hall for Sun Yat-Sen that competed with his tomb in Nanjing. (As noted, Chiang's wife was also Sun's sister-in-law, although her sister remained in Shanghai.)

This new Republic of China sought recognition as the "real" China as opposed to the Communist People's Republic of China. In Cold War Asia, the Straits of Taiwan could be drawn as a "neutralized" geopolitical moat and the Mainland excluded from the United Nations for decades. Taiwan's militarization (and America's support) meant that Mao Zedong never pressed any claim to the island too far.

Once installed in Taiwan, the ROC reformed landownership and created an inviting, stable climate for foreign investment, including nearly $2 billion from overseas Chinese between 1952 and 1989. It also sponsored infrastructural and technological development (Selya 1995: 10–15), even before U.S. aid ended in 1964. Taiwan's economic growth, like that of Hong Kong, was industrialized and export-driven. A cosmopolitan middle class would define economic and national futures that differed not only from those of Mainland China, but also from the nostalgic and displaced dictatorship of Chiang Kai-Shek, who ruled until his death in 1975.

Within the context of complex national and economic development, Taipei never became a stately city so much as a chaotically functional one with few monumental structures — museums, temples, markets, government buildings, the university, and the central train station — amidst rapidly built, uninspired modernist residential and office towers. As Roger Selya complained in 1995,

> the architectural mix of Taipei has been subject to frequent derision. For example, Herr (1968) has opined that "no matter how much you come to love Taipei, you will never think of it as beautiful." Glenn (1968) has disdainfully referred to the built landscape as "mongrelizing." He cites the negative aspects of Taipei's environment: the hills are too far off, it has no port, no spacious parks, and few imposing buildings. Glenn attributes the flavor and interest of the city to its noisy vitality — the hawkers' cries and the din of construction. (1995: 39)

Changes in life in Taiwan, however, also came from external developments. In 1972, the PRC replaced Taiwan in the UN. The thaw in U.S. relations with China under President Richard Nixon led to President Jimmy Carter's withdrawal of formal recognition from the ROC in 1979. An American Institute replaced the embassy in Taipei, part of a confusion of names and levels of contact that has played out through many subsequent venues. Taiwan, however, already was strong enough to forge a more independent economic and political path. Martial law ended in 1987 and the government slowly evolved toward more democracy and increasing recognition of the Taiwanese people, their heritage and their rights. Chiang Ching-Kuo, Chiang Kai-Shek's son, who ruled from 1978 to 1988, cracked down on corruption, incorporated Taiwanese into his ruling party and increased electoral participation. After his death, he was succeeded by Lee Teng-Hui, a native-born Taiwanese. In 1991, the planning commission for recovery of the mainland — a relic from the civil war — finally disappeared.

The reconciliation of multiple Taiwanese populations, movements toward democracy and democratic expression, and even the reconstruction of post-1971 global relations mean that Taiwan and Taipei, like Hong Kong, often challenge Mainland Chinese imaginations of the state and the world. As William Callahan concludes, "The issues have moved beyond unification/independence to more flexible notions of identity. . . . In this way, the real issue is not 'who will win in struggles of war and peace' — nationalist China or democratic Taiwan — but what form cosmopolitics will take in Greater China" (2004: 216–217).

Rethinking Taiwan as a state has led to the reform of Taipei, where administrations have grappled with pollution and green space and reconsidered history and memory in the fabric of the city. Taipei boasts vital institutions, artifacts of historical Chinese culture, and global connections. Government action also must meet the demands of increasingly wealthy citizens for space, quality of life, and consumption. The city's most recent project, Taipei 101, discussed below, provides both the tallest Finance Center in the world and a five-story luxury mall.

Economic developments and political changes have differentiated Taiwan from the Mainland, making any discussion of reunification complex despite the practice of "One Country, Two Systems" in Hong Kong. In the new millennium, for example, growing economic ties among China, Hong Kong, and Taiwan have not prevented Taiwanese threats of declarations of independence that would sever the ambiguous ties of the "two Chinas" and perhaps start a war. Speeches on independence by Taiwanese President Chen Shui Ban, who was reelected in 2004, provoked serious diplomatic conflicts. Opposition to his regime, in turn, has produced new Taiwanese contacts with the PRC, as leaders of other political parties (including the Guomindong!) have traveled, via Hong Kong, to Beijing for new conversations. At the same time, Taiwan's wealth allows it to invest in countries, such as those in Central America, in need of foreign aid and, in turn, to receive recognition from them. Thus, the ROC remains visible in global political and economic discussions through commerce, investment, friends, and émigrés.

While Hong Kong has long had a cultural Left (pro-PRC) and a cultural Right (pro–Republic of China), Taiwan did not figure in most citizen's political imaginations during the turbulent years of the 1960s, when many in Hong Kong were debating decolonization, nationalism, and a Hong Kong–Chinese identity. The moderate Hong Kong *Chinese Student Weekly*, for example, linked Chinese nationalism to the May 4 movement in 1919. Although this weekly was anti-Communist, it did not model itself on Taiwan, but chose a reformist procapitalist model. On the other hand, the Kwok Sui Pai (an informal designation of many pro-PRC activists) argued that to be nationalistic was to be like the Chinese in PRC. Since the "One Country, Two Systems" model was originally devised for Taiwan, the two areas have studied each other more carefully since negotiations for Hong Kong's Handover began.

Although Hong Kong and Taiwan did not converge politically, they have always shared cultural exchanges, especially in mass media. Growing up in the 60s in Hong Kong, Wong saw Mandarin-language films made in Taiwan, directed by people who had left Communist China, including Zhang Tui, Lee Han Chang, and King Hu. Meanwhile, from the 1950s until Taiwan joined the World Trade Organization in 2001, the government imposed strict quotas on foreign films. Hong Kong films, however, were certified by the Association of Freedom-Loving Dramatists so that they could be treated as Taiwan national films, creating an important market for Hong Kong films. The same Mainland exiles worked in both Hong Kong and Taiwan as directors, technicians, and actors; Brigitte Lin Chiang-Hsia, for example, started her career in Taiwan melodramas but gained international fame working in Hong Kong films with Tsui Hark and Wong Kar-Wai. Entertainment financing also has crossed national boundaries in transnational Chinese collaborations such as Ang Lee's *Crouching Tiger, Hidden Dragon* (2000).

Taiwanese popular songs have permeated Hong Kong airwaves as well. Singer Teresa Teng became the first "trans-Chinese" success: born and established in Taiwan, she triumphed in Hong Kong and became widely known as a symbol for the opening of Mainland China before her death in Thailand, recurring as an icon in Peter Chan's *Comrades* (see chapter 5).

Hong Kong and Taipei share many characteristic experiences of modernity as well as culture and media. As in Hong Kong, Taiwan's rapid industrialization produced social changes in families and lifestyles, especially for an urbane and cosmopolitan middle class. This has been chronicled, as in Hong Kong, in film and television, linking artistic expression by filmmakers like Hou Hsien-Hsiao and Tsai Ming-Liang with more popular media. Perhaps the epitome of cosmopolitan Taiwan filmmaking is Ang Lee (b. Taipei 1954). Lee dealt sensitively with issues of change in Taipei in *Eat Drink Man Woman* (1994), which plays with shifts in gender, generation, and culture (food), while one subplot on real estate speculation underscores the anxieties of rapid urban growth. Issues of transnational Taiwanese in the United States in *Pushing Hands* (1992) and *The Wedding Banquet* (1993) resonate with the experiences and sensibilities of many in Hong Kong. Lee has also shown himself adept with British period pieces (*Sense and Sensibility*, 1995), contemporary American social drama (*The Ice Storm*, 1993), Chinese myth (*Crouching Tiger, Hidden Dragon*, 2000), and action heroes (*The Hulk*, 2003).

Taipei thus is relevant to Hong Kong's status and connections in both its socioeconomic development and its difficult space inside and outside of China. Yet, at the same time, its roles as a capital — "imagined" and real — differentiate it from Hong Kong, as Selya observed a decade ago:

> As the locus of government and financial power, Taipei's status profited directly. For local entrepreneurs and foreign investors alike, Taipei became synonymous with access to decision makers and those individuals and institutions best placed to direct and oversee foreign trade. Taipei thus became a magnet for services as well as industry. As Taiwan's economy was restructured to reflect changing domestic and international conditions, Taipei again was the locus of both articulating and implementing change. Unfortunately Taipei also came to suffer from, and symbolize, the negative consequences of rapid development.

Some of these negative consequences, such as crowding, pollution, and traffic congestion are found virtually everywhere in the Republic of China. Other problems, such as crime and escalating housing prices, seem more restricted to Taipei City. Regardless of the geographical extent of the problems, however, the degree to which they can be solved in Taipei will not only determine the future of Taipei City, but the course of Taiwan's future social and economic development (1995: 16).

Connections, similarities, and differences become even clearer as we turn to another Chinese city to the south, Singapore.

SINGAPORE: THE OTHER CHINESE CITY–STATE

In many ways, Singapore seems to offer a laboratory comparison for Hong Kong. The two areas, often paired as Chinese city–states (for example, Yeung 1990: 167–212; Tu 1991: 10–13; Chiu, Ho, and Liu 1997; Meyer 2000), share important historical features. Founded by the British in 1819 on an island at the tip of the Malayan peninsula, Singapore grew as an entrepôt for opium and commerce, its population swelling through immigration dominated by Chinese, who today constitute 75 percent of the population (15 percent are Malay and 7 percent are Indian; see the Singapore Web site). Occupied by the Japanese in World War II, Singapore participated in the decolonization that transformed Asia. Yet, unlike Hong Kong, Singapore achieved independence in 1963 as part of the multiethnic and multicultural state of Malaysia. Shortly thereafter, it became an independent island city–state. At 240 square miles (622 square kilometers) with a population of roughly 3 million, it is a global city and competitor with Hong Kong in many of the same fields — shipping, manufacturing, global services, finance, and tourism. In short,

Singapore evokes what might have happened if Hong Kong Governor Trench's image of towing the island away from China and out to sea had come to pass.

Yet, Hong Kong people do not read Singapore through the prism of what might have been so much as they view it warily or even with disdainful humor. As Ezra Vogel wrote, "If Hong Kong entrepreneurs thought of Singapore as a bit dull, rigid and too tightly controlled, Singapore's leaders thought of Hong Kong as too speculative, decadent and undisciplined" (1991: 74). Singapore has pursued an economic and ideological system labeled variously as "inclusionary corporatist," "semi-democracy," "Asian democracy" or "technocratic authoritarian" (See Barr 2000: 226ff). Put simply, government, educated elites, entrepreneurs, and labor have been melded into a single state-building project, an ethos of pragmatism (Luck 2004) that contrasts with Hong Kong's stateless noninterventionism. While both cities have vaulted from Third to First World status through government action, civic drive, and global connectedness, they have distinct personalities.

As in Taiwan, the process by which Singapore came to independence entailed the construction of new citizenship. Prior to independence, the island's Chinese population was concerned about its minority status in Malaysia. Through the twentieth century, this Chinese population had grown in wealth and power, bound to China through business and family ties. Their support for the republic was solicited by Sun Yat-Sen himself. Singaporeans even adopted Mandarin as a unifying Chinese language that now sets them apart from other Chinese populations in Nanyang. After three years of Japanese occupation, though, the future of Singapore within the polyglot British possessions of Southeast Asia remained unclear.

Through the 1950s, British and Chinese politicians there focused on the development of political rights, with legislative elections arriving in 1955, decades before Hong Kong. Unlike Hong Kong, anticolonialism was a prominent theme in building local identity, helping to cement awkward relationships between Communists and non-Communists while appealing to Malays, working-class Chinese, and local elites.

The local government in Singapore sought, in turn, to transform its political status, moving through sometimes violent confrontations to a semiautonomous state of Singapore that held elections in 1959. Won by Lee Kuan Yew and his People's Action Party, the government began to change the economic role of the city-island from a port of trade for commodities to an independent production center where wealth would be channeled into housing, welfare, and education in ways that overlap with Hong Kong's emergence as a little dragon. This government balanced the different ethnic groups, valuing Malay, Tamil, Mandarin, and English as official languages and creating special aid programs for indigenous Malays.

Lee sought to link Singapore to Malaya, which concerned Muslim Malay leaders. So did the specter of a possibly communist state — "Cuba across the causeway" is an evocative phrase of the period. Eventually, a compromise created Malaysia from the British colonies of Malaya, Singapore, Sarawak, and North Borneo/Sabah in September 1963. The new state had a Malay population large enough to avoid a Chinese majority but also, made territorial claims that caused confrontations with Indonesia and the Philippines and damaged Singapore commerce and security. By August 1964, Singapore voted to opt out of the new confederation and become a multicultural republic under Lee Kuan Yew, an ideological and political leader over the next three decades (Lee 2000; Barr 2001).

Lee's policies in the city–state promised economic development and social unity. Negotiating with local leaders, Singapore was able to draw foreign investment, with the United States gradually replacing Britain as the primary investor and influence (Britain withdrew from its military bases in the late 1960s). To promote growth, the government increasingly regulated a previously unruly labor market and promoted business as it provided new social welfare programs, from housing to education. The resulting stability attracted corporate headquarters dealing with Southeast Asian petroleum and other sectors. Government-linked corporations became important players in local growth, and the state went so far as to mandate savings, which increased the amount of capital for further expansion. Singapore's manufacturing exports rose 2000 percent from 1969 to 1990, with notable strengths in chemicals and electronics. Its industrial workforce tripled to 447,436 (Meyer 2000: 230) and it moved ahead faster than Hong Kong in restructuring its economy for the service sector (Chiu, Ho, and Liu 1997). Singapore now claims one of the world's largest Gross Domestic Products relative to population size and is closely bound to regional and international markets through its tertiary expertise in the outsourcing of production to Malaysia, Thailand, and Indonesia.

As David Meyer points out, the question of both scale and success are important in any comparison of the Lion City and Hong Kong. Singapore's economy remains half the size of Hong Kong's and the scale of its global operations smaller. "Hong Kong importers and exporters participate in more-sophisticated trade networks, accumulate greater capital and develop higher levels of specialization in commodity trading. Most foreign multinationals market and distribute their goods in Asia from Hong Kong because they need access to these social networks" (2000: 230). Hong Kong has nearly ten times the regional headquarters that the smaller city–state has; Singapore even uses Hong Kong intermediaries for some participation in the growing Mainland economy, an ironic reversal of the meanings of distance. And its economy faced more serious and enduring problems in the Asian recessions of the late 1990s.

Nonetheless, Singaporeans seem to have a clearer ideology of citizenship. Lee Kwan Yew developed his Neo-Confucian ideas of order — scholarship, hierarchy, and harmony together — into a philosophy of "Asian values" that became a statement of identity in opposition to the West in the 1990s (2000). The Singapore 21 Committee has sought new visions of globalism and home, expressed through a richer cultural production (Lim 2003). Yet, Singaporean (Lee's) ideology has also drawn criticism; Tu Wei-Ming, in his analyses of Chinese identity, observed that "Singapore's Chineseness, in opposition to Hong Kong's, is not particularly pronounced; in a certain sense, it is artificially constructed" (1991: 12; see Yeo 2003; Lim 2003; Geh 2004, 2005).

The image of Singapore as a city is rarely one of excitement so much as ordered modernity, interspersed with a few colonial monuments and ethnic landscapes. In 1998, for example, 86 percent of Singapore's population lived in publicly subsidized housing (Kong and Yeoh 2003: 94), promoting high and somewhat uniform standards of living. Meanwhile, Singapore has gained a global reputation for limitations on media and dissent, eugenic rules prioritizing childbearing among educated elites, and harsh punishments for "quality of life" infractions — most famously, threatening a teenage expatriate vandal with caning.

We should also be careful not to reduce Singapore's varied citizenry to a hegemonic projection of its state project, which architect Rem Koolhaas and designer Bruce Mau suggests may underpin a Chinese vision of Singapore as a laboratory with the "exact dosage of 'authority, instrumentality and vision' necessary to appeal. . . . After the iconoclasm of communism there will be a second, more efficient Ludditism, helping the Chinese toward the 'desired land': market economy — but minus the decadence, the democracy, the messiness, the disorder, the cruelty of the West" (2000: 24–25).

Geographers Kong and Yeoh (1998), conclude that "daily life is, without conscious organization, seeping constantly out of the monolithic ideological and managerial structure of the Singapore state" (2003: 210). Still, the history and strategies it shares with Hong Kong and fundamental differences of independence, diversity, and social control in Singapore remind us of complexities in comparing dragons and lions (see Geh 2005).

BANGKOK: CHINESE AND THE THAI STATE IN NANYANG

Contemporary Bangkok and Thailand may, for some, raise the question of what actually constitutes an Asian tiger. Thailand is generally ranked among newly industrializing nations due to its roles in outsourced manufacturing from states like Singapore and its position in a global sex trade. It has other international roles as well — as a political center for nongovernmental organizations (NGOs) and as a cultural center with a rich national tradition. Moreover, the disparities between Bangkok's claims to be a world city and the problems of rural development (which drive migrants to the capital) distinguish it from more established and urbane economies that we have discussed so far. Thus, Thailand has more often been seen as an opportunity or a market for Hong Kong than a competitor.

Anthropologist Marc Askew (2002) has read Bangkok (known locally as Krung-Thep-Manakorn) as the embodiment of the nation's complex economic situation, with abandoned or uncompleted skyscrapers, luxurious malls, and gilded temples amid crowded streets of small shops, houses, and squatters in a vast urban web so dense that it becomes hard to move from place to place. In five decades, the city has grown from 1.6 million to 10 million, spread across 1570 square kilometers (see Web site for images and statistics). Bangkok brings together global wealth and shantytown poverty across sprawling neighborhoods, canals, and highways. Yet, unlike Hong Kong, Singapore, or even Taipei, Bangkok constitutes the center of a nation whose people have never been formally colonized. Moreover, Thai elites have linked cosmology and national history to the present and future of the city, building on a Buddhist ethos rather than a Confucian one (Askew 2002).

Throughout its history, the construction of a Thai Bangkok has played out in counterpoint to China, sometimes mediated, as in the rest of Indochina, through Hong Kong. In Thailand, Chinese emigrants over seven centuries have assimilated to a degree, but they have also clearly differentiated themselves from the emergent Thai state, China, and the colonial powers. The result has been a multiplicity of Sino–Thai identities and players who have become central to Thai development. Sino–Thais have also functioned as bridges to Hong Kong for a variety of commercial activities, many family-based.

The Thai people competed with neighboring realms while absorbing global movements, such as Buddhism, long before Western imperialism had reached Asia or Hong Kong existed. Chinese traders were present in the kingdom by the fourteenth century; their descendants became royal officials and magistrates. Indeed, King Taksin (reigned 1767–1782) was the son of a Chinese immigrant (Skinner 1958: 3; see 1–5).

Bangkok became a new capital for Siam in 1782. By the end of the century, perhaps half the population of Bangkok was of Chinese descent (Askew 2002: 29). These Chinese occupied a special economic and political niche, licensed to trade in ways that differentiated them from Thai subjects of the monarchy and linked them to China. Chinese immigrants took over opium farming, tax administration, and gambling. As they grew richer, the monarchy drew them into the nation–state project, paralleling some of the developments we have seen in Hong Kong. As the wealthiest Chinese gained noble titles, in fact, they assimilated to the Thai elite: "Their daughters, prized by the Thai for their light skin color, married into the Thai elite, and their sons, given a noble upbringing, often entered the government bureaucracy and earned noble titles themselves" (Skinner 1958: 8). Other Chinese used fictive associations with European colonial administrations in Hong Kong to gain extraterritorial status. Meanwhile, Chinese male laborers and traders intermarried with Thai women, producing the hybrid yet assimilated *lukchin*, one of the many regional, ethnic, and religious groups in the capital.

The multiple status of Chinese as immigrants, residents, citizens, and fathers of citizens shifted with changes in Thai nationalism and definitions of the state as G. William Skinner has shown (1957). A balance of assimilation incorporating difference achieved by the nineteenth century gave way to separation in the twentieth. In the late 1920s, as global economics challenged new Chinese immigration, the Chinese Republic made it easier for women to join their husbands abroad. This increased Chinese solidarity, but it also isolated them, as did schools and newspapers. At the same time, a growing Thai nationalism echoed European techniques of exclusion. A famous 1914 manifesto on "The Jews of the East," published under a pseudonym associated with the King (Rama VI) himself, decried Chinese racial loyalty (even in intermarriages), their sense of superiority, and their devotion to money and other stereotypes — identifying the Chinese as poisonous elements undermining "Thainess" (Landon 1941: 36).

After World War II, relations between the Thai and Chinese shifted frequently in relation to both local development and international politics, especially after China became Communist, an outcome that the Thais greatly feared. With the National Economic Development plan of 1961, the Thai government itself took on new economic roles, focusing on infrastructure while private enterprise moved ahead. With an average annual increase in its GDP of nearly 8 percent in its first decade, industry grew faster than agriculture, which had always dominated Thailand's economy. New ethnic and national patterns emerged, spurred in part by American investment during and after Vietnam, which favored the development of manufacturing.

Despite slower growth in the 1970s and the global recession of the early 1980s, Thai growth rebounded in the 1980s and 1990s. Bangkok became a more global city of skyscrapers and international headquarters — a city for tourists, bankers, and pleasure-seekers as well as Thais displaced by rural development (Krongkaew 1996). Here, the complexity of the views and positions of its Chinese residents — perhaps 25 percent of the metropolitan population — casts light on ambiguities of local and global development. Sino–Thais are involved in commerce and industry, but the Chinese are still associated with gambling and prostitution. A 1996 article in the *Far Eastern Economic Review* cited an ethnic pride within Sino–Thai identity that meant "Sino chic — suddenly it's cool to be Chinese" (Vatikiotis 1996: 22). That same year, however, campaigns against the Sino–Thai Prime Minister Banharn Silpa-Arch raised the issue of ethnic identity, which played a role in elections. Nevertheless, as Chinese have faced persecution in Indonesia, visits to Thailand by Chinese President Jiang Zemin (1999) and Premier Li Peng (2002) have elicited royal support for the integration of the Chinese in Thailand and a globalism that allows Sino–Thais to be a bridge between cultures while holding their place in the capitalist economy and statecraft of contemporary Thailand. Peter Chan, certainly a global Hong Kong film director, traces his origins to Bangkok as well.

Bangkok's urban form interprets global processes through the prism of its history. At the center of modern Bangkok, the religious–political complex of Krung Thep still embodies mythic dimensions of the monarchy and the state. Nearby, a "traditional Chinatown" plays host to overseas Chinese and attracts global tourism but more Chinese and lukchin (Sino–Thais) live throughout Bangkok, sometimes in shophouses that combine residence and workplace in largely Thai neighborhoods. Meanwhile, elegant malls with global brands have struggled through recessions while extensive building complexes reminiscent of Hong Kong's elite variations on New Towns sit next to traditional compounds. Caught in shifting opportunities and property markets, some Thais continue to live in squatter settlements facing clearance, while others of the growing middle class seek homes in suburbs, including gated communities further and further from the city (Askew 2002).

The growth of Bangkok and Thailand thus transcends the role of its Chinese citizens — yet Chinese people and Hong Kong have played critical roles in connecting the populations of Thailand to the rest of Southeast Asia. At the same time, Bangkok and Hong Kong are scarcely equal, as the presence of Thai maids in the SAR, Hong Kong people junketing to Pattaya beach resorts or joining Bangkok sex tours, or even Hong Kong's philanthropic roles after the 2004 Tsunami underscore. While Taiwan and Singapore are competitors — and perhaps cousins — of Hong Kong, Bangkok is perceived as an exotic other (despite the increasing frequency of labels reading "Made in Thailand"). Nonetheless, developments in Bangkok, from its economic growth to "Sino chic" and even its increasing visibility as a center for film production — including the newly launched Bangkok Film Festival — force us to consider the milieu of Asian competition within which Hong Kong now grows. With this variety of connections and competitions in mind, we return to East Asian cityscapes of globalization and change.

THE CREATIVE DESTRUCTION OF EAST ASIA: LANDSCAPE AND MEANING

On November 16, 2003, the mayor of Taipei and President of Taiwan opened a five-story mall at the base of the 508 meter (1667 foot) Taiwan Financial Center, inaugurating the tallest building in the world. Taipei 101 (nicknamed after its stories) was promoted by the mayor and the Taiwanese business elite, attracting international attention with its luxurious high-tech office spaces and designer stores such as Gucci, Prada, and Louis Vuitton. Defying local seismological conditions and a general Asian slump, this tower also made a strong architectural statement in a city shaped by colonialism and the transformations wrought by a displaced nationalist Chinese government (Hille 2003; "Large Crowd" 2003).

This skyscraper towers over an international landscape as well. Taipei 101 replaced Petronas Tower in Kuala Lumpur, Malaysia, a symbol of modernity (and oil) in a Muslim postcolonial state, as the tallest building in the world. Chicago's Sears Tower trails behind and New York's proposed Freedom Tower is still in the planning stage. Yet, Taipei 101's reign has already been threatened by proposals in India, Shanghai, and Guangzhou, often buildings designed to house World Financial or Trade Centers despite the fears associated with such structures after September 11 in the United States. While Hong Kong created and justified an aesthetics of density on the basis of limited buildable land (and offers one of the world's tallest office buildings in its International Financial Center, designed by Cesar Pelli), skyscrapers as symbols of modernity and power soar over sprawling Guangzhou, Shanghai, and Bangkok. This construction reminds us that "tigers" often compete for office clients using spatial symbols of power, and that Hong Kong has played an important role in all of this. Rereading the landscape of the Pacific Rim through the prism of its mega-projects (Olds 1995; Ford 2001) allows us to reassess meanings of globalization and power.

Urbanist Larry Ford, for example, has noted the dual value of skyscrapers within local and global webs of meaning:

This building trend in new financial centers of Asia has had both symbolic and pragmatic dimensions. The pragmatic — the simple need for lots of new space — is the easiest and most straightforward to discuss, but it is completely intertwined with the symbolic. Cities need major office buildings, first-class hotels and modern shopping facilities as well as improved infrastructure and housing; in addition, there is also a fascination in Asia with having the newest, fanciest, tallest and largest, and most modern and innovative buildings and landscapes in the world. The reasons for this are many and complex, including perhaps the response to colonial subjugation coupled with a strong work ethic and the perceived need to symbolically join the global economy. (2001: 124–125)

Some skyscrapers remain only partially completed, however — modernist skeletons recalling the region's economic volatility (Askew 2002).

Despite the meaning attributed to such buildings, these new mega-projects, often sponsored by governments in conjunction with local elites, are not always accepted by local populations. In Tokyo, neighbors have forced builders to remove the top stories of skyscrapers; in 2004, a Bangkok mall collapsed while undergoing renovation, killing some people trapped inside. In Shanghai and Beijing, resistance has been less successful, but environmentalists have argued that the former city, at least, needs to open human green space. Even in Singapore, a joint production of Singapore's Toy Factory Theatre Ensemble and Tokyo's Kageboushi Theatre company offered a multinational vision of the anguish of displacement by skyscrapers, billed as "Six Countries, Eight

Reflections, One Asian Soul in Crisis." As a reviewer writes, the play

> opens with a familiar premise: an urban planning official must be cleared to make way for new skyscrapers and a national defense plant. From that terse scenario dreamily unfolds in a wide-ranging rumination on the Asian condition. After encountering new perspectives of nation, society, family, sex, religion, ethnicity, fortune and occupation, the official discovers, just as the wrecking ball descends, that he has become part of the history being destroyed. (Smith 2003; see Yeo 2003)

In addition to skyscrapers mushrooming across Asia, three other ongoing Hong Kong projects typify the regional competition for global city status: the Hong Kong International Airport and SkyCity, Hong Kong Disneyland, and the new Cyberport.

As British and Chinese planners looked beyond the Handover, for example, the importance of a globally competitive airport to replace the cramped and aging Kai Tak facility, surrounded by urban high-rises, loomed large. Access has been a foundation for Hong Kong's global success and the territory needed an updated and smoothly functioning airport (Matsuda 1997: 81). In 1989, the government chose to build a new airport on two small islands off Lantau Island, creating a 1255 hectare site from landfill to hold a giant complex that could, with expansion, accommodate 87 million passengers by the time Hong Kong's special regime ends. Norman Foster, already known for his landmark Hongkong and Shanghai Bank building, became the project's architect. Lantau Island, actually larger than Hong Kong, was also more resistant to Britain, which gained control of the island with the 1898 lease of the

New Territories. Through the 1990s, it remained a peaceful place, connected to the rest of Hong Kong by ferry and used by locals for a day on the beach or sightseeing. Chek Lap Kok airport and the US$20 billion train, highway, and bridge system connecting it to Central have ended that isolation forever.

Construction was delayed by squabbles between the British and the Chinese, already irritated by colonial democratization. The Chinese were also worried about the debt such a project would leave for Hong Kong. It was not until 1994 that an agreement was reached, which meant that Kai Tak, in its eighth decade, was the airport of the Handover. Chek Lap Kok airport opened in 1998 and can now handle 45 million passengers each year with a capacity to cater 120,000 meals per day. The airport has sweeping vistas of Hong Kong through the terminal's soaring windows and 160 stores competing for consumer attention. Its arterial system of trains and highways link Lantau to Tsing Yi, Kowloon, and check-in services in Central, 34 kilometers away ("Hong Kong International Airport" 1998). Noanori Matsuda at Hong Kong University has claimed that this project represents more than a competitive economic strategy — it is a new urban model of Hong Kong itself as an "airport city" linking local and global spaces of transportation, capital, and exchange (1997: 83). Another critic highlights the "infrastructure of speed unique to Hong Kong — speed in which the city and the individual are one" (Kinoshita 1997: 80).

While these readings already recall the cyber-interpretation imposed on Kowloon's Walled City as an iconic place, the projects were only the beginning of development for Lantau. One of the current projects for development at the airport, for example, is the SkyCity, which will include a convention center, hotel, shopping, leisure/entertainment, and cross-border ferries to Guangdong. While airport construction already raised urban environmental concerns, exacerbated by increasing traffic, this project almost makes the city superfluous because visitors hardly need to leave the airport.

Hong Kong is scarcely unique in its emphasis on rapid international connections. Its airport faces regional competition from new airports in Guangzhou and Macau. Shanghai has also opened a new airport well in anticipation of its 2010 World's Fair, with a technologically sophisticated high-speed train. Bangkok, in turn, has a new US$5 billion airport scheduled to open in 2006; recognizing the traffic problems facing the metropolis, plans have also included housing for 10,000 families in its environs. In Thailand, public concerns have been raised about delays as well, lest this become another incomplete monument to modernity. The race for airports goes hand-in-hand with nationalist competition among flagship airlines like Hong Kong's Cathay Pacific, Singapore Air, or Thai Airways.

Development on Lantau today has also brought Disney to the SAR, exposing another competition among Asian tigers for leisure and tourism dollars. Disney brought its global corporation and symbols physically into Asia with the opening of Tokyo Disneyland in 1983. This mega-destination on reclaimed land in Tokyo Bay, with 17 million annual visitors, offers familiar landmarks like Cinderella's Castle. Its crowded version of Main Street was retooled as a World Bazaar with a Plexiglas canopy to adapt to the Japanese climate, and the company added animatronic depictions of Japanese history. In 2001, Disney also added an adjacent DisneySea complex that offers ports built around global (and Disneyfied) destinations.

Hong Kong's project would again make the city a bridge to China and Southeast Asia, eclipsing a local attraction (Ocean Park) on Hong Kong Island and Shenzhen transborder attractions that portray the "world in miniature" (see Holden 2004 for a cultural analysis of "worlds" in Shanghai and Singapore). In Hong Kong, Disney will combine Cinderella's Castle and jungle rides with dim sum and Asian food. The HKSAR government owns 57 percent of the operating company, expected to create 35,000 jobs and bring 5 million tourists each year after its scheduled September 2005 inauguration. As in the case of the airport, these promises have been offset by environmental complaints. Moreover, the projections have been challenged by Disney's plans to build another theme park in Shanghai (see BBC News Web site).

The physical recreation of Lantau around the airport complex, SkyCity and Disney faces intriguing competition from the proposed Norman Foster megaproject to remake West Kowloon, enclosing residential, commercial, and high cultural spaces in a bubble city, theming traditional urbanization in the center rather than around outlying spaces. Given the debates about place, history, and meaning resonating through these chapters, it is worthwhile to recall Larry Ford's comments on Singapore in the 1980s:

> Since tourists apparently were beginning to resist the idea of Singapore as a financial district and shopping mall, the government began to invest in rehabilitation programs for Chinatown, Little India, Arab Street, and the conversion of an old downtown market to a Victorian food hawker center. In addition, an old waterfront boat quay was turned into a picturesque restaurant row, and a former industrial area known as Clarke Quay

was redesigned by the American firm Elbasani and Logan to become Singapore's version of Quincy Market. . . . Many of the rehabilitated storefronts along commercial streets remain empty as locals flock to the malls. (2001: 143)

This vision also recalls the "sanitized Chineseness" Tu imputes to Singapore (1994: 12), and the problems of modernity, localism, and identity that critics such as Ackbar Abbas have posed to Hong Kong itself. (See Evans Chan Yiu Ping's meditations on Disneyland and other issues in *The Map of Sex and Love*, 2001).

A final Hong Kong project (on the island itself), focuses on a sort of "Virtual City," the US$2 billion Hong Kong Cyberport meant to turn Hong Kong into "Silicon Harbor." The Cyberport project began in 1999 as a joint venture of the Hong Kong government and Pacific Century CyberWorks Limited (PCCW) a company formed in 1994 by Richard Tzar-Kai Li, son of Li Ka-Shing. Having acquired Hong Kong Telecom in 2000, the company is the leading Internet provider in the SAR. Stock values have dropped, however, as the public has debated the viability of the Cyberport and a companion Science Park at Tai Po, near the Chinese border. Both projects depend on the value of physical proximity of telecommunications and electronic inventors and entrepreneurs, a need which some information scientists doubt, given Hong Kong's existing wiring (Lo 2002).

In addition to its business functions, the Cyberport offers elite residences, shopping, and a dinosaur museum, updating and upscaling New Towns while claiming a global scale rather than a local one (see Cyberport Web site). This has led to problems beyond slow growth amid an information economy bust:

Developers stood accused of selling fictional space. In 2003, for example, sales propaganda for "Bel Air Residences" used images of the Villa Ephrussi de Rothschild in Nice to sell its expensive apartments. A spokeswoman explained, "We wanted a Monte Carlo image, home to the rich and famous, glamourous lifestyle, shopping for brand names" (Fenton 2003).

This project also faces regional and global competition. Malaysia, for example, has promoted a series of Information Technology host zones with names like Cyberjaya. In Manila, Megaworld CyberCity and Fort Bonifacio Global City represent new commercial/residential complexes built around the state's attempt to position the city and country as the top service provider of the e-service industry, with call centers competing against both Western centers and South Asian competitors. That said, these are secondary niches, less ambitious than Hong Kong, which wants to be the regional leader (Silva 2000). Plans to create a new "intelligent island" in Singapore, meanwhile, have produced renewed global ties of investigation and entrepreneurship and motivated flows of people in and out of the city–state as "a prosthetically enhanced nation" (Ong 2004: 87).

All of these projects embody the changes, aspirations, and dilemmas of Hong Kong and its people in concrete places. They also make sense within the patterns of development of other cities and citizenries in China and the Pacific Rim, whether driven by information exchange, entertainment, or urban development. All local projects, yet global in their vision, their symbolism and the risk they assume. To complete this economic, political, and physical vision of global cities, however, we return to the human movements of global Hong Kong and its diasporic presence in people, goods, and media worldwide in our final chapter.

Diasporic Hong Kong
Seven

One day Heaven's eyes will no longer wink at me

And we'll go back to South China with enough money.

> — *Writing on the wall from Angel Island, 1910–1940*
> *(Hom 1991: 175)*

Since its foundation, Hong Kong has been a primary node for the flow of goods, services, beliefs, and people into and out of China. In this chapter, we explore globalization through the perspective of diaspora: the movement of peoples through and from Hong Kong and the transnational connections they may (or may not) maintain over time. The successes and failures of thousands of migrants have connected Hong Kong to the rest of the world via personal and family relationships for more than a century and continue to shape its future (see Ong 1999; Smith 2001; McKeown 2001; Goh and Wong 2004).

To explain the meanings and connections of global Hong Kong, this chapter begins with the local: Philadelphia's Chinatown, where diasporic presences can be illuminated in a single place. This specialization provides the opportunity to return to Hong Kong's history as a point of transit and connection that links destinations around the world. Changes in world immigration policies after World War II, especially in the 1960s and 1970s, intersected with postwar crowding and development in the colony and subsequent uncertainties about

Hong Kong's future to produce new patterns of international relations. While concentrating on Hong Kong immigrants in the United States, this chapter briefly discusses Britain, Canada, Australia, and Latin America, all of which offer different nodes in the world network of Hong Kong families, enterprise, and media.

Finally, this chapter explores Hong Kong's media landscape in relation to overseas Chinese populations and other global audiences. Technologies of connection and images of emigration reinforce the ties of diaspora for a people connected in so many ways to the world around them and allow the exploration of the imagination of these connections from multiple vantages as well.

THE GLOBAL AS LOCAL IN PHILADELPHIA CHINATOWN

We live in the suburbs ten miles northwest of Philadelphia, but that city's Chinatown is, for us, a place of social and cultural life as well as study, even if it lacks the dominant position and diversity of major Chinese enclaves in New York, San Francisco, Toronto, or Vancouver. Philadelphia's first Chinese establishments emerged more than 150 years ago and a Chinatown had coalesced by the turn of the century (Guan 2001). Yet, the 1937 Works Progress Administration (WPA) guide to Philadelphia depicted a sleepy bachelor community on one or two streets: "Placid Chinese, the younger in Western dress, tend novelty stores and serve in restaurants. The older generation, clinging to robes of the East, lounge about the sidewalks, smoking their long silver-handled pipes" (Federal Writer's Project: 387). While novelty stores and restaurants still abound, Chinatown has boomed since the 1960s, and women and families are as common as men on streets and in markets. Greater Philadelphia hosts roughly 20,000 inhabitants of Chinese ancestry, including descendants of older immigrant families, Hong Kong professionals, university students, working class immigrants, and Southeast Asian Chinese and refugees. They live throughout the city and its suburbs, but Chinatown offers a site to construct an ethnic identity and maintain ties to Greater Chinese culture and society.

Like many other global Chinatowns, Philadelphia's enclave lies "downtown" — drawing in luncheon patrons and tourists from the nearby Convention Center or Center City offices. This geography, however, has made many Chinatowns in North America vulnerable to urban renewal projects such as highways and public facilities; Philadelphia is no exception. In fact, different groups of Philadelphia Chinese Americans have united vocally in campaigns since the 1970s to resist such incursions — whether incursion has meant a highway, a prison, a baseball stadium, gentrification or casinos (Lin 2000; Guan 2001; Hunter 2004).

Vivid murals depicting the lives of Chinese American immigrants on buildings beside a major boundary street, Vine Street, greet those arriving by car from the suburbs. The sense of an entry by a back gate is reinforced by a wall to the north along Vine, decorated with Chinese motifs, that separates Chinatown from an interurban highway connector and buffers noise (the Vine Street Connector). The wall resulted from the 1960s activism to mitigate the impact of the highway, which led to active community organization in Chinatown. The connector nonetheless divides residences and commerce from the Chinese Catholic church, its school, and new commercial and public housing development to the north. It constitutes an urban edge, constraining growth in the area (see Goh 2004).

Three blocks to the south, near Center City, a stereotypical Chinese Gate again delineates an ethnic gateway, even though businesses have spilled onto adjoining streets before reaching the urban "wall" constituted by the downtown Galleria, an enclosed mall. To the East, Franklin Square, and a hospital turned condominium, parking, and various public buildings separate Chinatown from Independence Mall. A final "wall" took shape in the 1990s with construction of the Philadelphia Convention Center on the Western edge of Chinatown, giving the enclave a feeling of physical as well as ethnic separation from downtown.

Inside these "walls," Chinese and English signs call attention to restaurants, barbecue shops, Chinese markets, video and DVD stores, electronics shops, pharmacies, herbal shops, hairdressers, bakeries, novelty shops, religious establishments, banks, family and regional associations, and residential complexes (see Figure 7.1). Chinatown offers dense, lively, and sometimes chaotic streetscapes, though scarcely at the level of Hong Kong or Canal Street in New York. Still, fruits and vegetables spill out onto streets where people pause to greet friends and neighbors. Grandmothers tote babies in slings while children plead for meat-filled buns, bubble tea, or Hello Kitty stickers; teenagers chat on cell phones, tourists snap photos, and adults stop for tea or to meet with lawyers, doctors, and dentists offering bilingual services.

Based on goods, services, staffing, and our own experiences of different establishments, the primary regular and target clients of almost all businesses are greater Philadelphia Chinese American residents rather than non-Chinese tourists. Murals, bilingual street signs, and decorations in the sidewalk insist on the Chineseness of this space. Even the fire station identifies itself as the "House of Dragons." Meanwhile,

Figure 7.1
Philadelphia Chinatown 2004 (photograph by the authors).

Chinese bus companies offer cheap connections to New York and other Chinatowns, while travel agencies and phone cards speak to global connections that differentiate it as a place of recent immigration within the wider ethnic city.

What direct connections does this Chinatown have to Hong Kong today? People, products, and ideas travel here from Hong Kong, other parts of China, and global Chinese communities, making it difficult to distinguish Hong Kong ties per se. Cantonese barbecued meats, for example, are ubiquitous in Chinatowns worldwide; however, are their owners and cooks from Hong Kong, Guangdong, Vietnam, or the United States? Hong Kong people themselves may not seek or stress differences either. Just as Hong Kong appropriates practices from its regions and beyond, Chinatowns are crucibles of hybridity. Yet, this mixed formation still has some clear and important "Hong Kong" features.

Food has dominated Chinatowns all over the world; food practices in Philadelphia Chinatown attest to its central role in Chinese American communities, in both restaurants and home supplies. A few larger establishments, for example, serve dim sum daily, boasting their Hong Kong–style cuisine. Their Chinese names may copy more famous restaurants in Hong Kong and Guangdong, although this allusion may not carry over to their English names (which many Chinese ignore). "Hong Kong style" entails a mixture of food and quality. Decor is typically more subdued than in earlier Chinese American restaurants, relying on pastel tones, perhaps adorned with large photos of Hong Kong and multiple televisions mounted along the walls offering karaoke and satellite television fare. Tanks holding live seafood and Cantonese specialties complete the menu and decor.

Other restaurants specialize in rapid Southern Chinese fare — noodles and barbecue meats — that would be available in similar shops throughout Hong Kong. Vietnamese, Malay, and other Chinese cuisines (Shanghainese, Fukienese, and Sichuan) are also available, generally proffered by Cantonese-speaking servers. In Hong Kong, these would be "foreign" albeit familiar foods; in America, however, diners associate a wide range of Chinese and Asian cuisines with Chinatown. For dessert, several small shops offer sweet soups based on beans, sesame, taro, and nuts, again characteristic of Hong Kong. Bakeries display typical Hong Kong style breads and cakes to be consumed with milk tea or bubble teas. They frequently adopt names familiar to Hong Kongers like St. Honoré or *dai gal ok* ("big family happiness" — Hong Kong's fast food Cafe de Coral).

Food shops and larger grocery stores supply both families and restaurants. Few goods now come directly from or through

Hong Kong, apart from special sauces, Chinese wines, and seasonal goods like moon cakes for the mid-Autumn festival. More often, ingredients for home cooking equivalent to those used in a Hong Kong kitchen come from China, Southeast Asia (frozen and dried seafood), Japan (mushrooms), and Europe (cookies and candies that circulate as gifts in Hong Kong and the United States). Swimming fish and shellfish are available in many stores as well. The ability to shop *as if one lived* in Hong Kong has created new global ties with regard to fruits and vegetables that do not grow in the temperate mid-Atlantic. Crates of mangos, gail-lan (Chinese broccoli), persimmons, long beans, and other mainstays of Cantonese cuisine bear shipping labels from Mexico, Central America, and Chile (and are increasingly handled by Hispanic employees in Chinese-run shops). The Hong Kong/Chinese cook can reproduce the ingredients and conditions of Southern Chinese cuisine through a completely different geography of ingredients, although she may need to go to New York for fine teas or specialty items.

Novelty shops attract both Chinese and non-Chinese. Their tourist goods resemble items generally made in China and available in Hong Kong stores (or similar ones), worldwide. These items often pander to Western ideas of Chineseness or Asianness, foreign to the more sophisticated tastes of Chinese Hong Kong. More ambiguous are stores specializing in Japanese-style trinkets — Hello Kitty, "Snoopy," and the like — cherished by youths in Hong Kong and East Asia (Bosco 2001).

Other businesses have direct links to Hong Kong, such as the local HSBC branch, which competes with Chinese American banks headquartered in New York. Its Chinatown branch offers a Chinese staff and bilingual services under its familiar logo.

Travel agencies boast cheap airfares to Hong Kong and other Asian destinations for a transnational clientele; they also help diasporic Chinese obtain visas and U.S. travel documents.

Chinese bookstores and other shops sell newspapers that offer another connection to Hong Kong. Of the four most common major daily Chinese papers, two are affiliated with Hong Kong dailies (*Ming Pao* and *Sing Tao*), whose logo they display; another is more Taiwan-based, and the fourth, Mainland Chinese (Berger 2003). All have U.S. headquarters and newsrooms. Other newspapers, religious publications, and local announcements are distributed in stores and restaurants; still, the Chinese-linked newspapers hold sway at early morning dim sum in lively conversations. Stores often retain older newspapers for those who cannot go to Chinatown every day.

These papers provide news from Hong Kong, China, and Taiwan, devoting extensive layouts to Hong Kong celebrities. On December 30, 2003, for example, even the Taiwan-based *World Journal* devoted two full pages in the front and three in the entertainment section to the premature death of Hong Kong actress/singer Anita Mui, nearly 10 percent of the entire issue. *Sing Tao* and *Ming Pao* were even more lavish.

In addition, these papers report on U.S. and world issues for Chinese readers. American news is rarely "local." Instead, the papers pay special attention to Chinese Americans nationwide and political issues such as immigration. They sometimes provide stories ignored by the American press: during the Iraq War, many were more critical than the mainstream English language press. Even if Philadelphia coverage is scant, however, advertisements highlight restaurants, stores, and other services for the geographic market within which each edition is distributed. Outside major Chinatowns like New York or Los Angeles, "local" encompasses networks of cities and suburbs; for Philadelphia, these sprawl from New Jersey southward to Maryland. The bilingual *Chinese Yellow Pages* shows a similar breadth of connections, with a single volume covering New York, Pennsylvania, and New Jersey, and other national offices in San Francisco, Los Angeles, Houston, and Atlanta (*Chinese Yellow Pages* 2001: 18).

Chinatown shows an emphasis on global Chinese literacy in its book and magazine shops, with materials from Hong Kong, Taiwan, and China, including many celebrity periodicals. Hong Kong is a major publisher of Chinese news, expressing views that are more neutral and less censored than those published in China or Taiwan. The wall of one books and novelty shop also displays advertisements for employment and business opportunities that are crucial to immigrant networks.

In addition to print media, Chinatown video stores offer Hong Kong products, replacing the Chinese cinemas that once appeared in larger enclaves like Manhattan. A decade ago, Hong Kong films — popular works rather than the art films prized in the United States — were the staples of these stores. More recently, Hong Kong television soap operas of 30 to 50 episodes and Mainland dramas in Cantonese and Mandarin have become top rentals. As with newspapers, these stores cater to populations for whom Chinatown is a point of connection. Rentals for a week accommodate those who live in the suburbs.

All these Chinese-language businesses, including physicians and lawyers, banks and foodstores, change meanings over time with regard to the connections immigrants and their descendants maintain with Hong Kong or other points of origin. For many, these businesses establish places and networks in which immigrants know and support each other. They become less important as immigrants or their children learn language and skills to navigate their larger host society (see Kwong 1987; Lin 1998). Perhaps Chinese funeral homes most clearly evoke the ties of older immigrants to China, where bones were once returned, and the transition of generations commemorated and lived through Chinatown today.

Churches and schools reveal more about the social and cultural cohesion of Chinatown and its people. Philadelphia's Chinatown has had a large Christian population since the 1940s. The Roman Catholic church and school, Holy Redeemer, offers masses in Mandarin and Cantonese and classes in Chinese. Two Protestant churches also thrive; many friends of Wong's parents belong to the Baptist church in Chinatown, which has a very close-knit Hong Kong–based community that organizes formal and informal gatherings, ranging from religious and secular seminars on social issues to picnics and casual dinners. A new church had just opened in 2005 across Vine Street.

A Buddhist temple occupies an upper floor of an old industrial building, above a restaurant and surrounded by sweatshops; another has recently replaced a piano store, a relic of the area's prior economic base in textiles and light manufacturing. Many establishments distribute Buddhist literature. Family shrines also are ubiquitous in restaurants and stores. All these religious institutions offer diverse opportunities for interested people from Hong Kong, but should not be identified specifically with them.

Along with Catholic schools in the neighborhood, Chinese students attend downtown public schools. Here, English-language education may mean additional tutoring sessions for children in Chinese language and writing, including both Mandarin and Cantonese dominant families. Other part-time schools in suburban areas echo this cultural training (see below).

Chinatown hosts many additional important activities above street level. Upper stories house surname and regional associations linked to the Four Counties of nineteenth century emigration and central to older Chinatowns. Today, their mah jong games and personal networks are open to a wider — albeit Chinese-speaking — clientele. Factories occupy other floors, providing employment to many recent immigrants, sometimes under sweatshop conditions.

Many upper floors are residential, ranging from government-assisted apartments to workers sharing cramped housing to new condominiums selling a Center City location with only a slight evocation of any Chinatown context. Chinatown residents have expressed real concern over the incursions of non-Chinese who see these central residences as undervalued commodities in a booming real estate market (Lin 2000; Hunter 2004). Residents and activists now fight for rights to live and work in Chinatown itself. (See the documentary *Look Forward and Carry on from the Past,* 2002; *Voices of Chinatown,* 2005.)

These are not the only struggles that have shaped an urban political consciousness with Chinatown as a base since citizens fought against the Vine Street Connector. The Philadelphia Chinatown Development Corporation (PCDC, see Web site), which grew out of this struggle, has been active in housing and welfare issues. It now has its office in the senior citizen complex north of the highway, which emerged from such work. Asian Americans United guided later vocal public opposition to proposed stadium construction in the late 1990s. It also brought together Asian American teenagers to produce a video about their lives, *Face to Face: It's Not What You Think* (1997, with Wong's participation as facilitator). Yet, this group has now moved its offices to another Asian immigrant area in South Philadelphia. Many social, lobbying, and political groups, too, tend to work in larger categories of American public identity such as "Asian American" (Guan 2001).

Philadelphia's Chinatown is not the only metropolitan center for Chinese residence or activities. Another cluster of Chinese businesses and large grocery stores appears further south in the city near Philadelphia's historic Italian Market. While generally associated with Southeast Asian Chinese, its malls offer convenient free parking for suburban families in cars making purchases for the week. These shopping centers offer Vietnamese *pho*, dim sum, and even Chinese-Western items (*sai chan*) characteristic of Hong Kong cuisine. Another nucleus in northern Philadelphia has regular Chinese bus connections to Chinatown. Other Chinese restaurants are scattered across the city and suburbs. They vary in price, specialty, and quality, including many takeout stores in poor areas that provide a base for immigrant families. A pan-Chinese connection has been promoted by Philadelphia's active participation in Dragon Boat Festivals, celebrated globally in Hong Kong, China, Austrailia, and Europe.

Despite the opportunities of Chinatown, many middle-class Hong Kong immigrants — who predominate among those who left in the 1980s and 1990s — have settled in suburbia. For them, Chinatown remains a center for meetings, food, religion, and news, but parties and mah jong games take place in private homes while children attend local public and private schools. The Greater Philadelphia Cantonese Academy, a Saturday language school primarily run for the children of Hong Kong immigrants, has operated for many years in buildings rented from Main Line private schools and colleges, alongside similar schools for Japanese and Mandarin-speaking immigrants. Computers, telephones, and satellite dishes make it easy to keep in touch with Hong Kong itself, without the intermediary of any Chinatown, just as direct flights from Newark and JFK airports mean that Hong Kong is less than a day of airline travel away. Yet these suburban friends remind us that Chinatown also embodies Hong Kong in terms of people and networks. People meet one another at their jobs, restaurants, markets, churches, during Chinese New Year celebrations, and wedding or birthday banquets. They exchange news of family and friends, or views about Severe Acute Respiratory Syndrome (SARS), U.S. politics, and restaurants.

Maintaining a Hong Kong "space" in Chinatown, however, faces challenges as demanding as the gentrification facing Chinatown activists. A cultural marker as basic as language, for example, evolves in an immigrant community. Chinese immigrants speak different dialects of Chinese, although many are fluent in Cantonese and Mandarin or Cantonese and Fukienese. Mobility and success, however, are linked to English, whether learned in Hong Kong or after immigration. Young people born in the United States, in turn, favor English, despite demands of family and school that they practice their Cantonese. English is the lingua franca for non-Chinese tourists and for interactions with the burgeoning Hispanic workforce in menial jobs. The fully bilingual tend to speak their own Chinese language among themselves, with Hong Kong speakers sprinkling their conversations with Chinglish. Monolingual Chinese tend to be recent immigrants and the elderly.

Beyond the goods, services, and media of Chinatown, Hong Kong immigrants and their families form groups around personal connections and shared relations of class, experience, profession, and interests. These take shape within looser Hong Kong social and cultural networks that share customs with other Chinese and Asian immigrant communities, but are divided by class, immigration status, and opportunity. Hong Kong immigrants in Philadelphia are often cosmopolitan travelers who mingle with other Chinese from Taiwan, the Mainland, and Nanyang and polyglot citizens of the United States. Trips to Hong Kong to stay with relatives or visits to Chinese friends in Toronto's Chinatowns (for example) increase the complexity of their identities. While a mainland Chinese worker in a video about Philadelphia's Chinatown claims that leaving Chinatown is like "going to America" (*Look Forward*, 2002), such a stark delineation would be excessive for middle-class Hong Kong–linked families whom we know.

Philadelphia's Chinatown, in turn, is one of many across North America. Some are better known: New York's Chinatowns appear frequently in books, movies, and television (Kwong 1989; Lin 1998; Tchen 1999; and others), while San Francisco has been chronicled through historical works (Shah 1991), the lens of Hollywood musicals (*Flower Drum Song*, 1961), and the more ethnographic fictions of Wayne Wang (*Chan is Missing*, 1982; *Dim Sum — A Little Bit of Heart*, 1985). Other new Chinatowns, such as those in Houston and Atlanta, have taken shape in outlying malls and suburbia. Older Chinatowns such as New York, Los Angeles, and Toronto also have outlying counterparts in Flushing and Brooklyn or Richmond/Scarborough as well (Chen 1992). Such contemporary relations of diaspora, place, and identity, however, demand further examination of the history and people of Hong Kong amid changing Chinese globalism. While we cannot equate modern connections to Hong Kong with ghettoized identities of nineteenth-century Chinatowns, the stories of migration and acceptance are part of the history of global Chineseness in which Hong Kongers participate.

HONG KONG AND NINETEENTH-CENTURY CHINESE MIGRATIONS

Emigration from China preceded the foundation of the British colony in Hong Kong; Chinese, as we have seen in Thailand, have been present in Southeast Asia for centuries as traders and even officials. Although the Ming and Qing dynasties regarded those who left China as traitors, punishment only threatened those who returned — and even that threat faded in the nineteenth century. Meanwhile, in China, war, land pressures, and chronic instability fostered images, however fragmentary, of a better life elsewhere. Consequently, young Chinese men abandoned their homelands in increasing numbers. For Southern China, the Taiping rebellion, climatic disasters, and Guangzhou's decline all favored emigration, while the 1849 discovery of gold in California and other opportunities pulled Chinese to the Golden Mountain (*Gum San* = the United States). Hong Kong itself did not generate emigrants, but as Madeline Hsu shows in her study of ties between Taishan and the United States, it played a critical role in nineteenth-century movement:

> South Chinese had only to go to this nearby port city in order to find shipping companies, labor recruiters, friends, and business-men who could tell them about opportunities abroad and give them credit to buy the tickets to get there. Hong Kong supplied other links in the chain between Chinese in China and Chinese overseas by providing a secure and reliable channel for the back-and-forth flow of people, remittances, information, capital, political ideals, Chinese groceries, and technology (2000: 31).

Hong Kong was the bridge between worlds, with Chinese, rather than Western colonizers, as the transnational agents of mobility. As Hsu notes, between 1860 and 1874, 112,362 Chinese left Hong Kong for the United States alone. Ships left twice monthly by the end of this period, while Canadian and Japanese companies competed for passengers (2000: 32). Moreover, by the 1850s, Hong Kong entrepreneurs established export companies to provide goods to immigrant communities. They were known as Gold Mountain firms (jinshanzhuang/ Gum San Jang). These "made it possible for overseas Chinese to buy a tremendous variety of Chinese goods, including Chinese books and magazines, herbal medicines, fruits such as lychees, pineapples, ginger, water chestnuts, water lily roots, yuengans, pears, manis preserved in sugar syrup, seafood in the form of flower fish, black fish, eels and oysters as well as Chinese ducks, fried rice birds and quail" (Hsu 2000: 34). These items are still available in Chinatown stores. While these supplies were essential to maintaining Chinese knowledge, foodways, and healthways, Hsu argues that it was equally important that these firms "made it possible for Chinese living in urban centers like San Francisco, Chicago, Havana, Sydney, and Singapore to send letters, money, and information to villages in the backwaters of rural Guangdong" (2000: 35). Mail and remittances passed through Hong Kong via returning immigrants or couriers. Hong Kong became a crossroads in the two-way circulation of goods, cash, people, and stories.

Not all movement was voluntary. The Treaty of Nanjing permitted cheap export labor known as the "coolie trade": while ostensibly contract labor, conditions of recruitment, transport, and labor were often horrendous, as were conditions in the fields of Cuba, Peru, and the British Caribbean where they replaced (emancipated) African-American laborers (Look Lai 1993; McKeown 1996, 2001). In Hong Kong, British authorities soon sought to eliminate this trade, but the Portuguese permitted it through Macau until 1873 when Eça de Queiros, the Portuguese author, who had observed the cruelty of the coolie system in Cuba, fought to end it in the Portuguese Empire. Jonathan Porter notes that for roughly forty years, "the average price per head was about $50, including shipping costs. Prices of coolies at the point of sale in Cuba or Peru ranged from $120 to as much as $1,000. Between 1845 and 1873, of a total of 322,593 Chinese contract laborers exported from Chinese ports, 143,472 were exported through Macau alone" (1996: 57).

U.S. efforts to control the coolie trade soon gave way to restrictions on Chinese migration altogether, limits that would spread around the world over the next fifty years. In the United States, anti-Chinese rhetoric and riots led to racialized local, state, and national laws that limited Chinese claims for citizenship, despite occasional court victories to the contrary. The 1875 Page Act, for example, constrained the entrance of Chinese women under the guise of controls on prostitution. The 1882 Exclusion Act, negotiated with the Chinese government, finally suspended all labor immigration for a decade and made it impossible for Chinese to become naturalized citizens. Certain class exceptions survived: diplomats, merchants, ministers, and students could get through the bureaucratic obstacles. Yet, increasing nativist hostility — adopted by new European immigrants themselves — drove many Chinese out of rural and small town Western settings. By 1913, Chinese lost the right to own land in California — a provision in place until 1952 (Tong 2003). Meanwhile, "Health officials and politicians justified the idea of Chinatown as inherently pestilent, and they insisted on this idea, through the accumulation of these stereotyped images in their reports and rhetoric, with the value of natural truth." (Shah 2003: 44).

Racial discrimination also spread with American empire: Chinese in the Philippines found their status challenged as that colony passed from Spain to the United States. Chinese who had fled California for Cuba also faced new discrimination under American rule.

As Chinese dispersed to other American cities, by the 1930s tighter immigration controls, especially on women, meant the decline of many Chinatowns evoked in the WPA depiction of Philadelphia. (See Arkush and Lee 1993 for telling Chinese visions of the United States in this and later periods.)

Chinese inside and outside the United States reacted to limitations on their movement in various ways, from protest to evasion. The "paper son" tactic allowed Chinese to claim entry rights for male relatives through creative definitions of kinship. Chinatowns became places of refuge and conviviality for an aging, predominantly male population, constrained or scrutinized by a white-dominated society. When Japan became an official U.S. enemy in World War II, American Chinese used this shared foe to argue for new rights. In 1943, the Exclusion Act was repealed, although naturalizations were limited to 105 per year apart from military service and family reunification.

Similar restrictions faced Chinese migrants around the world. Exclusion grew more slowly in Canada, where Southern Chinese had migrated freely and established themselves in British Columbia before 1884, when a federal head tax was established. Chinese laborers were seen as an opportunity or a threat, depending on the position and politics of Canadian observers who frequently vilified them despite their contributions to railroad construction. On July 1, 1923, future Chinese immigrants were excluded by law, an event recalled by Canadian Chinese as "Humiliation Day." Chinatowns became aging bachelor refuges whose male/female ratio reached 12 to 1, although leaders protested discrimination.

In Australia, economic competition and racial stereotyping led to increasing restrictions on Chinese in the nineteenth century; policies constructing a "White Australia" were not eased until the postwar period. At the time of Australia's federation in 1901, there were 35,000 Chinese immigrants there (see Chinese Heritage of Australian Federation Web site and Ommundsen 2004), but the Chinese community would not again grow significantly until the 1970s. In Southeast Asia, as we have seen, Thailand also limited Chinese immigrations and status from the 1920s on.

In Latin America, finally, coolies had been vital to postslavery agricultural development in Peru, but in the late-nineteenth century, Japanese contract laborers increasingly replaced them. Peru gained a bad reputation in China that scarcely justified the cost and problems of a steam voyage from Hong Kong to San Francisco to Callao. In the early-twentieth century, new Chinese immigrants tended to enter urban commerce although they faced anti-Chinese sentiment in cities. By the 1930s, restrictions on immigration gradually moved toward a total ban on Chinese (McKeown 1996, 2001).

While Hong Kong was a primary point of connection for all these migrations, they were not simply extensions of Hong Kong. Most of those moving through Hong Kong came from elsewhere and their family ties and remittances bound them to Taishan or Guangzhou more than to Hong Kong. Given Hong Kong's role as a node, controls on immigration had less impact there than in populous rural counties. Golden Mountain firms such as regional and surname associations continued to be central to the lives of Chinese immigrants worldwide: Between 1922 and 1930, the number of these firms in Hong Kong increased from 116 to 290 (Hsu 2000: 34). Tung Wah Hospital and other Hong Kong associations dealt with diasporic Chinese, while, as we have seen, emigrants repatriated capital to Hong Kong for political activities and in businesses such as Wing On and Sincere Department Stores (see chapter 2) and Chinese from overseas could look to new locations, as did California Chinese who relocated to Cuba. These connective roles would increase with changes in Hong Kong and the world of global Chinese after World War II.

NEW DIASPORIC POPULATIONS: THE 1960S AND BEYOND

The globalization of production and exchange that accompanied Hong Kong's changing economy in the 1950s and 1960s opened new connections to the larger world. By the late 1960s, escorted tours to the United States and Europe were available to Hong Kongers, while study and business provided opportunities for a growing Chinese middle class there to travel abroad. For decades, Hollywood also flooded Hong Kong screens with images of the United States, even if these were more accessible to middle-class audiences than refugees and workers (McDonogh and Wong 2001; Choi 2002: 127). However, immigration demands not only increased international contact and a desire for mobility, but also expanded opportunities. The reshaping of global laws over the past

50 years has been especially significant to Hong Kong in this regard.

Great Britain provided an initial postwar destination for the people of Hong Kong who had emigrated there only in small numbers during the first century of the colony. The British Nationality Act of 1948 affirmed the right of Commonwealth and colonial citizens to become British subjects. In the 1950s, when rice farming faced competition from Southeast Asian production and mainland refugees flooded the colonies, Hong Kong–born people from the New Territories moved to the UK, as James Watson has shown in his study of the Man family. Most immigrants were peasants with little education; when they moved to England — primarily London — most worked in Chinese restaurant-related businesses (Watson 1975; Baker 1994; Parker 1995, 1998). The British government altered this primarily male labor immigration through the Commonwealth Immigration Act of 1962, which limited certain categories of migration but established rights of family reunification that fostered urban ethnic enclaves in the next decade, when a few thousand Hong Kong Chinese arrived each year. Uneasy reactions led to a new Immigration Act in 1971 and further legislation under the Thatcher government in 1981 that drew clear lines between citizenship in Britain and the Empire. The 1981 law created British Dependent Territory passports that were used in Hong Kong. In fact, many Hong Kong Chinese knew after 1962 that one strategy to gain dual citizenship was to claim a loss of one's passport in Great Britain and to seek a replacement there, resulting in a British passport. In later years, however, British Dependent Territory passports became more distinct, despite a confusing similarity of shape and cover that sometimes allowed Hong Kongers to enter Europe without visas.

After the Tiananmen Square protests in 1989, Britain bowed to international pressure and offered the right of abode in Britain for up to fifty thousand families. However, its point system favored bilingual, college-educated professionals and elites. This selection did not facilitate mass migration because an approved candidate might choose to stay and work in Hong Kong. Moreover, the British Nationality (Hong Kong) Act gradually eliminated Dependent Territory passports for those left behind. By the 1990s, roughly 150,000 Hong Kong people lived in Britain. Even more had the *right* to do so, but remained in Hong Kong or lived elsewhere.

Global waves of emigration from Hong Kong spread the impact of development and politics in the 1980s beyond this colonial bond. According to Wong Siu-Lun (1999), 22,400 people left Hong Kong in 1980, 30,000 in 1987. Their primary destinations were Canada, the United States, and Australia (Skeldon 1994: 125). In all three, the postwar thaw in restrictions on Chinese (and increasing American involvement in the region) had been followed by legal reforms such as the U.S. Immigration Act of 1965 that eliminated European-oriented quotas and facilitated a new influx of Asians and Latin Americans. More than 850,000 Chinese arrived in the United States between 1965 and 1990 (Tong 2003: 140). They included emigrants from Taishan, Vietnamese Chinese escaping the aftermath of the Vietnam War, and educated Hong Kongers, Taiwanese, and Mainlanders. Chain migration has been one important force in immigration as well, as one immigrant brings over family members as he/she gains residency or citizenship. In the United States, even green card lotteries sometimes have given preference to Hong Kong people.

Yet changes in reception are insufficient to explain Hong Kong emigration to these new worlds after the 1970s. For many Hong Kong residents, the major issues of migration were less opportunity than uncertainty, especially surrounding the negotiations of the 1997 Handover. After the Tiananmen protests in China in 1989, more people lost confidence. In 1992, 66,000 people left and only by 1995 did the number of migrants level out to around 40,300 (Wong 1999: 136).

In the 1990s, in fact, middle class Hong Kong residents had a deep knowledge of arcane immigration laws and loopholes beyond the longstanding traditions of chain migration (which were more likely to favor those who had passed through Hong Kong than Hong Kongers themselves). Visas for professionals favored doctors, scientists, and other educated professionals who wished to migrate. Given the colony's prosperity, investment visas also loomed large. These permitted emigrants to begin the trajectory to citizenship if they invested a certain amount in their new homeland, creating a fixed number of jobs. For the United States, the threshold was high — approximately US$1 million — but not impossible. Canada and Australia were less expensive, while nations in Central America, the Caribbean, and the South Pacific offered even cheaper havens.

Residencies and citizenship in other countries for many Hong Kong people have also been insurance measures rather than exile; the ability to travel between Hong Kong and a newly adopted homeland was an important consideration in moving. In some cases, the family would apply for immigration and moved there while the breadwinners, mostly fathers, returned to Hong Kong to work. These "astronauts" (*tai hong yan*) have built lives in both places, a strategy more prominent in the middle and upper middle class who have enjoyed Hong Kong prosperity, and more common in Australia and Canada than the United States because of less-stringent immigration and residency rules (Tam 2003).

The continuity of conditions in Hong Kong after 1997 and the relatively stable political climate of Mainland China have diminished this flow. In 2003, only 9,600 people left Hong Kong, the lowest number in twenty-three years (Lee 2004). Since 1997, the major global demographic concern in Hong Kong has been the issue of Mainland Chinese immigration, not emigration. The colonial administration had set Hong Kong people apart from their Chinese counterparts in Mainland China not simply by political boundaries, but also by wealth and a sense of superiority based on Hong Kong's connections to the rest of the world. Despite the contributions of postwar refugees to a new Hong Kong, neither the Chinese nor the Hong Kong Special Administrative Region government wanted an open border — so as to protect the prosperity and political differences of Hong Kong. However, as Hong Kong weathered the Asian Economic Crisis and the SARS scare and the Chinese economy has grown, Hong Kong's general attitude toward the Mainland Chinese has eased. The ailing tourist industry has worked to lure Chinese tourists and travel restrictions have been relaxed (although visas were limited before the July 1, 2004, demonstrations). This does not mean that either government is loosening immigration laws; however, Mainland Chinese represent an important human presence in shaping the Hong Kong economy and changing regional identities (Callahan 2004).

Today, Hong Kong Chinese have adapted and reproduced their families in new settings with new meanings. Around the world, they belong to populations identified as Chinese that have been characterized by, on the one hand, images of youth gangs and, on the other, the image of model minorities who turn Confucian values into educational and economic success. In Monterey Park, for example (outside Los Angeles), Hong Kong and Taiwan immigrants live in one of the first suburban cities in the United States where Asians constitute the majority population (Fong 1994; Zhou and Kim 2003). Justin Lin's 2002 *Better Luck Tomorrow* portrayed the tensions of model minority adolescents in Southern California suburbia. Suburbs of Toronto and Vancouver boast miles of Chinese malls and restaurants, where some developments have been funded by Li Ka-Shing himself (Delmont and Fennell 1989; Smart and Smart 1996). Chinese global citizens have gained elective and appointed roles in governments and achieved recognition in arts and culture.

Hong Kong diasporic identity also has become intertwined with social and cultural processes of difference, becoming part of larger social categories like "Asian Americans" or "peoples of color." As Benson Tong writes in his magisterial history of Chinese Americans, "Like African Americans and Native Americans, Chinese and other Asians were excluded from citizenship, since their nonwhiteness suggested the absence of the capacity for self-governance. Ascriptive exclusion and stratification have been central to the American past. Yet Chinese Americans have contested the boundaries of rights and obligations and continue to do so today" (2003: x). The people of global Hong Kong form part of this process and take on significant roles in shaping and communicating an image of themselves through their media (Christensen 1998; Ong 1999).

DIASPORA AND IMAGINATION

Diaspora involves not only the movement of peoples, but also the dissemination and interpretation of information by

Chinese and their descendants around the world. We have mentioned some of these works in film, both documentary (*Look Forward and Carry on from the Past; Face to Face*) and fiction (*Chan is Missing; Better Luck Tomorrow*). David Arkush and Leo Lee have assembled variegated interpretations of the United States by Chinese visitors and sojourners in their *Land without Ghosts* (1993) that complement an ever-growing production of Asian American literature (see Chan et al. 1991) and literary, social, and cultural studies. Rather than opening a new chapter (or new book), we close by refocusing on Hong Kong's longstanding central role as cultural producer and distributor in the press, movies, and television. These media create channels for global communication and, at the same time, explore different imaginations of what globalism means. As we conclude our examination of global Hong Kong, these cultural products offer both connections and commentaries on the processes we have discussed.

We have already introduced the availability and impact of Hong Kong newspapers in Chinatowns. This status clearly emerges from Hong Kong's hybrid history: as a British territory, Hong Kong was an attractive place for Chinese dissidents to express their views through the press. *Chung Kuo Jih Pao*, for example, which was published at the beginning of the twentieth century, called for the overthrow of the Qing and the formation of the republic (Tsai 1994; Lau 1997: 151–185). Despite colonial laws that limited freedom of the press and censored other media, Hong Kong newspapers were relatively free to express views critical of both the Left and the Right. Demonstrations have defended these rights in the HKSAR. Thus, Hong Kong–based newspapers (in hard copy and online) provide Chinatown residents of different backgrounds with news from a Hong Kong perspective. Magazines from major publishing groups like Ming Pao weeklies and monthlies provide gossip and political analysis.

More recently, Hong Kong television also has established global connections. Hong Kong was the first British colony to have television (via cable) in 1957; broadcast television arrived in 1967 (Wong and McDonogh 2001: 96–97). Television Broadcast Limited (TVB) offers two channels: Jade (Cantonese) and Pearl (English and some Mandarin since 1997); Asian TV (ATV) offers Cantonese and English/Mandarin Channels. Their programming has combined local soaps, melodramas, comedy, and news with programming imported from China, Britain, and the United States. Finally, Radio TV Hong Kong (RTHK) played an important role as a government production house for programs that commercial stations had to carry. Although part of the colonial administration, RTHK was modeled after the BBC, which had an independent editorial staff. During the 1970s, its newly established Public Affairs Television Unit became a training group for talented major filmmakers like Ann Hui, Tsui Hark, Ringo Lam, Patrick Tam, Clara Law, and other protagonists of the Hong Kong New Wave. Many of their programs dealt with sensitive local social issues, including housing and corruption (Ma 1999).

While television brought the world to Hong Kong, satellites today make Chinese television available worldwide *through* Hong Kong. TVB is "the world's largest producer and distributor of Chinese-language programmes" (see TVB Web site). Its network spans Thailand, Malaysia, Singapore, Indonesia, Europe, North America, Taiwan, and China. In the United States, Jadeworld TV (a subsidiary linked with Direct TV) offers a five-channel package that includes two Jade Channels in Cantonese, one Jade Super Channel in Mandarin (broadcast from Taiwan) a bilingual Cantonese/Mandarin movie channel, and CCTV, China Central TV from the People's Republic of China (PRC), recognizing the need to reach different kinds of Chinese through Hong Kong distribution. At least 24 satellite Chinese channels are available in the United States, including ATV, Zhujaing TV, Fujian TV, Guangdong TV, and Lotus (Macau) TV; except for CCTV, all broadcast from Southern China. Emigrants watch live Hong Kong, Taiwan, and Mainland Chinese news, offering an immediacy unheard of even ten years before. During the 2003 SARS crisis, for example, many Chinese Americans followed the global news so intently that some shopkeepers and restaurateurs believed that the drop in business in Chinatown was due more to a decrease in Chinese clients, whose fear resulted from their familiarity with Hong Kong/China news.

TVBI screens more than 6,000 hours of programming annually with a video library of 45,000 hours, all produced in Hong Kong. Since the 1970s, video, video compact disc (VCD), and DVD sales and rentals have brought Hong Kong media closer to the overseas Chinese. Hong Kong exports more of these to overseas Chinese communities than other Chinese producers, although VCDs have proven to be amenable to widespread piracy, eviscerating the video market in Hong Kong (Wong 1999).

Hong Kong cinema has had a long history of overseas distribution, especially through global Chinese enclaves that maintained their own theaters (Wong 1999). Wider distribution accelerated with Bruce Lee Siu-Lung (1940–1973), who became both the biggest star in Hong Kong and a worldwide phenomenon. Lee, himself transnational, was born in San Francisco while his father was on tour there. Lee himself later married an American. Even though Lee's martial arts prowess steadily grew, his works were often denigrated as B-movies in the West. Nonetheless, *Fists of Fury* (1972) raises questions about Chinese identity in addition to showcasing its martial arts artistry. While Lee would only be the sidekick on American television's *Green Hornet*, his films gained loyal followings in African American communities and in third world countries, where audiences identified with his heroic stand against his enemies — Japanese or whites — using his own body as the ultimate weapon, espousing an ethics of self-sufficient power (Joseph 1999).

After Lee's untimely death, Hong Kong's stylized action films continued to grow in international reputation and audience. Films like John Woo Yu Sen's *A Better Tomorrow* (1987) and *The Killer* (1989) or Ringo Lam Ling Tung's *City on Fire* (1987) and *Prison on Fire* (1987) were not only Hong Kong and Asian hits, but also built followings with U.S. college students, cutting-edge directors like Quentin Tarantino, French cinema clubs, and the international film festival circuit. This success changed Hollywood action films and translated into Hollywood opportunities for both directors. Yet Woo's star in these films, Chow Yun-Fat, while popular across Asia as a cool and sexy hero, has not found the same niche in Hollywood (see Teo 1997; Bordwell 2002; or others). Hong Kong actresses have found international success difficult to achieve as well, although the Malaysian Chinese Michelle Yeoh Chu Kheng has had some success in action films and the "trans-Chinese" *Crouching Tiger, Hidden Dragon* (2000). Maggie Cheung Man-Yuk, however, has starred in Hong Kong art and popular cinema, European cinema, and Wayne Wang's Hollywood film about the Handover, *Chinese Box* (1998). She became the first

Hong Kong woman to win the best actress prize at the Cannes Film Festival in 2004 (for a work made in France).

Jackie Chan seems to be an exception to these limits. Chan, blending martial arts and comedy, was already a star across Asia before he broke into the American mainstream with *Rumble in the Bronx* (1996), after some lesser action B-movies in the early 1980s. He has subsequently starred in Hollywood "buddy" productions, such as *Rush Hour* (1998) and *Shanghai Noon* (2000), in which he was paired with an American non-Chinese partner. Yet Chan remains anchored in Hong Kong as well: His new film releases appear each year in Hong Kong, where they are New Year's events and he acts as a spokesman for Hong Kong film and tourism abroad (Fore 1997; Wong 1999).

In addition to the global readings such films and actors elicit, Hong Kong film stories allow us to explore images of diaspora through concrete texts. In *Song of Exile* (1990), for example, a semi-autobiographical work by Ann Hui, a Chinese-Japanese woman (played by Maggie Cheung) explores her cultural affiliations and identity. Having left Hong Kong to work for the BBC, she returns from England to attend her sister's wedding. She then embarks on a journey to understand her Japanese mother and to negotiate her own relationship to China, exemplified by her grandparents who raised her in Macau and moved back to Guangzhou in the 1960s. In the end, both mother and daughter decide to stay in Hong Kong, affirming it as their homeland (Erens 2000). The film shows Hong Kongers with multiple connections to other places, where complex people make choices about their own destinies.

Other cinematic immigrants become totally lost due to conflicting goals and trajectories. In Clara Law's *Farewell My China* (1990), Maggie Cheung makes desperate attempts to gain a U.S. visa to leave China, but is rejected because of her attractiveness and potential to overstay her visa. Overcoming these obstacles and even having a child so that the consul would not think that she wants to stay in the United States, she arrives there only to experience America as a dystopia where crime, drugs, and prostitution run amok; the mise-en-scène captures an American that is dark and violent. She becomes schizophrenic, speaking Chinese to her immigrant husband one night and treating him as a stranger, speaking only English, the next morning. Finally, she kills him in Manhattan's Chinatown, in front of a replica of Tiananmen's Goddess of Liberty (see Evans Chan's 1996 *Crossings*).

In *Autumn Moon* (1992), Law follows a Hong Kong teenager about to go to Canada to join her parents, leaving her grandmother behind. The dialogue is in Cantonese, English, and Japanese, as the girl has a short platonic relationship with a Japanese tourist. The movie raises questions about movement, values, food, and family amid its ambience of silence and loss. Finally, in *Floating Life* (1995), Law, who emigrated to Australia with her husband, portrays a dysfunctional Hong Kong family in Australia and an extended family in Germany, exploring how immigration threatens the Chinese family. For Law, then, diaspora evokes mental dislocation and loss.

Perhaps the most complex of these films of diasporic imagination is Peter Chan Ho-San's *Comrades, Almost a Love Story* (1997; see chapter 5), which depicts multiple routes of migration from the Mainland through Hong Kong to New York's Chinatowns, interwoven with refractions of *The World of Suzie Wong*. Chan transforms the myth into something other than American, claiming it as part of Hong Kong history and identity as his characters carve out new lives in

New York City yet maintain shared memories and connections through Chinatown and transnational Chinese.

Other Hong Kong filmmakers have even recast the history of Chinese *in* America. In *Once Upon a Time in China and America* (1997) directed by Sammo Hung and produced and guided by Tsui Hark, the classic Hong Kong hero Wong Fei Hong finds himself in the American West. Wong, both a doctor of Chinese medicine and a kung fu master of the late-nineteenth century, was as localized a Cantonese hero as Roy Rogers or Superman for the United States and the hero of hundreds of Hong Kong films from the 1950s on. In various modern depictions, especially a series directed by Tsui Hark, he moves between worlds with authority, crossing the borders of imperial China and colonial Hong Kong, commenting on both.

By moving Wong Fei Hong to the American West, this film recaptures Chinese in the United States and reclaims a history as well as a place for Chinese in the "golden mountain." While Wong is a visitor, this cinematic West has a well-established — albeit segregated — bachelor Chinatown. After a series of struggles among Indians, bad guys, and Western and Chinese inhabitants of the town, it ends with the arrival of a Chinese woman, which foreshadows the eventual stabilization and reproduction of Chinese American lives.

Like Peter Chan's *Comrades*, this film raises questions about how Chinese have fit into the world of the Golden Mountain. Relationships between the Chinese and the non-Chinese, for example, are both stereotypical and surprising. Native Indians initially attack Wong, although he eventually is accepted into their lives (a scenario strongly echoed in Jackie Chan's Hollywood film *Shanghai Noon*). In *Once Upon a Time*, whites are generally racists, thieves, and fools who dominate a society in which Chinese characters are abused. Yet, stereotypical white prostitutes prove sympathetic allies for the Chinese and a white man who has learned from Wong eventually becomes the good mayor and racial harmonizer in the town. Illegal immigration is simply a way of life, a necessary act outside the law.

Tony Williams (2000) reads *Once Upon a Time* as the culmination of a sequence that "charts Huang's (Wong's) development from patriotic, monolingual Chinese hero to a figure who realizes the need for reintegration in the wider world of the twentieth century" (2000: 19) and a series that "attempts to construct a new version of an ethnic Chinese identity by moving beyond constricting definitions of nationhood and geographic territory to confront a wider Western world that encroaches on his homeland" (2000: 21). These readings posit an inevitable movement of China toward modernity, in which Hong Kong is a pivotal site, but American modernity an almost inevitable goal. Our reading takes America and diaspora as questions rather than the answer. Yet, as in *Comrades*, images of the continuity of Chinese place and lives in the United States embody an imagination of and for global Hong Kong, shared by Hong Kong citizens and others around the world.

All these Hong Kong films explore and project the choices that Hong Kong people may make in their individual lives. Rather than fearing movement or difference, as Clara Law suggests, or losing ties to Hong Kong, Peter Chan and Tsui Hark embrace movement and ambiguity while raising questions about global Hong Kong. This cinematic imagination of diaspora, like the readings of this imagination among global

Hong Kong descendants and a variety of other audiences worldwide, again reminds us of the human complexities of globalization that must be read alongside political and economic processes. While the place is small, and the people comparatively few, the intersections and connections that have created and renewed Hong Kong allow us to join these readings and to think critically about globalization as processes as well as human experiences.

Conclusion

The city of Hong Kong is, to a large extent, the product of human vision, endeavour and enterprise. It is a city that has a vibrancy that excites and stimulates the senses of local residents and visitors alike throughout each day and much of the night. It offers something of value for all in terms of places to visit, natural attractions to enjoy, things to do and customs to experience. It is forever changing in response to new ideas and technology. In a nutshell, Hong Kong has become a City of Vision and can be expected to use new challenges and opportunities in many diverse ways.

— *E.G. Pryor, "Foreword" to* Hong Kong: My City of Visions
[painting competition for primary and secondary students, 1996]
(Hong Kong: Hinge Marketing, 1996: 7)

In the introduction of this book, we presented Hong Kong as a microcosm through which to rethink global connections and identities from the perspectives of the political economics of space, historical processes, cultural production, people, and images. In the chapters that followed, we have explored not only these perspectives but also, in a sense, the experiences of the world mediated through Hong Kong and its people. Through these discussions, we have sought to present a vision of global Hong Kong that is multifaceted, complicated, and challenging both for our reading of this place and people and for other readings of global cities and their mobile, connected citizens.

We began with the immediacy of contemporary Hong Kong — the marches going on as we completed the manuscript, diseases we recall with a shudder — and the places that embody history and memory for us in Hong Kong, including the Kowloon Walled City. Yet, understanding this presence on a world stage also demands grounding in history: Globalization is not merely the creation of contemporary business or tele-communications. While the clash of empires may be the most compelling motif of Hong Kong's globalization, from the earliest contacts of Europeans and Chinese, globalization has also entailed human action, choice, belief, and interpretation. The people in — and eventually, of — Hong Kong have reconstituted the continuity of place through crises and dramatic transitions in the past half-century, from global, regional, and national events like World War II, the 1949 Chinese Communist Revolution, the Asian financial crisis, and SARS. More "domestic" events like Hong Kong's economic take off, 1960s disturbances, and the 1997 Handover that many world observers read as the "end" of Hong Kong entail local refractions of wider changes. We have shown the inextricable inter-connectedness of these events, using Hong Kong as a vantage point to explore and understand global relationships.

We also moved beyond Hong Kong to understand concurrent processes of globalization. The last three chapters thus balanced our exploration of the changing worlds of Hong Kong over time with a rethinking of space. Colonial Hong Kong, as many Chinese sources point out, was carved out of South China and, since the late 1970s, has played a central role in reconstructing that region. The tensions apparent in this "family reunion," become magnified as we link Hong Kong to a more competitive context, including Shanghai, its rival within a changing China, and other production centers of East Asia (which also invoke a Greater China). While we were able to talk about only three competing centers, we would hope readers would also think about relations to Japan, Korea, the Philippines, Malaysia, and Vietnam, which have appeared only in passing, to understand the complexity of networks and identities subsumed under the label "Pacific Rim."

Finally, we returned to the human stories of Hong Kong, present in various forms of diaspora and imagination. Chinatowns, commerce, news, and film all connect Hong Kong to people around the world who share family, culture, memory, and interest with the city and its future — an ongoing global connection, re-created daily and accessible to readers who may never visit the HKSAR. Once again, family, culture, and communication appear as foundations of globalization as much as features of the world city that are shaped by globalization. In this chapter, as throughout the text, we also have used place and film for insights into relations and beliefs, underscoring continuing values and practices that have reshaped global Hong Kong.

Globalization, in recent years, has become a conflictive reality for all citizens of the world. Economic opportunities for some represent patterns of exploitation for others, while human movements may mean escape, interest, consumption, or hope. Rather than promoting world unity or protesting insidious domination, we have read the stories of Hong Kong and its people as examples, offering answers and posing questions that go far beyond the crowded towers and bustling streets we have explored here. In this regard, we hope that this text and the resources of the bibliography and filmography that follow allow us all to learn *from* Hong Kong as well as learn about it.

Bibliography

This bibliography focuses on accessible English-language sources. Bilingual sources are indicated by an asterisk (*); sources in Chinese are provided with a Mandarin transliteration and English translation (as provided with other non-English sources). A select filmography and list of useful Web sites are cited in the text follow.

Abbas, A. (1997). *Hong Kong: Culture and the Politics of Disappearance.* University of Minnesota Press.

———. (1997). "Wong Kar-Wai + Speed," *SD Space Design* No. 394 (July): 36–39.

Abraham, T. (2004). *Twenty-First Century Plague: The Story of SARS.* Hong Kong: Hong Kong University Press.

Aijmer, C. (1980). *Economic Man in Sha Tin.* London: Curzon.

Akilli, S. (2003). "Chinese Immigration to Britain in the Post–WWII Period." <www.postcolonialweb.org/uk/mo/sakilli10.html> (accessed January 30, 2005).

American Chamber of Commerce in Hong Kong (1994). *Living in Hong Kong.* Hong Kong.

Appadurai, A. (1996). *Modernity at Large: Cultural Dimensions of Globalization.* Minneapolis: University of Minnesota Press.

Arkush, R. D., and Lee, L. O., eds. (1993). *Land without Ghosts: Chinese Impressions of America from the Mid-Nineteenth Century to the Present.* Berkeley: University of California Press.

Arnold, W. (2002). "Singapore Is Trying to Halt Slippage" *New York Times,* April 30: Wl 7.

Ash, R., Ferdinand, P., Hook, B., and Porter, R. (2000). *Hong Kong in Transition: The Handover Years.* New York: St. Martin's Press.

Askew, M. (2002). *Bangkok: Place, Practice, and Representation.* London: Routledge.

Atwell, P. (1985). *British Mandarins and Chinese Reformers: The British Administration of Weihaiwei (1898–1930) and the Territory's Return to Chinese Rule.* Hong Kong: Oxford University Press.

Baker, Hugh D. R. (1994). "Branches All Over: The Hong Kong Chinese in the United Kingdom." In R. Skeldon, ed. *Reluctant Exiles?: Migration from Hong Kong and the New Overseas Chinese.* Armonk, NY: M.E. Sharpe, 291–307.

Barboza, David (2005). "China, New Land of Shoppers Builds Malls on a Giant Scale," *New York Times* May 25: A1, C7.

Basler, Barbara. (1992). "The Walled City, Home to Huddled Masses, Falls." *New York Times,* June 16.

Benton, Gregor. (1983). *The Hongkong Crisis.* London: Pluto Press.

Berger, Joseph. (2003). "War, Waged a Character at a Time: Chinese-Language Dailies Battle Fiercely in New York." *New York Times,* November 10.

Bergère, Marie-Claire. (1998). *Sun Yat-Sen.* Stanford: Stanford University Press. Originally published as La Chine au Xxe. siècle. Paris: Librairie Fayard 1994.

"Betty." (1905). *Intercepted Letters: A Mild Satire on Hongkong Society.* Hong Kong: Kelly & Walsh.

Bickers, Robert M. (1997). "The Colony's Shifting Position in the British Informal Empire in China." In J. M. Brown and R. Foot, eds. *Hong Kong's Transitions, 1842–1997.* Oxford: St. Anthony's College, 33–61.

———. *Britain in China: Community Culture and Colonialism 1900–1949.* Manchester: Manchester University Press, 1999.

Bishop, Ryan, John Phillips, and Wei-Wei Yeo, eds. (2003). *Postcolonial Urbanism: Southeast Asian Cities and Global Processes.* New York: Routledge.

———. (2004). *Beyond Description: Singapore Space Historicity.* London: Routledge.

Blue, Gregory. (2000). "Opium for China: The British Connection." In T. Brooks and B. Wakabayashi, eds. *Opium Regimes.* Berkeley: University of California Press, 31–54.

Bordwell, David. (2000). *Planet Hong Kong.* Cambridge: Harvard University Press.

Bosco, Joseph. (2001). "The McDonald's Snoopy Craze in Hong Kong." In G. Mathews and T-L Lui, eds. *Consuming Hong Kong*. Hong Kong: Hong Kong University Press, 263–86.

Booth, Martin. (1996). *Opium: A History*. New York: St. Martin's Press.

———. (2004). *Gweilo: Memories of a Hong Kong Childhood*. London: Doubleday.

Boxer, C. R. (1968). *Fidalgos in the Far East, 1550–1770*. Hong Kong: Oxford University Press.

Bradsher, Keith. (2004a). "China Provinces form Regional Economic Bloc" *New York Times*, June 3: W1, 7.

———. (2004b). "City of Immigrants Begins to Find an Identity of its Own" *New York Times*, June 29: A4.

———. (2005a). "Arts Project Provokes Hong Kong Uproar" *New York Times*, January 4: E1.

———. (2005b). "Hong Kong's Leader Apologizes but Promises to Remain in Office" *New York Times*, January 13: A11.

Bristow, Roger. (1984). *Land Use Planning in Hong Kong: History, Policies and Procedures*. Hong Kong: Oxford University Press.

———. (1989). *Hong Kong's New Towns: A Selective Review*. Hong Kong: Oxford University Press.

———. (1996). "Hong Kong: A Political Economy of Waterfront Development." In P. Malone, ed. *City, Capital and Water*. London: Routledge, 110–33.

Brook, Timothy, and Bob Tadashi Wakabayashi, eds. (2000). *Opium Regimes*. Berkeley: University of California Press.

———. (2000). "Introduction: Opium's History in China." In T. Brook and B. Tadashi Wakabayashi, eds. *Opium Regimes*. Berkeley: University of California Press, 1–30.

Brown, E. Phelps. (1971). "The Hong Kong Economy: Achievements and Prospects." In K. Hopkins, ed. *Hong Kong: The Industrial Colony*. Hong Kong: Oxford University Press, 1–20.

Brown, Judith M., and Rosemary Foot, eds. (1997). *Hong Kong's Transitions, 1842–1997*. Oxford in Association with St. Anthony's College.

Boyden, S., S. Millar, K. Newcastle, and B. O'Neill. (1980). *The Ecology of a City and Its People*. Canberra: Australian National University.

Bun Fun Dik O-Mun [Colours of Macau]. (1999). Macau.

Callahan, William A. (2004). *Contingent Styles: Greater China and Transnational Relations*. Minneapolis: University of Minnesota Press.

Callick, Rowan. (1998). *Comrades and Capitalists: Hong Kong since the Handover*. Sydney: University of New South Wales.

Carroll, John M. (2005). *Edge of Empires: Chinese Elites and British Colonials in Hong Kong*. Cambridge: Harvard University Press.

Castells, Manuel. (1996). *The Rise of Network Society*. Cambridge: Blackwell.

———. (1997). *The Power of Identity*. Malden, MA: Blackwell.

———. (1998). *The End of the Millennium*. Malden, MA: Blackwell.

Cayrol, Pierre. (1998). *Hong Kong in the Mouth of the Dragon*. Rutland, VT: Charles E. Tuttle.

Chako, Sussy. (1994). *Chinese Walls*. Hong Kong: Asia 2000.

Chan, Anson Fang On-Sang (2000). "Hong Kong Gears up for a World without Walls." *Hong Kong Report 1999*. Hong Kong: Government Printing Office, 1–7.

Chan, Anthony. (1996). *Li Ka-Shing: Hong Kong's Elusive Billionaire*. Hong Kong: Oxford University Press.

Chan, Cecilia and Peter Hills, eds. (1993). *Limited Gains: Grassroots Mobilization and the Environment in Hong Kong*. Hong Kong: Centre of Urban Planning and Environmental Management, Hong Kong University.

———. (1993). "The Context" in *Limited Gains*. C. Chan and P. Hills, eds. Hong Kong: Centre of Urban Planning and Environmental Management, Hong Kong University: 1–14.

Chan, Cheung Ming, Alfred, Au Chor Fai, and Choy Bing Kong. (1991). *A Longitudinal Study on the Kowloon Walled City Clearance: The Pattern of Service Utilization, Community Identity, and Life Satisfaction of the Residents*. Report from the Center for Hong Kong Studies, Chinese University of Hong Kong.

Chan, David Ka-Ho Mok, and Tung Anguo. (2004). In L. Wong, L. White, and S. Gui, eds. "Education" in *Social Policy Reform in Hong Kong and Shanghai: A Tale of Two Cities*. Armonk, NY: M.E. Sharpe, 85–126.

Chan, J. P., F. Chin, L. Inada, and S. Wong, eds. *The Big AIIIEEEEE!: An Anthology of Chinese American and Japanese American Literature*. New York: Penguin, 1991.

Chan, Kai Cheung. "History." *The Other Hong Kong Report 1993*. In Choi Po-King and Ho Lok-Sang, eds.. Hong Kong: Chinese University Press, 1993, 455–84.

Chan, Lau Kit-Ching. *China, Britain, and Hong Kong 1895–1945*. Hong Kong: Chinese University Press, 1990.

Chan, Ming, and Alvin Yo, eds. (2002). *Crisis and Transformation in Hong Kong's China*. Armonk, NY: M.E. Sharpe.

Chan, Wai Kwan. (1991). *The Making of Hong Kong Society: Three Studies of Class Formation in Early Hong Kong*. Oxford: Clarendon.

———. (1997). "Trade and Service Industries." In J. Y. S. Cheng, ed. *The Other Hong Kong Report 1997*. Hong Kong: Chinese University Press, 305–26.

Chen, E.K.Y., Jack F. Williams, and Joseph Wong, eds. (1991). *Taiwan: Economy, Society, and History*. University of Hong Kong: Center for Asian Studies.

Chen, Hsiang-Shui. (1992). *Chinatown No More: Taiwan Immigrants in Contemporary New York*. Ithaca: Cornell University Press.

Cheng, Helen Hau-Ling. (2001). "Consuming a Dream: Homes in Advertisements and Imagination in Contemporary Hong Kong." In G. Mathews and T. L. Lui, eds. *Consuming Hong Kong*. Hong Kong: Hong Kong University Press, 205–36.

Cheng, Irene. (1976). *Clara Ho Tung: A Hong Kong Lady, Her Family and Her Times*. Hong Kong: Chinese University Press.

Cheng, Joseph Y. S., ed. (1999). *Political Participation in Hong Kong*. Hong Kong: City University of Hong Kong Press.

Cheng Miu Bing, Christina. (1997). "Resurgent Chinese Power in Postmodern Disguise: The New Bank of China Buildings in Hong Kong and Macao." In G. Evans and M. Tam. S. M., eds. *Hong Kong: The Anthropology of a Chinese Metropolis*. Hong Kong: Curzon Press, 102–23.

Cheng Po Hung. (2003). **Early Hong Kong Brothels*. University of Hong Kong Museum and Art Gallery.

Cheng, Sea-Ling. (2001). "Consuming Places in Hong Kong: Experiencing Lan Kwai Fong" In G. Mathews and T. L. Lui, eds. *Consuming Hong Kong*. Hong Kong: Hong Kong University Press, 263–86.

Cheng, S. K. and Chow, Y. Y. (1997). "Opening Alternative Working Spaces: Analysis of a Group of Street Hawkers." In Law Wing Sang, ed.. *Whose City. Hong Kong: Oxford University Press, 141–60.

Cheung, Anthony, and Gu Xingyuan. (2004). "Health Finance." In L. Wong, L. White, and Gui S., eds. Social Policy Reform in Hong Kong and Shanghai: A Tale of Two Cities. Armonk, NY: M.E. Sharpe, 23–52.

Cheung, Gary. (2003a). "Hong Kong-Shenzhen Trade Zone Endorsed." South China Morning Post, October 27: 2.

———. (2003b). "Hong Kong Firms Eye Guangzhou Investment." South China Morning Post, November 15: 2.

———. (2004). and Chow Chung-Yan. "Let HK Play Key Role in Delta Region, Tung Urges." South China Morning Post, June 1.

Cheung, Peter T. Y. (1994 [1998]). "Changing Relations between the Central Government and Guangdong." In Y. M. Yeung and David K. Y. Chu, eds. Guangdong. Hong Kong: Chinese University Press.

———. (1999). "Guangzhou and Tianjin: The Struggle for Development in Two Chinese Cities." In J. H. Chung, ed. Cities in China: Recipes for Economic Development in the Reform Era. London: Routledge, 18–53.

Ching, Frank. (1999). The Li Dynasty: Hong Kong Aristocrats. New York: Oxford University Press.

Ching, Maybo. (1996). "Literary, Ethnic, or Territorial: Definitions of Guangdong Culture in Late Qing and the Early Republic." In T. T. Liu and D. Faure, eds. Unity and Diversity: Local Cultures and Identities in China. Hong Kong: Hong Kong University Press, 51–66.

Chiu, Stephen W. K., K. C. Lo, and Tai-luk Loi. (1997). City States in a Global Economy: Industrial Restructuring in Hong Kong and Singapore. Boulder, CO: Westview.

Choa, G. (2002). The Life and Times of Sir Kai Ho Kai. Hong Kong: Chinese University Press.

Choi, Po-King, ed. (2002). Wanwan Liu Dain Ban [6:30 Every Night: 70s Women Workers Who Went to Evening School]. Hong Kong: Step Forward Multimedia Ltd.

Choi, Pauline. (1993). "Environmental Protection in Hong Kong: An Historical Account." In C. Chan and P. Hills. Limited Gains. Centre of Urban Planning and Environmental Management, Hong Kong University: 29–40.

Chow, Larry Chuen-Ho, and Yiu-Kwan Fan, eds. (1999). *The Other Hong Kong Report 1999*. Hong Kong: Chinese University Press.

Chow, Rey. (1993). *Writing Diaspora: The Tactics of Internvention in Contemporary Cultural Studies*. Bloomington: Indiana University Press.

——— "King Kong in Hong Kong: Watching the 'Handover' from the U.S.A." *Social Text 55*, 16, 2 (Summer): 93–108.

Chu, Cindy Yik-Yi. (2004). *The Maryknoll Sisters in Hong Kong, 1921– 1969: In Love with the Chinese*. New York: Palgrave MacMillan.

Chu, David K. Y. (1996). "The Hong Kong-Zhujiang Delta and the World City System." In F. C. Lo and Y. M. Yeung, eds. *Emerging World Cities in Pacific Asia*. Tokyo: United Nations University Press, 465–97.

Chu, David Y. K. (1998). "Synthesis of Economic Reforms and Open Policy." In Y. M. Yeung and D. K. Y. Chu, eds. *Guangdong*. 2d ed. Hong Kong: Chinese University Press, 485–504.

Chugani, Michael. (1978). "No Place for History in Money-Conscious HK." *Hong Kong Standard*, June 8.

———. (1979). "The Hong Kong Club: Thumbs Up . . . or Down?" *Hong Kong Standard*, March 30.

Chun Beng Hunt and Kwok Kian-Woon. (2001). "Social Pluralism in Singapore." In R. Hefner, eds. *The Politics of Multiculturalism: Pluralism and Citizenship in Malaysia, Singapore, and Indonesia*. Honolulu: University of Hawaii Press, 86–118.

Chung Chihua Judy, Jeffrey Inaba, Rem Koolhaas, and Sze Tsung Leong, eds. (2001). *Great Leap Forward: Harvard Design School Project on the City*. Cambridge: Harvard Design School.

Chung, Stephanie Po-Yin. (1998). *Chinese Business Groups in Hong Kong and Political Change in South China, 1900–1925*. Basingstoke: MacMillan.

Chung, Wah Nan. (1998). *Contemporary Architecture in Hong Kong*. Hong Kong: Joint Publishing.

Clark, David. (1996). *Urban World/Global City*. London: Routledge.

Clifford, Nicholas. (1991). *Spoilt Children of Empire: Westerners in Shanghai and the Chinese Revolution of the 1920s*. Hanover: Middlebury College Press.

Clift, Winifred Lechmere. (1927). *Looking on in Hong Kong*. Hong Kong: Messrs Kae Shean.

Coates, Austin. (1978). *A Macau Narrative*. Hong Kong: Heinemann.

Cody, Jeffrey W. (2005). "Heritage as Hologram: Hong Kong after a Change of Sovereignty, 1997–2001." In W. Logan, ed. *The Disappearing Asian City: Protecting Asia's Urban Heritage in a Globalizing World.* Oxford: Oxford University Press, 185–208.

Commission of Inquiry. (1967). *Report of . . . Kowloon Disturbances 1966.* Hong Kong: J/H/Lee at the Government Press.

Committee of Hongkong-Kowloon Compatriots of All Circles for the Struggle against Persecution by the British Authorities in Hong Kong. (1967). *The May Upheaval in Hong Kong: N.p.*

Conceição, Deolinda da. (1956). *Cheong-Sam.* Macau: Instituto Cultural.

Constable, Nicole. (1994). *Christian Souls and Chinese Spirits: A Hakka Community in Hong Kong.* Berkeley: University of California Press.

———, ed. (1996). *Guest People: Hakka Identity in China and Abroad.* Seattle: University of Washington Press.

———. (1996). "Introduction: What Does It Mean to Be Hakka?" In N. Constable, ed. *Guest People.* Seattle: University of Washington Press, 1996, 3–35.

———. (1997). *Maid to Order in Hong Kong: Stories of Filipina workers.* Ithaca, NY: Cornell University Press.

Coonts, Stephen. (2000). *Hong Kong.* New York: St. Martin's Press.

Copper, John F. (1999). *Taiwan: Nation-State or Province?* Boulder, CO: Westview.

Correia, António. (1996). *Contos de Ou-Mun* [Macau Stories] Macau: Livros do Oriente.

Dalziel. (1907). *Chronicle of a Crown Colony.* Hong Kong: Semos.

Darwin, John. (1997). "Hong Kong in British Decolonisation" In J. M. Brown and R. Foot, eds. *Hong Kong's Transitions, 1842–1997.* Oxford: St. Anthony's College Press, 16–32.

Delmont, John, and Thomas Fennell. (1989). *Hong Kong Money: How Chinese Families and Fortunes are Changing Canada.* Toronto: Key Porter Books.

Deng, Xiaoping. (1993). *On the Question of Hong Kong.* Beijing: New Horizon.

Dimbley, Jonathan. (1997). *The Last Governor: Chris Patten & the Handover of Hong Kong.* Boston: Little, Brown and Company.

Drakakis-Smith, David. (1979). *High Society: Housing Provision in Metropolitan Hong Kong, 1954–1979. A Jubilee Critique.* Hong Kong: Centre of Asian Studies, Hong Kong University.

Echenberg, Myron J. (2002). "Pestis Redux: The Initial Years of the Third Bubonic Plague Pandemic 1894–1901." *Journal of World History* 13 (2) Fall: 429–4n9.

Edmonds, Richard Louis. (1996). "Geography and Natural Resources." In B. Hook, ed. *Guangdong: China's Promised Land*. Hong Kong: Oxford University Press, 71–116.

Eitel, E. J. (1983 [1895]). *Europe in China*. Hong Kong: Oxford University Press.

Endacott, G. B. (1958). *A History of Hong Kong*. London: Oxford University Press.

———. (1982). *Government and People in Hong Kong, 1845–1962: A Constitutioal History*. Westport, CT: Greenwood Press.

Erens, Patricia Brett. (2001). "The Film Work of Ann Hui." In P. Fu and D. Desser, eds. *The Cinema of Hong Kong*. Cambridge: At the University Press, 176–99.

Erni, John Nguyet. (2001). "Like a Post-Colonial Culture: Hong Kong Re-Imagined." *Cultural Studies* 15 (3, 4): 389–418.

Escoda, Isabel Taylor. (1994). *Letters from Hong Kong*. Hong Kong.

———. (1994). *Hong Kong Postscript*. Hong Kong: Media Mark.

Evans, Grant, and Maria Tam, eds. (1997). *Hong Kong: The Anthropology of a Chinese Metropolis*. Hong Kong: Curzon Press.

Fanon, Frantz. (1963). *The Wretched of the Earth*. New York: Grove Press.

Faure, David. (1986). *The Structure of Chinese Rural Society: Lineage and Village in the Eastern New Territories, Hong Kong*. Hong Kong: Oxford University Press.

———. (1996a). "History and Culture." In B. Hook, ed. *Guangdong: China's Promised Land*. Hong Kong: Oxford University Press, 1–30.

———. (1996b) "Becoming Cantonese, the Ming Dynasty Transition." In T. T. Lui and D. Faure, eds. *Unity and Diversity*. Hong Kong: Hong Kong University Press, 37–50.

———, ed. (1997). Society (*A Documentary History of Hong Kong*). Hong Kong: Hong Kong University Press.

——— and Helen Siu, eds. (1995). *Down to Earth: The Territorial Bond in South China*. Stanford: Stanford University Press.

———, J. Hayes, and A. Birch, eds. (1984). *From Village to City: Studies in the Traditional Roots of Hong Kong*. Hong Kong: Hong Kong University Press.

Federal Writer's Project. (1937). Works Progress Administration for the Commonwealth of Pennsylvania. *Philadelphia: A Guide to the Nation's Birthplace*. Philadelphia: William Penn Foundation.

Fenton, Anna. (2003). "Clamour of French Riviera Used to Sell Flats in Pokfulam." *South China Morning Post*, February 24.

Fishman, Robert. (1987). *Bourgeois Utopias*. New York: Basic Books.

Fitzpatrick, Laim. (2003). "The Long March." TimeAsia online. http://www.time.com/time/asia/covers/501030714/story2.html. (accessed January 2004).

Flowerdew, John. (1998). *The Final Years of British Hong Kong: The Discourse of Colonial Withdrawal*. London: MacMillan.

Fong, Timothy. (1994). *The First Suburban Chinatown: The Remaking of Monterey Park, California*. Philadelphia: Temple University Press.

Fore, Stephen. (1996). "Jackie Chan and the Dynamics of Global Entertainment." In S. Lu, ed. *Transnational Chinese Cinemas*. Honolulu: University of Hawaii, 239–62.

Freedman, Maurice. (1966). *Chinese Lineage and Society: Fukien and Kwantung*. London: The Athlone Press.

Friedmann, John. (1986). "The World City Hypothesis" *Development and Change* 17: 69–74.

Fu, Poshek. (2003). *Between Shanghai and Hong Kong: The Politics of Chinese Cinemas*. Stanford: Stanford University Press.

———— and David Desser, eds. (2000). *The Cinema of Hong Kong: History, Arts, Identity*. Cambridge: Cambridge University Press.

Fung, Anthony. (2001). "What Makes the Local? A Brief Consideration of the Rejuvenation of Hong Kong Identity." *Cultural Studies* 15 (3, 4): 591–602.

Ga Cheun Chao/Hong Kong Home: Multistories. (2001). Hong Kong Heritage Museum.

Geiger, Theodor, assisted by Frances M. Geiger. (1973). *Tales of Two City-States: The Development and Progress of Hong Kong and Singapore*. Washington: National Planning Association.

Gibson, William. (1993). *Virtual Light*. London: Penguin.

————. (1997). *Idoru*. New York: G.P. Putnam

————. (1999). *All Tomorrow's Parties*. New York: G.P. Putnam.

Gillingham, Paul. (1983). *At the Peak: Hong Kong Between the Wars*. London: MacMillan.

Girard, Greg, and Ian Lambot. (1993). *City of Darkness: Life in Kowloon Walled City*. Hong Kong: Watermark.

Goh, Robbie. (2004). "Diaspora and Violence: Cultural/Spatial Products, Abjection and Exchange." In R. Goh and S. Wong, eds. *Asian Diasporas*. Hong Kong: Hong Kong University Press, 33–52.

———. (2005). *Contours of Culture: Space and Social Difference in Singapore*. Hong Kong: Hong Kong University Press.

———, and Shawn Wong, eds. (2004). *Asian Diasporas*. Hong Kong: Hong Kong University Press.

Gunn, Geoffrey. (1996). *Encountering Macau: A Portuguese City-State on the Periphery of China, 1557–1999*. Boulder, CO: Westview.

Gittins, Jean. (1982). *Stanley: Behind Barbed Wire*. Hong Kong University Press.

Guan, Jian. (2001). "Ethnic Consciousness Arises on Facing Spacial Threats to Philadelphia Chinatown" In A. Erdentug and F. Colombijn, eds. *Urban Ethnic Encounters: The Spatial Consequences*. London: Routledge: 126–141.

Gutierrez, Laurent, and Valerie Portefaix. (2000). *Mapping Hong Kong*. Hong Kong: Map Book Publishers.

———, and Ezio Manzini, eds. (2002). *HK Lab*. Hong Kong: Map Book Publishers.

Halter, Seth. (2000). "Hong Kong's Dirty Little Secret: Clearing the Walled City of Kowloon." *Journal of Urban History* 27 (1): 92–113.

Hall, Peter. (1992). *In the Web*. London: Basingstoke.

Hamilton, Gary G. (1999). "Hong Kong and the Rise of Capitalism in Asia." In G. Hamilton, ed. *Cosmopolitan Capitalists*. Seattle: University of Washington Press, 14–34.

———, ed. (1999). *Cosmopolitan Capitalists: Hong Kong and the Chinese Diaspora at the end of the Twentieth Century*. Seattle: University of Washington Press.

Hammond, Stefan, and Mike Wilkins. (1996). *Sex and Zen and a Bullet in the Head*. New York: Fireside.

Han, Su-yin. (1952). *A Many-Splendoured Thing*. Boston: Little Brown.

Hase, R. H., and Elizabeth Sinn, eds. (1995). *Beyond the Metropolis: Villages in Hong Kong*. Hong Kong: Joint Publishing Company.

Hayes, James. (1977). *The Hong Kong Region, 1850–1911*. Hamden, CT: Shoestring Press.

———. (1983). *The Rural Communities of Hong Kong.* Hong Kong: Oxford University Press.

———. (1994). *Tsuen Wan: Growth of a "New Town" and Its People.* New York: Oxford University Press.

Hills, Peter. (1996). "Is Hong Kong's Development Sustainable?" In A. Yeh, ed. *Hong: Planning Hong Kong for the Twenty First Century.* Centre of Urban Planning and Environmental Management, University of Hong Kong, 274.

Hing Lo Shun. (1995). *Political Development in Macau.* Hong Kong: Chinese University Press.

Hinton, H. J. (1941). "Hong Kong's Place in the British Empire." (Notes on Luncheon Lecture): n.p.

Holden, Philip. (2004). "At Home in the World: Community and Consumption in Urban Singapore." In R. Bishop, J. Phillips and W. Yeo, eds. *Beyond Description: Singapore Space Historicity.* London: Routledge, 79–94.

Hom, Marion K. trans. and ed. (1991). "Poems from Songs of the Golden Mountain." In J. P. Chan, F. Chin, L. Inada, and S. Wong. *The Big AIIIEEEEE!: An Anthology of Chinese American and Japanese American Literature.* New York: Penguin, 140–77.

Hong Kong. (1924). Hong Kong: Kelly & Walsh.

Hong Kong Centenary Commemorative Talks, 1841–1941. (1941). Hong Kong: World News Service.

Hong Kong Reports. (1949–). Hong Kong: Government Printing Office.

Ho Ching-Inn and Rosa Yau. (1999). **City of Victoria.* Hong Kong Museum of History.

Ho, Suenn. (1993). "An Architectural Study on the Kowloon Walled City: Preliminary Findings." Hong Kong.

Hong Kong Going and Gone. (1980). Hong Kong Branch of Royal Asiatic Society.

*Hong Kong: My City of Visions (Painting Competition). (1996). Hong Kong: Hinge Marketing.

Hong Kong 1997: The Accelerating City Space and Design. (1997).

"Hong Kong International Airport" Special Issue of *Building Journal and Construction and Contract News.* (1988). Hong Kong.

Hong Kong Reports (various years). Hong Kong: Government Printing Office.

*Hong Kong Urban Council *Cantonese Melodrama 1950–1969*. (1986). Hong Kong.

———. (1992). **Overseas Chinese Figures in Cinema*. Hong Kong.

———. (1994). **Cinema of Two Cities: Hong Kong—Shanghai*. Hong Kong.

———. (1996). **The Restless Breed: Cantonese Stars of the Sixties*. Hong Kong.

Hong Kong Film Archive *The Cathay Story*. (2002). Hong Kong.

Hong Kong Museum of Art. (1991). *Historical Pictures*. Hong Kong.

Honig, Emily. (1986). *Sisters and Strangers: Women in the Shanghai Cotton Mills, 1919–1949*. Stanford: Stanford University Press.

Hook, Brian, ed. (1996). *Guangdong: China's Promised Land*. Hong Kong: Oxford University Press.

———, and Lee Wing On. (1996). "Human Resources and the Impact of Reform." In B. Hook, ed. *Guangdong: China's Promised Land*. Hong Kong: Oxford University Press, 117–48.

———. (1997). "National and International Interests in the Decolonisation of Hong Kong, 1946–1997" In J. M. Brown and R. Foot, ed. *Hong Kong's Transitions, 1842–1997*. Oxford: St. Anthony's College Press, 84–102.

Hopkins, Keith, ed. (1971). *Hong Kong: The Industrial Colony: A Political, Social, and Economic Survey*. Hong Kong: Oxford University Press.

———. (1971). "Introduction." In K. Hopkins, ed. *Hong Kong: The Industrial Colony*. Hong Kong: Oxford University Press, xi–xv.

Hsu, Madeleine Yuan-Yin. (2000). *Dreaming of Gold, Dreaming of Home: Transnationalism and Migration between the United States and South China, 1882–1943*. Stanford: Stanford University Press.

Huang, Tsung-Yi Michelle. (2004). *Walking Between Slums and Skyscrapers: Illusions of Open Space in Hong Kong, Tokyo and Shanghai*. Hong Kong: Hong Kong University Press.

Hughes, Richard. (1976 [1968]). *Borrowed Place, Borrowed Time: Hong Kong and its Many Faces*. London: Andre Deutsch.

Hung, Wing Fat. (1993). "The Politicization of the Environment." In C. Chan and P. Hills, ed. *Limited Gains*. Centre of Urban Planning and Environmental Management, University of Hong Kong: 41–50.

Hui, Bo-Kung. (2004). "Asian Financial Crisis and the Analysis of Developmentalism." In ed. K. Y. Law and K. M. Lee. **The Economy of Hong Kong in Non-economic Perspectives*, Hong Kong: Oxford University Press, 281–91.

Hunter, Anna. (2004). "Big Trouble in Little Chinatown" *Philadelphia Weekly*, September 1–7.

Ikels, Charlotte. (1996). *The Return of the God of Wealth: The Transition to a Market Economy in Urban China*. Stanford: Stanford University Press.

"Inside the Forbidden City." *The Guardian* July 21, 2004. <http://books.guardian.co.uk/firstchapters/story/0,6761,1272847,00.html> (accessed August 2005).

Ip, Inn Cheng. (2002). "The Sanitary City: The Colonial Formation of Hong Kong and Early Public Housing." *EHKCSS (Hong Kong Culture and Social Studies)* 2 <www.hku.hk/hkcsp/ccex/3hkcss/01> (accessed February 2005).

Jarvie, Ian. (1977). *Window on Hong Kong: A Sociological Study of the Hong Kong Film Industry and Its Audience*. Hong Kong: Centre for Asian Studies, Hong Kong University Press.

———, and Joseph Agassi, eds. (1968). *Hong Kong: A Society in Transition*. New York: Praeger.

Jaulin, Jean, and Jean-François Huchet. (2004). "Growth Models Fail to Deliver." In K. Y. Law and K. M. Lee. *The Economy of Hong Kong in Non-economic Perspectives*. Hong Kong: Oxford University Press, 257–70.

Jones, P. (1967). "Productivity Counts." *Far Eastern Economic Review* 56 (13) June: 725.

Joseph, May. (199). *Nomadic Identities: The Performance of Citizenship*. Minneapolis: University of Minnesota Press.

Joanilho, Marcel. (2004). "SAR Losing 'Dragon Head' Status." *Evening Standard*, May 17.

Kahn, Joseph. (2004). "Police Raid Chinese Newspaper that Reported New SARS Case." *New York Times*, January 8: A7.

Kelly, Ian. (1986). *Hong Kong: A Political Geographic Analysis*. Honolulu: University of Hawaii Press.

Kim, Eun Mee. (1998). *The Four Asian Tigers: Economic Development and the Global Political Economy*. San Diego: Academic Press.

King, Anthony. (1990). *Global Cities: Post-Imperialism and the Internationalization of London*. London: Routledge.

———. (2003). "Actually Existing Postcolonialisms: Colonial Urbanism and Architecture after the Post-Colonial Turn." In ed. R. Bishop, J. Phillips, and W. W. Yeo. *Postcolonial Urbanism*. New York: Routledge, 167–86.

Kinoshita, Hikaru. (1997). "The Significance of Designs Apposite to Hong Kong." *SD Space Design* 394 July: 80.

Knight, Alan. (1999). "Washing Away 100 Years of Shame." In A. Knight and Y. Nakano, eds. *Reporting Hong Kong*, London: Curzon Press, 72–98.

Knight, Alan and Yoshiko Nakano, eds. (1999). *Reporting Hong Kong: Foreign Media and the Handover*. London: Curzon Press.

Kojima, Kazuhiro. (1997). "The Future Reveals Itself in Hong Kong." *SD Space Design* 394 (July): 50.

Kong, Lily, and Brenda S. A. Yeoh. (2003). *The Politics of Landscape in Singapore: Constructions of "Nation."* Syracuse: Syracuse University Press.

Koolhaas, Rem, and Bruce Mau. (2000). "Singapore Songlines: Portrait of a Potemkin Metropolis . . . or Thirty Years of Tabula Rasa." In M. Miles, T. Hall, and I. Borden, eds. *The City Cultures Reader*. London: Routledge, 22–25.

Kristof, Nicholas. (2003). "Ringing China in from the Cold." *New York Times,* June 3: A31.

Krongkaew, Medhi. (1996). "The Changing Urban System in a Fast Growing City and Economy: The Case of Bangkok and Thailand." In F.C. Lo and Y. M. Yeung, eds. *Emerging World Cities in Pacific Asia*. Tokyo: United Nations University Press, 286–334.

Kueh, Y. Y. and Robert F. Ash. (1996). "The Fifth Dragon: Economic Development." In B. Hook, ed. *Guangdong: China's Promised Land*. Hong Kong: Oxford University Press, 149–92.

Kwok, Edmund S. T. (1982). "From 'The Campaign for Chinese to Be an Official Language' to 'The Second Chinese Language Campaign'." In J. Cheng, ed. *Hong Kong in the 1980s*. Hong Kong: Somerson, 32–44.

Kwok, Kwok-chuen. (1997). "Money and Banking." In J. Cheng, ed. *The Other Hong Kong Report 1997*. Hong Kong: Chinese University Press, 327–40.

Kwok, Reginald Yin-Wang, and Alvin So, eds. (1995). *The Hong Kong–Guangdong Link: Partnership in Flux*. Armonk, NY: M.E. Sharpe.

Kwong, Kai-Sun. (1997). *Tourism and the Hong Kong Economy*. Hong Kong: Hong Kong University Press.

Kwong, Peter. (1987). *The New Chinatown*. New York: Noonday Press.

Kwong, Sunny Kai-sun. (1997). "Technology and Industry." In J. Cheng, ed. *The Other Hong Kong Report 1997*. Hong Kong: Chinese University Press, 283–305.

Lam, Cissy K. S. (1985). "Sovereignty over Hong Kong" *The Cambrian Law Review* <http://home.navigator.com/~cissylam/HongKong.htm> (accessed December 2003).

Lam, Pun-Lee, and Yue Cheong Chan. (1998). *Privatizing Water and Sewage Systems*. Hong Kong: City University Press of Hong Kong.

Lam, Shui-hum, ed. (2002). *Xianggong Bianyuan Laogon Koushu [Oral histories of Hong Kong fringe labor]*. Hong Kong: Oxfam Publishing.

Lambot, Ian, and Gillian Chambers. (1986). *One Queen's Road Central*. Hong Kong.

Landon, Kenneth Perry. (1941). *The Chinese in Thailand*. London: Oxford University Press.

Lau, Chi Kuen. (1997). *Hong Kong's Colonial Legacy*. Hong Kong: Chinese University Press.

Lau, Kwok-yu, James Lee, and Zhang Yongyue. (2004). "Housing." in L. Wong, L. White, and S. Gui, eds. Social Policy Reform in *Hong Kong and Shanghai*, Armonk, NY: M.E. Sharpe, 53–84.

Lau Siu-Kai. (1962). *Society and Politics in Hong Kong*. Hong Kong: Chinese University Press.

———. (1977). *Utilitarian Familiarism: An Inquiry into the Basis of Political Stability*. Hong Kong: Chinese University of Hong Kong Social Research Centre.

——— and Kuan Hsin-Chi. (1988). *The Ethos of the Hong Kong Chinese*. Hong Kong: Chinese University Press.

Lau, Y. W. (2002). *A History of the Municipal Councils of Hong Kong, 1883–1997*. Hong Kong: Leisure and Cultural Services.

Lau Yee-cheung. (1998). "History." In Y. M. Yeung and David K.Y. Chu, eds. *Guangdong*. Hong Kong: Chinese University Press, 465–84.

Law Kam Yee, and Lee Kam Ming, eds. (2004). *The Economy of Hong Kong in Non-economic Perspectives. Hong Kong: Oxford University Press.

Law Kar, and Stephen Teo, eds. (1997). *Gwongying Bunfan Nghsap Nihn/ Fifty Years of Electric Shadows*. Hong Kong: Urban Council.

Law Society of Hong Kong. (2003). "The Law Society's Comments on the Proposed Committee Stage Amendments to the Article 23 Blue Bill."

Law Wing-Sang, ed. (1997). *Whose City? Analysis of Post-War Hong Kong Citizenship and Politics*. Hong Kong: Oxford University Press.

Lee. Chin-Chuan, Joseph Man Chan, Zhongdang Pan, and Clement Y.K. So, eds. (2002). *Global Media Spectacle: News War over Hong Kong*. Albany: State University of New York Press.

Lee Ching Kwan. (1998). *Gender and the South China Miracle: Two Worlds of Factory Women*. Berkeley: University of California Press.

Lee, Eliza W.Y., ed. (2003). *Gender and Change in Hong Kong: Globalization, Postcolonialism and Chinese Patriarchy*. Hong Kong: Hong Kong University Press.

Lee Gan Wei. (2004). "Emigration in Hong Kong Last Year was the Lowest in 23 years." *Sing Tao Daily*, January 15.

Lee, Gregory. (2003). *Chinese Unlimited: Making the Imaginary of China and Chineseness*. Honolulu: University of Hawaii Press.

Lee Ho Yin, and Lynne D. Distefano. (2002). *A Tale of Two Villages: The Story of Changing Village Life in the New Territories*. New York: Oxford University Press.

Lee Ing-Kwan, and Leung Sai-Wing. (1995). *Democracy, Capitalism, and National Identity in Public Attitudes*. Occasional Papers Series No. 4, Department of Applied Social Sciences. Hong Kong Polytechnic University.

Lee Kwan Yew. (2000). *From Third World to First: The Singapore Story, 1965–2000*. New York: Harper Collins.

Lee, Leo Ou-Fan. (1999). *Shanghai Modern: The Flowering of a New Urban Culture in China 1930–1945*. Cambridge: Harvard University Press.

Lee, Martin. (2003). "China's Censors Extend their Reach" *New York Times* June 3, A31.

Lee, S. H. (2003). "The SARS Epidemic in Hong Kong." *Journal of Epidemiology and Community Health* 57 (652, 3) (September).

Lethbridge, Henry. (1978). *Hong Kong Stability and Change*. Hong Kong: Oxford University Press.

Leu Siew Yung. (2003). "Extra Police for Crime-Hit Guangzhou." *South China Morning Post,* September 9: 2.

Leung, Benjamin K. P. (1994). "Social Inequality and Insurgency in Hong Kong." In ed. B. K. P. Leung and T. Y. C. Wong, eds. *Twenty-Five Years of Social and Economic Development in Hong Kong*. Hong Kong: Hong Kong University Press, 117–98.

———. (1996). *Perspectives on Hong Kong Society*. Hong Kong: Hong Kong University Press.

——— and Teresa Y.C. Wong, eds. (1994). *Twenty-Five Years of Social and Economic Development in Hong Kong*. Hong Kong: Hong Kong University Press.

Leung Ping-Kwan. (2000). "Urban Cinema and the Cultural Identity of Hing Kong." In P. Fu and D. Desser, eds. *The Cinema of Hong Kong*. Cambridge: Cambridge University Press, 227–51.

Lim, Shirley Geok-Lin. (2003). "Regionalism, English Narrative, and Singapore as Home and Global City." In R. Bishop J. Phillips and W. W. Yeo, eds. *Postcolonial Urbanism*. New York: Routledge, 205–26.

Lin, Jan. (1998). *Reconstructing Chinatown: Ethnic Enclave, Global Change*. Minneapolis: University of Minnesota Press.

Lin, Jennifer. (2000). "Chinatown Fears It Will Lose Its Way." *The Philadelphia Inquirer*, June 14.

Liu Shuyong. (1997). *An Outline History of Hong Kong*. Beijing: Foreign Languages Press.

Liu Tao Tao and David Faure, eds. (1996). *Unity and Diversity: Local Cultures and Identity in China*. Hong Kong: Hong Kong University Press.

Lo Fu-Chen, and Yue-Man Yeung, eds. (1996). *Emerging World Cities in Pacific Asia*. Tokyo: United Nations University Press.

Lo Hsiang-Lin, et al. (1959). *Yiba Sier Nian Yiqian Xianggang Jie qi Duiwei Jiantong. [Hong Kong and its external communication before 1842]*. Hong Kong: Privately Printed.

Logan, John, ed. (2002). *The New Chinese City: Globalization and Market Reform*. Malden, MA: Blackwell Publishers.

Loh, Christine. (2002). "Ports, Airports, and Bureaucrats: Restructuring Hong Kong and Guangdong." CLSA. <www.civic-exchange.org/publications/ 2002/PAB%20report.pdf> (accessed January 2005). Hong Kong: Hong Kong University Press.

——— and Civic Exchange. (2004). *At the Epicentre: Hong Kong and the SARS Outbreak*. Hong Kong: Hong Kong University Press.

Look Lai, Walton. (1993). *Indentured Labor, Caribbean Sugar: Chinese and Indian Migrants to the British West Indies, 1838–1918*. Baltimore, MD: The Johns Hopkins University Press.

Lu, Sheldon Hsiao-ping, ed. (1997). *Transnational Chinese Cinemas: Identity, Nationhood, Gender*. Honolulu: University of Hawaii Press.

———. (2000). "Filming Diaspora and Identity: Hong Kong and 1997." In P. Fu and D. Desser, eds. *The Cinema of Hong Kong*. Cambridge: Cambridge University Press, 273–88.

Luck, Kwok Mean (2004). "Singapore: A Skyline of Pragmatism." In R. Bishop, J. Phillips, and W. Yeo, eds. *Beyond Description: Singapore Space Historicity*. London: Routledge, 112–124.

Lui, Hon-Kwong. (1997). *Income Inequality and Economic Development*. Hong Kong: City University of Hong Kong Press.

Lui, Tai-Lok. (1997). "The Hong Kong New Middle Class on the Eve of 1997." In J. Cheng, ed. *The Other Hong Kong Report 1997*. Hong Kong: Chinese University Press, 207–26.

———. (2001). "The Malling of Hong Kong." In G. Mathews and T.-L. Lui, eds. *Consuming Hong Kong*. Hong Kong: Hong Kong University Press, 23–46.

Ma, Jiewei. (2001). "Re-Advertising Hong Kong: Nostalgia Industry and Popular History." *Positions* 9, 1 (Spring): 131–39.

Ma, Kit-Mai. (1999). *Culture, Politics and Television in Hong Kong*. London: Routledge.

Ma, Kit-Mai. (2002). "An Historical Analysis of Television Culture" (Din See Man Fa Dik Liksi Fan Sik. In T. Ng and T. Cheng, eds. *Yue Du Xianggang Po Kue Wan Qua (Reading Hong Kong Popular Culture)*. Hong Kong: Oxford, 681–694.

Madancy, Joyce. (2003). *The Troublesome Legacy of Commissioner Lin: The Opium Trade and Opium Suppression in Fujian, 1820s to 1920s*. Cambridge: Harvard University Asia Center.

Made in Hong Kong: A History of Export Design In Hong Kong. (1990). Hong Kong: Museum of History.

Magnago Lampugnani, Vittorio, ed. (1993). *Hong Kong: The Aesthetics of Density*. New York: Prestag-Verlei.

Marchetti, Gina. (1993). *Romance and the "Yellow Peril": Race, Sex, and Discursive Strategies in Hollywood Fiction*. Berkeley: University of California.

————. (2000). "Buying American, Consuming Hong Kong." In P. Fu and D. Desser, eds. *The Cinema of Hong Kong*. Cambridge: Cambridge University Press, 289–313.

Marks, Robert. (1998). *Tigers, Rice, Silk, and Silt: Environment and Economy in Late Imperial South China*. Cambridge: Cambridge University Press.

Marshall, Tyler. (2003). "Wal-Mart Dazzles Chinese Shoppers." *Los Angeles Times*, November 27: F13.

Matsuda, Naonori. (1997). "Airport City" *SD Space Design* 394 (July): 78–83.

Mathews, Gordon, and Tai Luk Loi, eds. (2001). *Consuming Hong Kong*. Hong Kong: Hong Kong University Press.

McDonogh, Gary W. (1997). "Citizens of Tomorrow: Citizenship, Identity, and Urbanism in the Twenty-First Century." *City & Society Annual Review*: 5–34.

———— and Cindy Hing-Yuk Wong. (2001). "Orientalism Abroad: Hong Kong Readings of the World of Suzie Wong." In D. Bernardi, ed. *Classic Hollywood, Classic Whiteness*. Minneapolis: University of Minnesota Press, 210–44.

McKeown, Adam. (1996). "Inmigración China al Peru, 1904–1937: Exclusión y negociación" *Histórica* 20 (1) (Julio): 59–91.

————. (2001). *Chinese Migrant Networks and Cultural Change: Peru, Chicago, Hawaii 1900–1936*. Chicago: University of Chicago Press.

Meyer, David R. (2000). *Hong Kong as a Global Metropolis*. Cambridge: Cambridge University Press.

Milligan, Barry. (1995). *Pleasures and Pains: Opium and the Orient in Nineteenth-Century British Culture*. Charlottesville: University of Virginia.

Miners, Norman. (1987). *Hong Kong under Imperial Rule, 1912–1941*. Hong Kong: Oxford University Press.

Mintz, Sidney W. (1985). *Sweetness and Power: The Place of Sugar in Modern History*. New York: Penguin.

Mitchell, Katharyne. (1999). "Hong Kong Immigration and the Question of Democracy: Contemporary Struggles over Urban Politics in Vancouver, B.C." In G. Hamilton, ed. *Cosmopolitan Capitalists*. Seattle: University of Washington Press, 152–66.

Mitchell, Tom. (2003). "Why Shenzhen's Reforms Are Not Aimed at Undermining the Party." *South China Morning Post*, January 24: 20.

McLean, John. (1996). *Tartan Dragon*. Jersey: Winter Productions.

Morley, David, and Kevin Robins. (1995). *Spaces of Identity: Global Media, Electronic Landscapes, and Cultural Boundaries*. London: Routledge.

Morris, Jan. (1997). *Hong Kong: Epilogue to an Empire*. New York: Vintage.

———. (2003). *The World*. New York: W.W. Norton.

Munn, Christopher. (2000). "The Hong Kong Opium Revenue, 1845–1885." In T. Brook and B. Wakabayashi, eds. *Opium Regime*. Berkeley: University of California Press, 105–26.

———. (2001). *Anglo-China: Chinese People and British Rule in Hong Kong, 1841–1880*. Richmond: Curzon Press.

Neller, R. J., and K. C. Lam. (1998). "The Environment." In ed. Y. M. Yeung and David K. Y. Chu, eds. *Guangdong*. Hong Kong: Chinese University Press, 435–65.

New, Christopher. (2000). *A Change of Flag*. Hong Kong: Asia.

Ng, Cho-Nam, and Ng Ting-Leung. "The Environment." In J. Y. S. Cheng, ed. *The Other Hong Kong Report 1997*. Hong Kong: Chinese University Press, 483–504.

Ng, Chun-Hung, and Cheng Sei-Wei, eds. (2002). **Reading Hong Kong Popular Cultures, 1970–2000*. Hong Kong: Oxford University Press.

Ng, Hang Sau. (1993). "Mobilizing Tsing Yi Residents against Housing for Low-income groups." In C. Chan and P. Hills, ed. *Limited Gains*. Centre of Urban Planning and Environmental Management, Hong Kong University, 63–82.

Ng, Tseun-Hong and Cheng Tse-Wai, eds. (2002). *Yue Du Xianggang Po Kue Wan Qua (Reading Hong Kong Popular Culture)*. Hong Kong: Oxford.

Ng, Yiu Fai. (1993). "The Environment and Grassroots Participation in Squatter Areas." In C. Chan and P. Hills, eds. *Limited* I. Centre of Urban Planning and Environmental Management, University of Hong Kong: 99–116.

Norman, Jerry. (1988). *Chinese*. Cambridge: Cambridge University Press.

*Of Hearts and Hands: Hong Kong's Traditional Trades and Crafts. (1995). Hong Kong: Urban Council.

O'Donnell, Mary Ann. (1999). "Path Breaking: Constructing Gendered Nationalism in the Shenzhen Special Economic Zone." *Positions* 7 (2) (Fall): 343–75.

———. (2001). "Creating Hong Kong, Razing Baoan, Preserving Xin'an: An Ethnographic Account of Urbanization in the Shenzhen Special Economic Zone" *Cultural Studies* 15 (3, 4): 419–43.

O'Toole, James. (2003). "China's Fantastic Growth Is Revolutionary in All Ways" *Pittsburgh Post-Gazette*, November 2: World A1.

Olds, Kris. (1995). "Globalization and the Production of New Urban Spaces: Pacific Rim Megaprojects in the Late-Twentieth Century." *Environment and Planning A* (27): 1713–43.

Ommundsen, Wenchi. (2004). "Cultural Citizenship in Diaspora: A Study of Chinese Australia." In R. Goh and S. Wong, eds. *Asian Diasporas*. Hong Kong: Hong Kong University Press, 77–94.

Ong, Aihwa. (1999). *Flexible Citizenship: The Cultural Logics of Transnationalism*. Durham, NC: Duke University Press.

———. (2004). "Intelligent Island, Baroque Ecology." In R. Bishop, J. Phillips, and W. Yeo, eds. *Beyond Description: Singapore Space Historicity*. London: Routledge, 176–189.

Page, Max. (1999). *The Creative Destruction of Manhattan, 1900–1940*. Chicago: University of Chicago Press.

Parker, David. (1995). *Through Different Eyes: The Cultural Identities of Young Chinese People in Britain*. Aldershot: Avebury.

———. (1998). "Chinese People in Britain: History, Futures, Identities." In G. Benton and F. N. Pieke, *The Chinese in Europe*. New York: St. Martin's Press, 67–95.

Património Arquitectónico Macau [Macau architectural patrimony]. (1988). Macau: Instituto Cultural.

Patten, Christopher. (1998). *East and West: China, Power, and the Future of Asia*. London: Times Books.

Peplow, S. H. and M. Barker. (1931). *Hongkong Around and About*. Hong Kong: Ye Old Printerie.

Pierson, Herbert. (1992). "Cantonese, English, or Putonghuam — Unresolved Communicative Issues in Hong Kong's Future." In G. Postiglione, ed. *Education and Society in Hong Kong*. Hong Kong: Hong Kong University Press, 183–202.

Piña-Cabral, João de. (2002). *Between China and Europe: Person, Culture, and Emotion in Macao*. London: Continuum.

——— and Nelson Lourenço. (1991). "A questão das origenes: Família e etnicidade macenses" *Antropologia* (Macau) 16: 104–25.

Planning, Environment, and Lands Branch, Government Secretariat. (1989). "Pollution in Hong Kong — A Time to Act." Hong Kong.

———. (1991). "Saving Our Environment: First Review of the 1989 White Paper Pollution in Hong Kong — A Time to Act." Hong Kong.

Pope-Hennessey, James. (1964). *Verandah: Some Episodes in the Crown Colony*. London: George Allen and Unwin.

Porter, Jonathan. (1996). *Macau: The Imaginary City Culture and Society 1551 to the Present*. Boulder, CO: Westview.

Pryor, Ted, and Peter Cookson Smith. (2000). "What Kind of Harbour City Do We Want?" In W. S. Wong and E H.W. Chan, eds. *Building Hong Kong: Environmental Considerations*. Hong Kong: Hong Kong University Press, 61–80.

Rafferty, Kevin. (1993). *City on the Rocks*. New York: Penguin.

Richardson, Tim. (1977). *North Point*. Hong Kong.

Ritzer, George. (2004). *The Globalization of Nothing*. Thousand Oaks, CA: Sage.

Roberts, J. A. G. (2002). *China to Chinatown: Chinese Food in the West*. London: Reaktion Books.

Rock, Michael T. (2000). "Thailand's Old Bureaucratic Polity and Its New Semi-democracy." In M. Khan and J. K. Sundaram, eds. *Rents. Rent-Seeking and Economic Development: Theory and Evidence in Asia*. Cambridge: Cambridge University Press, 182–206.

Rooney, Nuala. (2003). *At Home with Density*. Hong Kong University Press.

Rosen, Sharon. (1976). *Mei Foo Sun Chuen: Middle Class Chinese Families in Transition*. Taipei: Oriental Cultural Service.

Rosenthal, Elisabeth. (2003). "The SARS Epidemic: The Path from China's Province, a Crafty Germs Breaks Out." *New York Times*, April 27: 1.

Ruggeri, Laura. (2002). "Prisoners of the Californian Dream." In L Gutierrez, E. Manzini, and V. Portefaix, eds. *HK Labs*. Hong Kong: Map Books, 258–70.

Salaff, Janet. (1988). *State and Family in Singapore*. Ithaca, NY: Cornell University Press.

———. (1993). *Working Daughters of Hong Kong: Filial Piety or Power in the Family*. New York: Columbia University Press.

Sassen, Saskia. (1994). *Cities in a World Economy*. London: Pine Forge.

———. (2002). *Global Networks, Linked Cities*. New York: Routledge.

Sayer, Geoffrey R. (1975). *Hong Kong 1862–1919: Years of Discretion*. Hong Kong: Hong Kong University Press.

————. (1980 [1937]). *Hong Kong 1841–1862: Birth, Adolescence, and Coming of Age*. Hong Kong: Hong Kong University Press.

Schiffrin, Harold Z. (1968). *Sun Yat-Sen and the Origins of the Chinese Revolution*. Berkeley: University of California Press.

Scott, Ian. (1989). *Political Change and the Crisis of Legitimacy in Hong Kong*. Hong Kong: Oxford University Press.

Selya, Roger. (1995). *Taipei*. Chichester: John Wiley.

Shah, Nayan. (1991). *Contagious Divides: Epidemics and Race in San Francisco's Chinatown*. Berkeley: University of California Press.

Shipp, Steve. (1997). *Macau, China: A Political History of the Portuguese Colony's Transition to Chinese Rule*. Jefferson, NC: McFarland.

Shohat, Ella and Robert Stam. (1995). *Unthinking Eurocentrism*. London: Routledge.

Shuman, Michael. (2004). "Macau's Big Score." *TimeAsia*. May 24, 2004. http://www.time.com/time/asia/magazine/article/0,13673,501040531-641209,00.html.

Siddall, Linda. (1991). "The Environment." In Y. W. Sung and M. Y. Lee. *The Other Hong Kong Report 1991*. Hong Kong: Chinese University Press, 403–20.

Silva, Veronica. (2000). "Philippines to Focus on E-Service Niche" *I.T. News Daily* July 14. <itmatters.com.ph/giic/news_07142000d.html> (accessed May 15, 2002).

Sinn, Elizabeth. (1988). *Power and Charity: The Early History of the Tung Wah Hospital*. Hong Kong: Oxford University Press.

———— ed. (1990). *Between East and West: Aspects of Social and Political Development in Hong Kong*. Centre of Asian Studies, Hong Kong University.

Siu, Fong Hong. (2002). "Xianggang Zaizo" (Remaking Hong Kong). In Ng T. and Cheng Tse-Wai, eds. *Yue Du Xianggang Po Kue Wan Qua (Reading Hong Kong Popular Culture)*. Hong Kong: Oxford, 703–714.

Siu, Helen. (1996). "Remade in Hong Kong: Weaving into the Chinese Cultural Tapestry." In T. T. Lin and D. Faure, eds. *Unity in Diversity*. Hong Kong: Hong Kong University Press, 177–97.

————. (1999). "Hong Kong: Cultural Kaleidoscope on a World Landscape." In G. Hamilton, ed. *Cosmopolitan Capitalists*. Seattle: University of Washington Press, 100–17.

———— and David Faure. (1995). "Introduction." In D. Faure and H. Siu, eds. *Down to Earth: The Territorial Bond in South China*. Stanford: Stanford University Press, 1–20.

Siu, Margaret. (1997). *Her Majesty the Comrade: A Novel of Hong Kong 1997*. Hong Kong: Marsell Enterprises.

Skeldon, Ronald. (1997). "Hong Kong Communities Overseas." In J. M. Brown and R. Foot, eds. *Hong Kong's Transitions, 1842–1997*. London: MacMillan Press, 121–48.

Skinner, G. William. (1957). *Chinese Society in Thailand: An Analytical History*. Ithaca, NY: Cornell University Press.

————. (1958). *Leadership and Power in the Chinese Community of Thailand*. Ithaca, NY: Cornell University Press.

———— ed. (1977). *The City in Late Imperial China*. Stanford: Stanford University Press.

————. (1999). "The Difference a Century Makes." In G. Hamilton, ed. *Cosmopolitan Capitalists*. Seattle: University of Washington Press.

Smart, Alan. (1992). *Making Room: Squatter Clearance in Hong Kong*. Centre of Asian Studies, Hong Kong University.

————. (2002). "The Hong Kong/Pearl River Delta Urban Region: An Emerging Transnational Mode of Regulation or Just Muddling Through?" In J. Logan, ed. *The New Chinese City*. Malden, MA: Blackwell, 92–100.

———— and Josephine Smart. (1996). "Monster Homes: Hong Kong Immigration to Canada, Urban Conflicts, and Contested Representations of Space." In J. Caulfield and L. Peak, eds. *City Lives and Forms*. Toronto: University of Toronto Press, 33–47.

Smart, Josephine. (1989). *The Political Economy of Street Hawkers in Hong Kong*. Centre of Asian Studies, Hong Kong University.

———— and Alan Smart. (1999). "Personal Relations and Divergent Economies: A Case Study of Hong Kong Investment in South China." In S. Low, ed. *Theorizing the City*. New Brunswick, NJ: Rutgers University Press, 169–200.

Smith, Carl T. (1995). *A Sense of History: Studies in the Social and Urban History of Hong Kong*. Hong Kong: Hong Kong Educational Publishing Company.

Smith, Michael Peter. (2001). *Transnational Urbanism: Locating Globalization.* Malden, MA: Blackwell.

Smith, Peter C. (2000). "Sustainability and Urban Design." *Building Hong Kong: Environmental Considerations.* W. S. Wong and E. H. W. Chan, eds. Hong Kong: Hong Kong University Press, 27–42.

Snow, Philip. (2004). *The Fall of Hong Kong: Britain, China, and the Japanese Occupation.* New Haven, CT: Yale University Press.

Sum, N. L. (2002). "Globalization and Hong Kong's Entrepreneurial City Strategies: Contested Vision and the Remaking of City Governance in (Post)–Crisis Hong Kong." In J. Logan, ed. *The New Chinese City.* Malden, MA: Blackwell, 74–91.

Sun Yat-Sen. (1994). *Prescriptions for Saving China: Selected Writings of Sun Yat-sen.* Eds. J. Wei, R. H. Myers and D. G. Gillin. Stanford: Hoover Institution Press.

Sung Yun-Wing. (1991). "Introduction." In Sung Y-W and Lee Ming-Kwan, eds. *The Other Hong Kong Report.* Hong Kong: Chinese University Press, xix–xxvi.

Sweeting, Anthony. (1990). "Controversy over the Reopening of Hong Kong University, 1942–1948." In E. Sinn, ed. *Between East and West.* Hong Kong: Center of Asian Studies, 25–46.

———. (1992). "Education within Historical Processes." In G. Postiglione, ed. *Education and Society in Hong Kong.* Hong Kong: Hong Kong University Press, 39–82.

———. (1993). *Phoenix Transformed: The Reconstruction of Education in Post-War Hong Kong.* Hong Kong: Oxford University Press.

Swyngedouw, Erik, and Guy Baeten. (2001). "Selling the City: The Political Economy of 'Glocal' Development — Brussel's Conundrum." *European Planning Studies,* October: 827–49.

Tam, S. Maria. (2003). "Empowering Mobility: 'Astronaut's Wives' Women in Australia." In Lee, E. ed. *Gender and Change in Hong Kong: Globalization, Postcolonialism and Chinese Patriarchy.* Hong Kong: Hong Kong University Press, 177–199.

Tang, Kwong-Leung. (1998). *Colonial State and Social Policy: Social Welfare Development in Hong Kong, 1842–1997.* Lanham, MD: University Press of America.

Tchen, John Kuo-Wei. (1999). *New York Before Chinatown: Orientalism and the Shaping of American Culture, 1776–1882*. Baltimore, MD: The Johns Hopkins University Press.

Thayer, James. (2002). *The Gold Swan*. New York: Simon & Schuster.

Teo, Stephen. (1997). *Hong Kong Cinema*. London: BFI.

Tong, Benson. (2003). *The Chinese Americans*. Boulder, CO: University of Colorado Press.

Torgrimson, John. (1991). "Vietnamese Boat People." In Y. W. Sung and M. Y. Lee, eds. *The Other Hong Kong Report 1991*. Hong Kong: Chinese University Press, 103–16.

Traver, Harold. (1992). "Opium to Heroin: Restrictive Opium Legislation and the Rise of Heroin in Hong Kong." *Journal of Policy History* 4: 307–74.

Tsai, Jung-Fang. (1993). *Hong Kong in Chinese History: Community and Social Unrest in the British Colony, 1842–1913*. New York: Columbia University Press.

Tsang, Steve. (2004). *A Modern History of Hong Kong*. London: I. B. Tauris.

Tu, Wei-Ming ed. (1994). *The Living Tree: The Changing Meaning of Being Chinese Today*. Stanford: Stanford University Press.

———. (1994). "Cultural China: The Periphery as Center." In W. M. Tu, ed. *The Living Tree*. Stanford: Stanford University Press, 1–34.

Turner, J. A. (1982 [1884]). *Kwang Tung or Five Years in South China*. Hong Kong: Oxford University Press.

Turner, Matthew. (1996). "60s/90s." In M. Turner and I. Ngan, eds. *Hong Kong 60s/90s: Designing Identity*. Hong Kong: Center for Performing Arts.

Vaid, K. N. (1972). *The Overseas Indian Community in Hong Kong*. Centre of Asian Studies, Hong Kong University.

Vicente, Manuel, Manuel Graça Dias, and Helena Rezende. (1991). *Macau Gloria: A glória do vulgar*. Macau: Instituto Cultural de Macau.

Vogel, Ezra F. (1969). *Canton under Communism: Programs and Politics in a Provincial Capital, 1949–1968*. Cambridge: Harvard University Press.

———. (1989). *One Step Ahead in China*. Cambridge: Harvard University Press.

———. (1991). *The Four Little Dragons: The Spread of Industrialization in East Asia*. Cambridge: Harvard University Press.

Wallerstein, Immanuel. (1974). *The Modern World System: Capitalist Agriculture and the European World Economy.* New York: Academic Press.

Wang, Ling-chi. (1994). "Roots and Changing Identity of the Chinese in the United States." In W. Tu, ed. *The Living Tree.* Stanford: Stanford University, 185–212.

Wang, Wang-Chi. (2000). *Lishi de chenzhong Cong: Xianggang kan Zhongguo dalu de Xiannggang shi lunshu [The burden of history: historical narrative on Hong Kong in Mainland China].* Hong Kong: Oxford University Press.

Ward, Barbara E. (1989). *Through Other Eyes: An Anthropologist's View of hong Kong.* Hong Kong: Chinese University Press.

Warren, William. (2002). *Bangkok.* London: Reaktion.

Watson, James L. (1975). *Emigration and the Chinese lineage: The Mans in Hong Kong and London.* Berkeley: University of California Press.

———. (2000). "Food as a Lens: The Past, Present, and Future of Family Life in China." In Jun Jing, ed. *Feeding China's Little Emperors: Food, Children, and Social Change.* Stanford: Stanford University Press, 199–212.

"We Shall Win! British Imperialism in Hong Kong Will Be Defeated." (1967). Hong Kong.

Wei, Betty Peh-T'i. (1987). *Shanghai: Crucible of Modern China.* Hong Kong: Oxford University Press.

Welsh, Frank. (1993). *A Borrowed Place: The History of Hong Kong.* New York: Kodansha International.

Wesley-Smith, Peter. (1990). *Unequal Treaty, 1898–1997: China, Britain, and Hong Kong's New Territories.* Hong Kong: Oxford University Press.

———. (1992). "Identity, Land, Feng Shui, and the Law in Traditional Hong Kong." Paper delivered at the Commission on Folk law and Legal Pluralism in Wellington, NZ, August 27–30.

Whisson, Michael G. (1968). "Some Sociological Aspects of the Illegal Narcotics in Hong Kong." In I. Jarvie and J. Agassi, eds. *Hong Kong: A Society in Transition.* London: Praeger, 299–316.

White, Barbara Sue. (1994). *Turbans and Traders: Hong Kong's Indian Communities.* Hong Kong: Oxford University Press.

Wilbur, C. Martin. (1976). *Sun Yat-Sen: Reluctant Revolutionary.* New York: Columbia University Press.

Wilkinson, Judith. (1993). "A Chinese Magistrate's Fort." In G. Girard and I. Lambot, eds. *City of Darkness: Life in Kowloon Walled City*. London: Watermark, 60–73.

Williams, Stephanie. (1989). *Hong Kong Bank: The Building of Norman Foster's Masterpiece*. Boston: Little, Brown and Company.

Williams, Tony. (2000). "Under 'Western Eyes': The Personal Odyssey of Huang Fei-Hongin Once Upon a Time in China." *Cinema Journal* 40, 1 (Fall): 3–24.

Wils, John E. Jr., and Paul Van Dyke. (2000). "Strange Shores: 442 Years of Anomaly in Macau and Counting." *Harvard Pacific Review* (Summer) <http://hcs.harvard.edu/~hapr/summer00_tech/macau.html> (accessed February 2005).

Wong, Bib. (2000). "Opium and Modern Chinese State-Making." In T. Brook and B. Wakabayashi, eds. *Opium Regimes*. Berkeley: University of California Press, 189–211.

Wong Cheuk Yin. (2004). "The Leftist Riots and Regime Legitimacy in Hong Kong." *EHKCSS*: E-Journal on Hong Kong Cultural and Social Studies <www.hku.hk.hkcsp.ccex.ehkcss01> (accessed June 6, 2005).

Wong, Cindy Hing-Yuk. (1999). "Cities, Cultures, and Cassettes: Hong Kong Cinemas and Transnational Audiences." *Postscript* 19: 87–106.

——— and Gary McDonogh. (2001a). "The Mediated Metropolis: Reflections on Anthropology and Communication." *American Anthropologist* 103, 1 (March): 96–111.

——— and Gary McDonogh. (2001b). "Consuming Cinema: Reflections on Movies and Marketplaces in Contemporary Hong Kong." In ed. G. Mathews and T.-L. Lui, eds. *Consuming Hong Kong*. Hong Kong: Hong Kong University Press, 81–114.

Wong, David O.Y. (1996). *Environmental Conservation and Planning: Hong Kong and Overseas Encounters*. Hong Kong: Woods Age.

Wong Koon-Kwai, and Man Chi-Sum. (1998). "Environment: Will Hong Kong Become Greener Tomorrow?" In L.C-H. Chow and Y-K Fan, eds. *The Other Hong Kong Report 1998*. Hong Kong: Chinese University Press, 383–402.

Wong, Linda, and Gui Shixun. (2004). "Introduction." In L. Wong, L. White, and Gui S., eds. *Social Policy Reform in Hong Kong and Shanghai*. Armonk, NY: M.E. Sharpe, 1–22.

Wong, Linda, Lynn White, and Gui Shixun, ed. (2004). *Social Policy Reform in Hong Kong and Shanghai: A Tale of Two Cities*. Armonk, NY: M.E. Sharpe.

Wong, Shirley. (2002). "Colonialism, Power, and the Hongkong and Shanghai Bank." In I. Borden, J. Kerr and J. Rendell, eds., with A. Pivaro. *The Unknown City: Contesting Architecture and Social Space*. Cambridge: MIT Press, 160–75.

Wong Siu-Lun. (1999). "Deciding to Stay, Deciding to Move, Deciding Not to Decide." In G. Hamilton. *Cosmopolitan Capitalists*. Seattle: University of Washington Press, 135–51.

Wong, Wah Sang, and Edwin H. W. Chan. (2000). *Building Hong Kong: Environmental Considerations*. Hong Kong: Hong Kong University Press.

Wong Wai King. (2000). *Tai O, Love Stories of the Fishing Village*. HK: 1920–2000.

Wong, Yue-Chim, Richard. (1998). *On Privatizing Public Housing*. Hong Kong: City University of Hong Kong Press.

Wong Yui-Tim. (1997). "Labour and Employment." In J. Cheng, ed. *The Other Hong Kong Report 1997*. Hong Kong: Chinese University Press, 341–56.

Woo, Edward S. W. (1998). "Urban Development." In Y. M. Yeung and David Chu, eds. *Guangdong*. Hong Kong: Chinese University Press, 355–84.

Xiong Yuezhi. (1996). "The Image and Identity of the Shanghainese." T. T. Liu and D. Faure, eds. *Unity and Diversity*. Hong Kong: Hong Kong University Press, 99–106.

Yahuda, Michael. (1996). *Hong Kong: China's Challenge*. London: Routledge.

Yardley, J. (2005). "As Quickly as it Appears — SARS Disappears — for Now." *New York Times*, May 16.

Yatso, Pamela. (2001). *New Shanghai: The Rocky Rebirth of China's Legendary City*. New York: John Wiley and Sons.

Yau, Esther. (1999). *At Full Speed: Hong Kong Cinema in a Borderless World*. Minneapolis: University of Minnesota Press.

Yeh, Anthony Gar-On, ed. (1996). *Planning Hong Kong for the Twenty-First Century*. Center for Urban Planning and Environmental Management, Hong Kong University.

Yeh, Catherine. (1996). "Creating a Shanghai Identity — Late Qing Courtesan Handbooks and the Formation of the New Citizen." In T. T. Liu and D. Faure, eds. *Unity and Diversity*. Hong Kong: Hong Kong University Press, 107–24.

Yeo, Wei-Wei. (2003). "City as Theatre: Singapore, State of Distraction." In R. Bishop, J. Phillips, and W. W. Yeo, eds. *Postcolonial Urbanism*. New York: Routledge, 245–64.

Yep, Ray, King-Lun Ngok, and Zhu Baoshu. (2004). "Migration and Competitiveness." In L. Wong, L. White, and Gui S., eds. *Social Policy Reform in Hong Kong and Shanghai*. Armonk, NY: M.E. Sharpe, 217–38.

Yeung, Y. M. (1990). *Changing Cities of Pacific Asia: A Scholarly Interpretation*. Hong Kong: The Chinese University Press.

———. (1998). "Introduction." Y. M. Yeung and David Chu, eds. *Guangdong*, Hong Kong: Chinese University Press, 1–21.

——— and David K.Y. Chu, eds. (1998). *Guangdong: Survey of a Province Undergoing Rapid Change*. Hong Kong: Chinese University Press.

——— and Sung Yun-wing, eds. (1996). *Shanghai: Transformation and Modernization under China's Open Policy*. Hong Kong: Chinese University Press.

Young, John. (1981). "China's Role in Two Hong Kong Disturbances: A Scenario for the Future?" *Journal of Oriental Studies* 19: 1.

Yu Qun and Cheng Shuwei. (2004). "Meiguo de Xianggang Zhengce 1942–1960 [United States policies toward Hong Kong (1942–1960)]." In K. L. Law and K. M. Lee, eds. *The Economy of Hong Kong in Non-Economic Perspectives*. Hong Kong: Oxford University Press, 27–40.

Yu Shengwu, and Liu Cuakuan, eds. (1993). *Shijiu shijide Xianggang [Nineteenth century Hong Kong]*. Beijing: Zhonggua Shinju.

Yu Shegwu, and Liu Shuyong. (1995). *Ershu shijide Xianggong [Twentieth Century Hong Kong]*. Beijing: Grand Encyclopedia.

SUGGESTED FILMOGRAPHY

This list cannot provide complete references or interpretations, which are available in Teo (1997), Fu and Desser (2000), etc. Instead, it should remind researchers about films we have discussed that illustrate Hong Kong life and explore global Hong Kong identities.

2046. (2004). Wong Kar-Wai. Stories of love and memory interwoven from 1960s to the imaginary future. Sequel to *In the Mood for Love*.

Autumn Moon. (1992). Dir. Clara Law Cheuk-Yiu. Floating encounters between Japanese visitor and Chinese student about to depart for Canada to join her family.

Batman Begins. (2005). Christopher Nolan. Occassionally sinicized Batman, with possible references to Walled City according to industry powers.

Better Luck Tomorrow. (2002). Justin Lin. Suburban Asian Americans torn between model minority and violence.

Better Tomorrow, A. (1986). John Woo. Classic choreographed story of crime, family and change.

Boat People. (1982). Ann Hui On-Wah. Vietnamese refugees.

C'est La Vie, Mon Cheri. (1993). Derek Yee Tung-Sing. Urban melodrama with many scenes of night market in Temple Street.

Chan is Missing. (1982). Wayne Wang. Low-budget saga of San Francisco Chinatown.

Chinese Box. (1998). Wayne Wang. Hollywood version of the Handover, with interesting historical errors amid general paranoid climate.

Chungking Express. (1994). Wong Kar-Wai. Hong Kong as postmodern and multicultural setting with vivid interpretation of Chungking Building, Kowloon.

Citizen Hong Kong. (1999). Ruby Yang. Documentary on the experience of transition.

Comrades, Almost a Love Story. (1996). Peter Chan Ho Sun. Love story of two star-crossed modern mainland immigrants in Hong Kong and the United States.

Dim Sum — A Little Bit of Heart. (1985). Wayne Wang. Mother and daughter in San Francisco Chinatown.

Durian, Durian. (2000). Fruit Chan Gwa. Parallel stories of a family from Shenzhen and a prostitute from inland China in their lives in Mong Kok (Hong Kong) and on their returns to China.

Face to Face: It's Not What You Think. (1997). Scribe Video, Philadelphia. Grassroots dialogues by Asian American youth in Philadelphia, covering school, racism, gangs, and hopes.

Farewell, My China. (1990). Clara Law. Dystopic visions of Chinese in America.

Fathers and Sons. (1980). Alan Fong. Semi-autobiographical story of Hakka squatters in 1960s Hong Kong.

Fists of Fury. (1972). Wei Lo. Classic Bruce Lee work also raising issues of Chinese identity.

Floating Life. (1966). Clara Law Cheuk-Yiu. Hong Kong emigrants displaced and dysfunctional in Australia.

Gen-X Cops. (1999). Benny Chan. Teen flick with transnational heroes and villains.

Hollywood Hong Kong. (2002). Fruit Chan Gwa. Squatters in contemporary HK.

Hong Kong Story, The. (1997). Libby Halliday. An historical overview with strong English presence.

In the Face of Demolition. (1953). Lee Tit. Lives of Hong Kong residents in a crowded postwar housing conditions.

In the Mood For Love. (2001). Wong Kar-Wai. Reflections on 1960s Hong Kong.

Journey to Beijing. (1998). Evans Chan Yiu Shing. Four month walk from Hong Kong to Beijing with reflections on Hong Kong society.

The Killer. (1989). John Woo. Classic Hong Kong gangster film.

Lee Rock, The $500,000 Detective. (1991) and *Lee Rock Part II* (1992). Lau Kwok-Cheung. Semi-historical rise and fall of Hong Kong police officer, telling story of corruption and ICAC.

Little Cheung. (1999). Fruit Chan Gwa Lives centered on a cha-chaan-teng in Mong Kok and the people who intersect there.

Long Arm of the Law. (1984). Johnnie Mak Tong-Hung. Transborder crime spree with shootout in the Walled City of Kowloon.

Longest Summer. (1998). Fruit Chan Gwa. Displaced Chinese soldiers of the British Army await the Handover.

Look Forward and Carry on from the Past: Stories from Philadelphia's Chinatown. (2002). Philadelphia Folklore Project.

Love Is a Many-Splendoured Thing. (1959). Henry King. Based on Han Suyin; race and class in Hong Kong seen through American eyes.

Made in Hong Kong. (1997). Fruit Chan Gwa. Gang life in housing projects before the Handover: first part of Chan's Handover trilogy.

Map of Sex and Love. (2001). Evans Chan Yiu Shing. Global love stories with wry commentary on Hong Kong and Macau.

Once Upon a Time in China and America. (1997). Dir. Sammo Hung; Prod. Tsui Hark. Hong Kong hero Wong Fei Hung in the West.

Opium War. (1997). Xie Jin. Chinese recreation of seminal events in Hong Kong history.

Rouge. (1987). Stanley Kwan. A nostalgic vision of 1930s Hong Kong.

Rumble in the Bronx. (1996). Stanley Tong. Jackie Chan crossover film, set in New York's Chinatown although shot in Vancouver.

Shanghai Noon. (2000). Tom Dey. Jackie Chan and buddy in Old West.

Song of Exile. (1990). Ann Hui. Semi-autobiographical exploration of the roots of a Japanese Chinese woman moving through Hong Kong and China.

Soong Sisters. (1997). Mabel Cheung. All-star biography of family central to 20th century China.

Summer Snow. (1995). Ann Hui. Working woman struggling with job and family in contemporary Hong Kong.

To Liv(e). (1992). Evans Chan Yin-Shing. Meditations on Hong Kong partially in response to Liv Ullman's critique of situation of Vietnamese Boat People in Hong Kong.

Wicked City. (1992). Dir. Michael Mak; Prod. Tsui Hark. Monsters attack Hong Kong; based on Japanese anime.

World of Suzie Wong. (1960). Ray Stark. Classic Hollywood vision of Hong Kong.

Young and Dangerous I-IV. (1996–1998). Peter Chan; highly popular youth/crime dramas.

WEB SITES

Bangkok: www.bma.gov.th

Chinese Heritage of Australian Federation (Latrobe): www.chaf.lib.latrobe.edu.au

Civic Exchange, Hong Kong: www.civic-exchange.org

Cyberport, Hong Kong: www.cyberport.com.hk

Dark Horizons (movie previews): www.darkhorizons.com

Discover Hong Kong: www.discoverhongkong.com

EHKCSS: E-Journal on Hong Kong Cultural and Social Studies: www.hku.hk/hkcsp/ccex/ehkcss)1/index.htm

Friends of the Harbour, Hong Kong: www.friendsoftheharbour.org

Guangdong News: www.newsgd.com, for individual cities and towns, e.g., Shenzhen, see: www.newsgd.com/citiesandtowns/shenzhen

Hong Kong and Shanghai Bank: www.hsbc.com

Hong Kong Cricket Club: www.hkcc.org/club/history.htm

Hong Kong Special Administrative Region: www.info.gov.hk

Immigration, Hong Kong: www.immd.gov.hk

Museu de Macau: www.macaumuseum.gov.mo

"Opium Wars" (film and war): www.cyber.law.harvard.edu/ChinaDragon/opiumwar.html

Philadelphia Chinatown Development Corporation (PCDC): www.chinatown-pcdc.com

Shanghai Disney (BBC News): news.bbc.co.uk/1/hi/business/2137993.stm

Shanghai Information Resources Network: www.libnet.sh.cn/newsirn/english/indexen.htm

Taipei/Taiwan: www.taipei.org

Television Broadcast Limited (TVB): www.tvb.com/affairs/faq/tvbgroup/tvbi.html

Tung Wah Hospital: www.tungwah.org.hk

Virtual Walled City: www.flex.co.jp/kowloon/home (inactive as of 2005)

World Health Organization (WHO), SARS: www.who.int/csr/sars

Index

Abbreviations after places refer to Hong Kong locations: HKI
(Hong Kong Island), K (Kowloon) and NT (New Territories).

279 **Index**

Dickinson Report (HK 1966) 88
Dim sum 141–142, 154, 195, 204,
    206, 210
"Disappearance" 112, 115, 116, 122
Discovery Bay (Lantau) 22
Disease 1, 3–5, 48–49, 66, 79,
    119, 131, 139, 158, 209,
    220, 223, 234; see also
    Bubonic Plague; Influenza;
    Pneumonia; SARS
    Western perceptions 3, 48–49
Disney theme parks xvi, 22, 112,
    171, 192–196
    Disney Sea 192
    HK Disneyland xviii, 21, 111,
        169, 192–193
    Shanghai 192
    Tokyo 192
District Watch Force (HK) 48
Divorce 88
Dongguan (China) 144, 157
Downtowns 12–14, 54, 71,
    121–128, 142, 157,
    161–162, 183, 193,
    196–201, 207, 210;
    see also Central (HK)
Dragon Boat Festival 210
Dragons 127, 159, 167, 181, 202
    Asian Dragons 157, 165, 181
    Feng Shui 127–128
Drugs and alcohol 25–30, 36–43,
    229
    addiction 38–43
Durian, Durian (film F Chan 2000)
    20

E

East Asia 43, 63, 70, 71, 167–197
East River (China) 83, 135

Eat Drink Man Woman (film Lee
    1994) 178
Eça de Queiros, José Maria 215
Education 7, 11, 35, 48, 66, 81–82,
    98, 100–101, 113, 117,
    144, 172, 180–183
    colonial 7, 35, 48, 81–82, 98,
        100–101, 113, 117, 172
Eiffel Tower (Paris France) 20
Eisenhower, Dwight David
    (U.S. President) 70
Elbasani and Logan (architects) 196
Electronics 73, 76, 142, 182,
    194–195
Elderly (including grandparents)
    23, 90, 175–176, 198,
    201, 211, 214, 228
Elections (HK) 10, 78, 88, 104–105,
    108, 110–111, 155
    Singapore 9, 181
    Taiwan 173–174
Elites 14, 19, 20, 36, 45, 47, 48–49,
    54, 55, 57–60, 84, 86, 87,
    95, 96, 105, 122–123,
    132, 157, 158, 160, 171,
    173, 177, 178, 181, 183,
    184, 187, 189, 213
    Chinese 35, 36, 45, 48–49,
        57–60, 105, 122–123,
        132, 171, 183–184
    Eurasian 47, 57–59
Elliott, Captain Charles 39, 40, 44
"end-game syndrome" 90
Emigration 67, 84, 101, 104, 106,
    115, 131–132, 137,
    142, 200, 209, 213,
    216, 220–222; see also
    Immigration; Migration
England 1, 35, 39, 46, 219, 228